BRITISH&AMERICAN CULTURE

了解英美 汉英对照

一本就够

郑杰 编著

中国纺织出版社

图书在版编目（CIP）数据

了解英美一本就够：汉英对照 / 郑杰编著. —北京：中国纺织出版社，2017.1（2024.7重印）
ISBN 978-7-5180-3000-2

Ⅰ.①了… Ⅱ.①郑… Ⅲ.①英语–汉语–对照读物②英国–概况③美国–概况 Ⅳ.①H319.4：K

中国版本图书馆CIP数据核字（2016）第237594号

策划编辑：张向红　　　　责任编辑：张向红
责任设计：林昕瑶　　　　责任印制：储志伟

中国纺织出版社出版发行
地　　址：北京市朝阳区百子湾东里A407号楼　邮政编码：100124
销售电话：010—67004422　传真：010—87155801
http://www.c-textilep.com
E-mail: faxing@c-textilep.com
中国纺织出版社天猫旗舰店
官方微博http://weibo.com/2119887771
永清县晔盛亚胶印有限公司印刷　各地新华书店经销
2017年1月第1版　2024年7月第3次印刷
开　本：880×1230　1/32　印张：13.5
字　数：350千字　定价：88.00元

凡购本书，如有缺页、倒页、脱页，由本社图书营销中心调换

前言
Preface

畅游世界，揭秘西方，"英美文化"为你打开第一道门。每天读点英美文化，雕刻文化时光，茗品西方文化中英美味道的最精髓：

从英语世界古老的牛津大学，到创造多名富豪的哈佛大学；

从纯粹自然的黄石国家公园，到高贵典雅的海德公园；

从大英博物馆的奢华，到大都会艺术博物馆的现代；

从充满神秘色彩的巨石阵，到见证过历史风云的威廉古堡；

从伦敦眼到百老汇；

从唐宁街十号到白宫……

这里采集了英美范围内将近百个流传于人间的伟大的文化结晶，让你在学习英文的同时，来一次彻彻底底的文化洗礼和心灵震撼之旅。

本书的亮点是"全"：它选材广泛，英美文化的要点无不涉及，涵盖名牌大学、地标建筑、旅游胜地、特色美食、知名品牌、名人明星、特色节日等，纵述英美国家自古至今种种文化积淀。这些文化符号无不曾对英美的兴衰、发展起过重要作用，至今仍和现实生活密不可分。如今，它们已经不再只属于英国和美国，现代化的交通和信息传输把它们传播到世界的各个角落。本书的编者们花费了大量的时间和精力搜集资料，整理文字，最终将这财富呈现在读者面前。

该书不仅适合英语专业学生用作学习辅助材料，同时，也适合各个层次、各个年龄阶段的非专业读者阅读。这是一本浓缩英美文化知识精粹的良书。它将散如繁星的文化常识聚集一起，力求贴近生活，让读者足不出户，便可领略英美国家的文化魅力，轻松学到知识。用地道英语呈现的文化经典，能很好地帮读者提高语言能力和阅读水平，

  这是一本集阅读性、休闲性和学习性为一身的英文休闲读物。

  英美文化的历史上缔造了很多经典，这些经典包括建筑、美食、节日、文学等等，无疑不是人类文化历史上的奇葩。《了解英美一本就够》使经典成为通识——它用地道的英语、凝练的中文与精美的图片，诠释着文化经典之最。

编者
2016.6

目录 Contents

前言

Section 1-1（英）享誉世界的名牌大学 1

1. 剑桥大学 University of Cambridge——全世界最顶尖的大学 2
2. 牛津大学 University of Oxford——英语世界中最古老的大学 5
3. 圣安德鲁斯大学 University of St. Andrews——苏格兰最古老的大学 8
4. 帝国学院 Imperial College——专精于科学技术的大学 11
5. 杜伦大学 University of Durham——享有极高美誉的大学 14
6. 巴斯大学 University of Bath——英国大学中规模较小的一所 18
7. 埃克塞特大学 University of Exeter——花园式的大学 21
8. 华威大学 University of Warwick——英国名门大学 24
9. 约克大学 University of York——风景秀丽的大学 27
10. 兰卡斯特大学 Lancaster University——最佳研究型的大学 30
11. 伯明翰大学 University of Birmingham——英国"红砖大学"之一 32
12. 爱丁堡大学 University of Edinburgh——英国第四大难以申请的大学 36

Section 1-2（美）享誉世界的名牌大学 41

1. 哈佛大学 Harvard University——美国思想源泉的诞生地 42
2. 耶鲁大学 Yale University——未来领袖人物的实验室 45
3. 普林斯顿大学 Princeton University——充满朝气的圣学天堂 48
4. 哥伦比亚大学 Columbia University——匠心独运的帝王学院 51
5. 达特茅斯学院 Dartmouth College——全美无线化做得最好的高校 54
6. 康奈尔大学 Cornell University——真正意义的全民大学 57
7. 麻省理工学院 MIT——全球高科技人才的摇篮 60

I

目录 Contents

8. 斯坦福大学 Stanford University——象征21世纪科技精神的名校............63

9. 布朗大学 Brown University——美国学术界精英的伊甸园................66

Section 2-1（英）叹为观止的地标建筑................69

1. 伊丽莎白塔 Elizabeth Tower——英国古典文化的代表..................70
2. 伦敦眼 London Eye——飞翔在伦敦上空的"胶囊"....................73
3. 白金汉宫 Buckingham Palace——全球最昂贵的豪宅..................75
4. 伦敦塔桥 The Tower of London——拥有"伦敦正门"之美称............79
5. 国会大厦 The Houses of Parliament——英国政治的中心舞台...........82
6. 威斯敏斯特教堂 Westminster Abby——不简单的宗教场所..............85
7. 哈罗德百货公司 Harrods——英国的百年老店......................88
8. 圣保罗大教堂 St. Paul's Cathedral——世界著名的宗教圣地............91
9. 大英博物馆 British Museum——古代文明的汇聚地..................94
10. 伦敦碎片大厦 The Shard——欧洲第一高楼......................97

Section 2-2（美）叹为观止的地标建筑................101

1. 白宫 White House——美国政府的代名词........................102
2. 帝国大厦 Empire State Building——美国经济复苏的象征..............104
3. 世贸中心 World Trade Center——美国人心中永远的伤痛..............107
4. 林肯纪念堂 Lincoln Memorial——美国永恒的塑像..................110
5. 金门大桥 The Golden Gate Bridge——进入古稀之年的大桥............113
6. 拉什莫尔山 Mount Rushmore——被全球人"玩坏"了的圣山............116

7. 自由女神像 Statue of Liberty——美利坚民族和美法人民友谊的象征....... 118
8. 纽约中央车站 Grand Central Terminal——见证了岁月流逝的大中央火车站 .. 121
9. 联合国总部大厦 The United Nations Headquarters——世界上唯一的一块"国际领土".. 124

Section 3-1（英）流连忘返的旅游胜地............... 127

1. 巨石阵 Stonehenge——怪异的史前文明遗址.................. 128
2. 温莎古堡 Windsor Castle——见证老天荒爱情故事之地............ 130
3. 唐宁街 Downing Street——世界上出镜率最高的街道............. 133
4. 诺森伯兰国家公园 Northumberland National Park——宛如仙境的国家公园.. 136
5. 尼斯湖 Loch Ness——充满谜团的湖泊..................... 138
6. 泰晤士河 Thames River——英国著名的"母亲"河.............. 140
7. 布莱尼姆宫 Blenheim Palace——英国园林的经典之作............ 143
8. 锡辛赫斯特 Sissinghurst——见证爱情的玫瑰花园.............. 146
9. 杜莎夫人蜡像馆 Madame Tussaud's——英国古今名人集合之地....... 148
10. 特拉法尔加广场 Trafalgar Square——观光客的必到之地.......... 150

Section 3-2（美）流连忘返的旅游胜地............... 153

1. 时代广场 Times Square——世界的十字路口.................. 154
2. 科罗拉多大峡谷 Grand Canyon National Park——切割出来的奇迹..... 158
3. 尼亚加拉大瀑布 Niagara Falls——震撼人心的跨国瀑布........... 161
4. 黄石国家公园 Yellowstone National Park——地球上最独一无二的神奇.. 164
5. 好莱坞环球影城 Universal Studios Hollywood——造梦机器的聚集地... 167

III

6. 大都会博物馆 Metropolitan Museum of Art——引人入胜艺术的殿堂 170

7. 圣地亚哥海洋世界 Sea World San Diego——人与动物共享的水上乐土 172

8. 大雾山国家公园 Great Smoky Mountains National Park——迷雾中的人间仙境 174

Section 4-1（英）垂涎欲滴的特色美食 177

1. 哈吉斯 Haggis——苏格兰的"国菜" 178

2. 炸鱼薯条 Fish and Chips——英国美食的"国粹" 181

3. 鳗鱼冻 Jellied Eels——黑暗料理的奇葩 184

4. 苏格兰蛋 Scotch Eggs——三百年历史的苏格兰美食 187

5. 皮夹克土豆 Jacket Potato——英国特有的土豆吃法 189

6. 烤豆子 Baked Beans——英式早餐不可缺少的一道菜 192

7. 血肠 Black Pudding——人类最早自制的菜肴 195

8. 康沃尔馅饼 Cornish Pasty——英国传统的矿工食品 197

9. 约克郡布丁 Yorkshire Pudding——英国人周日晚餐的重要组成部分 200

10. 司康饼 Scone——英式的快速面包 202

11. 奶酪蛋糕 Cheesecake——令人欲罢不能的美味 204

12. 苏格兰鲜鱼浓汤 Cullen Skink——经典的苏格兰风味 206

Section 4-2（美）垂涎欲滴的特色美食 209

1. 鲁本三明治 Reuben Sandwich——让人欲罢不能的三明治 210

2. 烘肉卷 Meatloaf——一道纯正的西餐狠菜 213

3. 巴法罗鸡翅 Buffalo Wings——一道地道的纽约州美味 216

IV

4. 芝加哥式比萨 Chicago-style Pizza———极致奢华的芝加哥式馅饼 219

5. 贝奈特饼 Beignet———一道受人欢迎的开胃菜 222

6. 龙萨饼 Runza———一种伏尔加德意志移民的民族美食 224

7. 斯派蒂斯 Spiedies———一种传统的意大利烤肉串 226

8. 牛油蛋糕 Butter Cake———不自觉流口水的美食 229

9. 新泽西猪肉卷 Pork Roll———特色的新泽西早餐 231

10. 巧克力豆曲奇 Chocolate Chip Cookie———龙卷风般的味觉感受 233

Section 5-1（英）受人追捧的知名品牌 237

1. 皇家壳牌石油 Royal Dutch Shell———油气行业领导者 238

2. 阿斯顿马丁 Aston Matin———英国豪华跑车制造商 241

3. 宾利 Bentley———熠熠生辉顶级英国豪华汽车 244

4. 巴宝莉 Burberry———极具英国传统风格的奢侈品牌 246

5. 特易购 Tesco———英国最大的零售公司 248

6. 吉百利 Cadbury———老牌糖果制造商 251

7. 联合利华 Unilever———为世人带来美好生活 254

8. 君皇仕 Gieves & Hawkes———为欧洲的贵族量身打造 257

9. 芝华士 Chivas Regal———威士忌三重调和的创造者 259

Section 5-2（美）受人追捧的知名品牌 261

1. 微软 Microsoft———PC 机软件开发的先导 262

2. 可口可乐 The Coca-Cola Company———让碳酸饮料深入人心 265

V

目录 Contents

3. 迪斯尼 The Walt Disney Company——因一只老鼠而成为传奇............ 267
4. 耐克 Nike Inc.——给体育界带来了一场革命.................... 271
5. 星巴克 Starbucks——将丑小鸭变成白天鹅的奇迹............... 274
6. 雅诗兰黛 Estée Lauder Companies——奉行为每个女性带来美丽的原则..... 277
7. 克莱斯勒 Chrysler——汽车工业的领导性品牌.................. 279
8. 苹果 Apple Inc.——砸醒世人的第三颗苹果.................... 281
9. 肯德基 KFC——一只鸡,改变了人们的饮食世界................. 284
10. 沃尔玛 Walmart——世界上最大的连锁零售企业................ 287

Section 6-1（英）影响世界的励志名人............ 291

1. 查尔斯·狄更斯 Charles Dickens——展现英国底层生活的文学巨匠....... 292
2. 简·奥斯汀 Jane Austin——独立自主的"道德教育家"............... 295
3. 威廉·莎士比亚 William Shakespeare——被喻为"人类文学奥林匹斯山上的宙斯".. 297
4. J.K. 罗琳 J.K. Rowling——挥动魔法棒的"灰姑娘"................ 301
5. 查尔斯·卓别林 Charles Chaplin——奠定了现代喜剧电影的基础......... 304
6. 费雯丽 Vivien Leigh——妩媚动人的"好莱坞的珍珠"............... 307
7. 休·格兰特 Hugh Grant——风度翩翩的英伦绅士.................. 309
8. 温斯顿·丘吉尔 Winston Churchill——大英帝国的"帝国之心"......... 311
9. 撒切尔夫人 Margaret Hilda Thatcher——英国永远的"铁娘子"........ 314
10. 艾萨克·牛顿 Isaac Newton——百科全书式的"全才"............... 317
11. 斯蒂芬·威廉·霍金 Stephen William Hawking——最杰出的"宇宙之王".. 321

12. 弗朗西斯·培根 Francis Bacon——英国唯物主义和整个现代实验科学的真正始祖 324

Section 6-2（美）影响世界的励志名人 327

1. 亚伯拉罕·林肯 Abraham Lincoln——洋溢神性光辉的政客 328
2. 埃尔维斯·普雷斯利 Elvis Presley——世界人民眼中永远的猫王 331
3. 迈克尔·杰克逊 Michael Jackson——心怀大爱的流行天王 335
4. 伊丽莎白·泰勒 Elizabeth Taylor——好莱坞性感端庄的代名词 338
5. 拉尔夫·爱默生 Ralph Emerson——美国孔子般的灵魂人物 341
6. 迈克尔·乔丹 Michael Jordan——飞起来的23号球衣 344
7. 伊利莎白·雅顿 Elizabeth Arden——让世界充满了芬芳 347
8. 阿尔伯特·爱因斯坦 Albert Einstein——震撼世界的超级大脑 349
9. 乔治·华盛顿 George Washington——全世界第一位以"总统"为称号的国家元首 352
10. 约翰·D. 洛克菲勒 John D. Rockefeller——全球历史上除君主外最富有的人 355

Section 7-1（英）独具特色的当地节日 359

1. 圣帕特里克节 St. Patrick's Day——爱尔兰的国庆节 360
2. 彭斯晚宴 Burns Night——名副其实的狂欢酒筵 363
3. 威尔士诗歌音乐会 The Eisteddfod——英国威尔士民谣之夜 366
4. 情人节 St. Valentine's Day——爱情见证之时 369
5. 耶稣受难日 Good Friday——纪念耶稣生命中最高潮的一周 372

目录
Contents

6. 圣灵降临日 Pentecost——圣灵浇灌的神圣时刻 375

7. 女王诞辰日 Queen's Birthday——英国举国欢庆的国庆日 378

8. 五朔节 May Day——古老的春之节日 380

9. 烟火节 Guy Fawkes Day——英国最美的夜晚 383

Section 7-2 （美）独具特色的当地节日 387

1. 美国独立日 Independence Day——通过《独立宣言》的这一天 388

2. 马丁·路德金日 Martin Luther King, Jr. Day——唯一一个纪念美国黑人的联邦假日 391

3. 复活节 Easter Day——象征着重生与希望的节日 394

4. 华盛顿诞辰日 Washington's Birthday——美国的"总统日" 398

5. 美国阵亡将士纪念日 Memorial Day——展现爱国情操的重要节日 ... 401

6. 感恩节 Thanksgiving Day——是美国人民独创的一个古老节日 404

7. 万圣节 Halloween——"Trick or Treat"捣蛋鬼们的狂欢节 407

8. 圣诞节 Christmas Day——美国庆祝圣人诞生的节日 411

Section 1-1　（英）享誉世界的名牌大学

英国是欧洲最古老的国家之一，亦是欧洲高等教育最发达的国家之一。英国的高等学府历史悠久，文化底蕴深厚，为英国乃至世界培养了大批的杰出人物。他们被视为世界高等教育的鼻祖，他们的教育理念、方式、内容都与时俱进，成为真正屹立不倒的鲜明旗帜。

1 剑桥大学 University of Cambridge
——全世界最顶尖的大学

◆ History

Founded in 1209, Cambridge is the second-oldest university in the English-speaking world and the world's fourth-oldest surviving university. The monks from nearby Ely, Cambridgeshire, which was a bishopric church, were thought to have been responsible for the scholarly and **ecclesiastical**（教会的）reputation that served in the foundations of the university. The university was established by scholars from Oxford in 1209, although, in order to claim precedence, it is common for Cambridge to trace its founding to the 1231 charter from King Henry III granting it the right to discipline its own members and an **exemption**（豁免）from some taxes. It grew out of an association of scholars who left the University of Oxford after a dispute with townsfolk. The two ancient universities share many common features and are often jointly referred to as "Oxbridge".

【阅读辅助】
剑桥大学始创于1209年，是英语世界中第二历史悠久的大学，亦为全球第四古老并幸存的高校。该大学的前身是剑桥市的学者协会。协会的创办者原为牛津大学的成员，在与当地居民发生冲突后移居到剑桥，并希望延续他们的传统与精神。这使得两所古老的大学在包括办学模式等多方面都非常相似，而且这两所学校相互间也展开了历史相当悠久的竞争。

✦ Summary

Cambridge is formed from a variety of institutions which include 31 **constituent**（构成的）colleges and over 100 academic departments organized into six schools. The university occupies buildings throughout the town, many of which are of historical importance. The colleges are self-governing institutions founded as integral parts of the university. The central university and colleges have a combined **endowment**（捐赠）of around £4.9 billion, the largest of any university outside the United States. Cambridge is a member of many associations and forms part of the "golden triangle" of leading English universities and Cambridge University Health Partners, an academic health science centre. The university is closely linked with the development of the high-tech business cluster known as "Silicon Fen".

Students' learning involves lectures and **laboratory**（实验室）sessions organized by departments, and supervisions provided by the colleges. The university operates eight arts, cultural, and scientific museums, including the Fitzwilliam Museum and a botanic garden. Cambridge's libraries hold a total of around 15 million books, 8 million of which are in Cambridge University Library which is a legal deposit library. Cambridge University Press, a department of the university, is the world's oldest publishing house and the second-largest university press in the world. Cambridge is regularly placed among the world's best universities in different university rankings. Besides academic studies, student life is centered on the colleges and numerous pan-university artistic activities, sports clubs and societies.

阅读辅助

剑桥大学由多个成员机构组成，培养了众多著名人士。该大学现共有31所书院及6所学术学院。剑桥大学现有100多个院系部门，它们都被归入6所学术学院。这些机构遍布剑桥市的不同角落，为学生提供不同的教学及娱乐设施。剑桥大学所收到的捐款馈赠为全欧最多。剑桥大学共有114所图书馆。其中大学中央图书馆有800万馆藏量，馆方有复印所有在英国或爱尔兰出版的书刊的权利。

◆ Notable alumni

Over the course of its history, a sizeable number of Cambridge University academics and alumni have become notable in their fields, both academic, and in the wider world. Former undergraduates of the university have won a grand total of 61 Nobel prizes, 13 more than the undergraduates of any other university. Cambridge academics have also won 8 Fields Medals and 2 Abel Prizes.

Cambridge has many notable alumni, including several eminent mathematicians, scientists, politicians, and Nobel laureates who have been **affiliated**（附属的）with it. Throughout its history, the university has featured in literature and artistic works by numerous authors including Geoffrey Chaucer, E. M. Forster and C. P. Snow.

阅读辅助

纵观剑桥史，剑桥大学培养了众多著名人士。包括数十位诺贝尔得奖者，这些人现在或曾经在剑桥大学学习或工作。另外，剑桥大学校友还包括多名数学界及科学界的名人，更有诸多校友在其各自领域独领风骚。

2. 牛津大学 University of Oxford
——英语世界中最古老的大学

✧ History

While having no known date of foundation, there is evidence of teaching as far back as 1096, making it the oldest university in the English-speaking world, and the world's second-oldest surviving university. It grew rapidly from 1167 when Henry II banned English students from attending the University of Paris. After **disputes**（争论）between students and Oxford townsfolk in 1209, some academics fled northeast to Cambridge where they established what became the University of Cambridge. The two "ancient universities" are frequently jointly referred to as "Oxbridge".

The students associated together on the basis of geographical origins, into two "nations", representing the North and the South. In later centuries, geographical origins continued to influence many students' affiliations when membership of a college or hall became **customary**（习惯的）in Oxford. In addition to this, members of many religious orders, including Dominicans, Franciscans, Carmelites, and Augustinians, settled in Oxford in the mid-13th century, gained influence, and maintained houses or halls for students. At about the same time, private **benefactors**（捐助者）established colleges to serve as self-contained scholarly communities. Among the earliest such founders were William of Durham, who in 1249 endowed University College, and John Balliol, father of a future King of Scots; Balliol College bears his name. Another founder, Walter de Merton, devised a series of regulations for college life; Merton College thereby became the model for such establishments at Oxford, as well as at the University of Cambridge.

> **阅读辅助**
>
> 虽然牛津大学的实际创立日期仍不清楚,但有记录的授课历史可追溯到1096年。牛津的师生人数自1167年亨利二世禁止英国学生前往巴黎大学就学后,就开始迅速上升。1209年,牛津师生与镇民的冲突使一些牛津学者各辟蹊径。他们迁离至东北方的剑桥镇并成立了后来的剑桥大学,因此这两所古老的大学在办学模式等各方面都非常相似。

◇ Summary

The University is made up of a variety of institutions, including 38 constituent colleges and a full range of academic departments which are organized into four divisions. All the colleges are self-governing institutions as part of the university, each controlling its own membership and with its own internal structure and activities. Being a city university, it does not have a main campus; instead, all the buildings and facilities are scattered throughout the **metropolitan**（大都市的）centre.

Most undergraduate teaching at Oxford is organized around weekly tutorials at the self-governing colleges and halls, supported by classes, lectures and laboratory work provided by university faculties and departments. Oxford is the home of several notable scholarships, including the Clarendon Scholarship which was launched in 2001 and the Rhodes Scholarship which has brought graduate students to read at the university for more than a century. The university operates the largest university press in the world and the largest academic library system in the United Kingdom.

> **阅读辅助**
>
> 牛津大学由38所书院及4所学术学院组成。各个书院为独立的行政机构并隶属于大学。它们有自己的管理框架、招生标准以及学生活动安排。牛津并没有自己的主校区,其各学院的大楼和设施分散

于市中心的各个角落里。牛津大学同时为两个著名奖学金计划的举办地：一个为克拉伦登奖学金；另一个为过去一个多世纪里吸引了不少杰出研究生前来学习的罗德奖学金。牛津同时拥有全球最具规模的大学出版社及全英最大型的大学图书馆系统。

◆ Notable alumni

Throughout its history, a **sizeable**（相当大的）number of Oxford alumni, known as Oxonians, have become notable in many varied fields, both academic and otherwise, ranging from T. E. Lawrence, British Army officer known better as Lawrence of Arabia to the explorer, courtier, and man of letters, Sir Walter Raleigh. Moreover, 58 Nobel prize-winners have studied or taught at Oxford, with prizes won in all six categories.

26 British prime ministers have attended Oxford, over 100 Oxford alumni were elected to the House of Commons in 2010. At least 30 other international leaders have been educated at Oxford. The University is associated with eleven winners of the Nobel Prize in Chemistry, five in physics and sixteen in medicine. Oxford has also produced at least 12 saints, and 20 Archbishops of Canterbury, the most recent Archbishop being Rowan Williams, who studied at Wadham College and was later a Canon Professor at Christ Church. They had a long list of writers associated with Oxford.

阅读辅助

牛津大学培养了众多社会名人，其中包括26位英国首相，几乎所有二战后当选的首相均毕业于牛津。截至2010年，逾100位牛津人获选入下议院。牛津同时也是30位他国首领的母校。众多著名文学家均为牛津出身。至于科学界的名人则包括了数名诺贝尔化学、物理学及生理或医学奖的得主。另外共有12名圣人及20位坎特伯雷大主教诞生于此校。

3 圣安德鲁斯大学 University of St. Andrews
——苏格兰最古老的大学

◇ **History**

It is the oldest of the four ancient universities of Scotland, and the third oldest university in the English-speaking world. The university was founded in 1410 when a group of Augustinian clergy, driven from the University of Paris by the Avignon schism and from the universities of Oxford and Cambridge by the Anglo-Scottish Wars, formed a society of higher learning in St. Andrews, which offered courses of lectures in divinity, logic, philosophy, and law. A charter of privilege was bestowed upon the society of masters and scholars by the Bishop of St. Andrews, Henry Wardlaw, on 28 February, 1411. Wardlaw then successfully **petitioned**（祈求）the Avignon Pope Benedict XIII to grant the school university status by issuing a series of papal bulls, which followed on 28 August, 1413. King James V also later lent his support by granting the university a royal charter in 1532.

A college of theology and arts called St. John's College was founded in 1418. St. Salvator's College was established in 1450, by Bishop James Kennedy. St. Leonard's College was founded in 1511 by Archbishop Alexander Stewart, who intended it to have a far more monastic character than either of the other colleges. St. John's College was refunded by Cardinal James Beaton under the name St. Mary's College in 1538 for the study of **divinity**（神学）and law.

阅读辅助

圣安德鲁斯大学建立于1410年到1413年，是苏格兰第一所大学，同时也是英语世界中第三古老的大学，仅次于牛津大学与剑桥大学。1410年，一群很有可能毕业于巴黎大学的学生在圣安德鲁斯创立了一所高等院校。1413年，本笃十三世为圣安德鲁斯大学正式颁布教宗诏书，标志着圣安德鲁斯大学正式拥有大学身份。同年第一位毕业生以文学学士的身份毕业。

◇ **Summary**

St. Andrews is made up of a variety of institutions, including three constituent colleges and 18 academic schools organized into four faculties. The university occupies historic and modern buildings located throughout the town. The academic year is divided into two terms, Martinmas and Candlemas. In term time, over a third of the town's population is either a staff member or student of the university. The student body is notably diverse: over 30% of its intake come from well over 100 countries, 15% from North America. The university's sport teams compete in BUCS competitions, and the student body is known for preserving ancient traditions such as Raisin Weekend, May Dip, and the wear of **distinctive**（与众不同的）academic dress.

National league tables currently rank St. Andrews as the third best university in the United Kingdom. The Schools of Physics and Astronomy, International Relations, Computer Science and Mathematics are ranked first in the United Kingdom by The Guardian. International league tables rank St. Andrews less highly, though The Times Higher Education World Universities Ranking names St. Andrews among the world's Top 20 Arts and Humanities universities. St. Andrews has the highest student satisfaction (joint first) amongst all multi-faculty universities in the United Kingdom.

> **阅读辅助**
>
> 圣安德鲁斯大学包括3个学院和18个学术机构。作为苏格兰历史最悠久的大学,学校自然保留了不少的传统。最有名的特色传统之一便是学生长袍。另外,该大学还拥有全英最高的美国学生比例。圣安德鲁斯大学多次被评为英国年度优秀大学,在苏格兰更是长期占据第一名,是英国的顶级学府之一。

◆ **Notable alumni**

St. Andrews has many notable alumni and affiliated faculty, including eminent mathematicians, scientists, theologians, philosophers, and politicians. Recent alumni include the former First Minister of Scotland Alex Salmond, Secretary of State for Defence Michael Fallon, HM British Ambassador to China Barbara Woodward, United States Ambassador to Hungary Colleen Bell, Olympic gold medalist Chris Hoy and royals Prince William, Duke of Cambridge, and Catherine, Duchess of Cambridge. It boasts five Nobel Laureates: two in Chemistry and one in Physiology or Medicine and one each in Peace and Literature.

> **阅读辅助**
>
> 圣安德鲁斯大学有许多著名的校友,其中包括著名的数学家、科学家、神学家、哲学家和政治家。大学共培养了5名诺贝尔奖获得者,其中两名是诺贝尔化学奖获得者、一名是诺贝尔生理学或医学奖获得者、还有就是诺贝尔文学奖和诺贝尔和平奖获得者。

4 帝国学院 Imperial College
——专精于科学技术的大学

◇ History

Imperial began with Queen Victoria's husband, Prince Albert, who had a vision that Britain would advance from public education in the sciences, industry, and arts. He **envisioned**（预期）a small area celebrating the grandeur of Britain as a world-class cultural hub including the Natural History Museum, Victoria and Albert Museum, Science Museum, Royal Albert Hall and Imperial College London. The university has grown through **mergers**（合并）, including with St. Mary's Hospital Medical School, the National Heart and Lung Institute and Charing Cross and Westminster Medical School. Queen Elizabeth II opened the recently established Imperial College Business School building in 2004. A former constituent college of the University of London, Imperial became independent during its centennial celebration in 2007.

The Royal College of Chemistry was established by private **subscription**（签署）in 1845 as there was a growing awareness that practical aspects of the experimental sciences were not well taught and that in the United Kingdom the teaching of chemistry in particular had fallen behind that in Germany. The Royal School of Mines was established by Sir Henry de la Beche in 1851, developing from the Museum of Economic Geology, a collection of minerals, maps and mining equipment. The Royal College of Science was established in 1881. The main objective was to support the training of science teachers and to develop teaching in other science subjects alongside the Royal School of Mines earth sciences specialities.

> **阅读辅助**
>
> 帝国学院于1907年由维多利亚女王和阿尔伯特亲王将1845年建立的皇家科学院、大英帝国研究院、皇家矿业学院和伦敦城市与行会学院合并而成,尽管这几所学院仍然在宪制上保留着自己的实体,但是帝国学院已在1907年7月获得了皇家特许状,成为一个统一的实体。随后,圣玛丽医院医学院、国家心脏和肺学会、查令十字和西敏寺学校先后并入帝国学院,组建大学的医学院,并作为帝国学院的第四个宪制学院而被纳入。2007年,在学院成立100周年之际,帝国学院终成为一所独立的大学。

◇ Summary

Imperial is organized into four faculties - science, engineering, medicine and business - within which there are more than 40 departments, institutes and research centers. The main campus is located in Kensington with additional campuses in Chelsea, Hammersmith, Paddington, Berkshire and in Singapore. Imperial is a major centre of **biomedical**(生物医学的) research and is part of the Imperial College Healthcare academic health science centre. It is a member of numerous university associations including the Association of Commonwealth Universities, European University Association, G5, Association of MBAs, League of European Research Universities and Russell Group and forms part of the golden of leading English universities.

Imperial is consistently included among the world's top universities, ranking 2nd in the 2014 QS World University Rankings and 9th in the 2014 Times Higher Education World University Rankings. According to a corporate study in The New York Times, its graduates are among the 10 most valued in the world.

(英)享誉世界的名牌大学 Section 1-1

> **阅读辅助**
>
> 帝国学院提供本科和研究生教育，共设有四个学院：工程学院、医学院、自然科学院和商学院。帝国学院的本部校园位于伦敦市中心的南肯辛顿，另设切尔西、哈默史密斯、帕丁顿、丝木园及怀学院校区。大学各个学系与研究中心被归入四大学术学院。这里通常被认为是英国最严格的大学，它授予一等学位的比例和每年的淘汰率都十分引人瞩目，所以它也是英国入学标准最高的大学之一。

◇ **Campus**

Imperial's main campus is located in the South Kensington area of central London. It is situated in an area of South Kensington, known as Albertopolis, which has a high concentration of cultural and academic institutions, including the Natural History Museum, the Science Museum, the Victoria and Albert Museum, the Royal College of Music, the Royal College of Art, the Royal Geographical Society and the Royal Albert Hall. The Imperial Institute was constructed in South Kensington between 1888 and 1893. Its central tower **survives**（幸存）. There were smaller towers at the east and west end, a library, laboratories, conference rooms and exhibition galleries with gardens at the rear.

> **阅读辅助**
>
> 帝国学院的本部校园位于伦敦市中心的南肯辛顿，它是一个开放式的大学，由众多分散的校区组成，其中包括自然历史博物馆、科学博物馆、维多利亚和阿尔伯特博物馆、皇家艺术学院、皇家音乐学院以及皇家地理协会等。南肯辛顿校区中央的女王塔则是校园里的标志性建筑。

5 杜伦大学 University of Durham
——享有极高美誉的大学

✧ History

The strong tradition of theological teaching in Durham gave rise to various attempts to form a university there, notably under King Henry VIII and Oliver Cromwell, who issued letters patent and **nominated**（被提名的）a proctor and fellows for the establishment of a college in 1657. Indeed were it not for the "sheltered" position of Oxbridge, the university system in the UK would perhaps look very different today. Consequently, it was not until 1832 when Parliament, at the **instigation**（煽动）of Archdeacon Charles Thorp and with the support of the Bishop of Durham, William van Mildert, passed an act to enable the Dean and Chapter of Durham Cathedral to appropriate part of the property of their church to fund a new university, which came into being as the "Warden, Masters and Scholars of the University of Durham". Durham University was founded by Act of Parliament in 1832 and granted a Royal Charter in 1837. On the accession of Queen Victoria, an order of the Queen-in-Council was issued granting the use of Durham Castle as a college of the university. It was one of the first universities to **commence**（着手）tuition in England for more than 600 years and claims to be the third oldest university in England.

(英) 享誉世界的名牌大学　Section 1-1

> **阅读辅助**
>
> 杜伦大学的教学与科研历史可以追溯到600多年前，它属于英格兰最早开设的一批大学，由于杜伦郡有着深厚的神学教育传统，因此这个城市一直孕育着一个大学的诞生计划——特别是在国王亨利八世以及奥利弗·克伦威尔时期。奥利弗·克伦威尔于1657年颁发特许状，并任命一位学监和其他相关人员共同负责着手在杜伦郡建立一所大学。但直到1832年，在助理主教查尔斯·索普的鼓励和杜伦教区主教威廉·范·米尔德特的支持下，国会才通过一项法案允许分配部分教会的财产用于在当地兴建一所大学，并给予其扶持。这样，一所新的大学才得以在杜伦诞生，成为仅次于牛津大学和剑桥大学的英格兰第三古老的大学。

◆ Campus

Durham University owns a 227.8 hectare estate which includes part of a UNESCO world heritage site, one ancient monument, five grade-one-listed buildings and 68 grade-two-listed buildings along with 44.9 ha of woodland. The estate is divided across two separate locations: Durham City and Queen's Campus, Stockton.

Durham University has a unique estate, which includes 63 listed buildings, ranging from the 11th-century Castle to a 1930s Art Deco Chapel. The university also owns and manages the World Heritage Site in partnership with Durham Cathedral. The university's ownership of the World Heritage Site includes Durham Castle, Palace Green, and the surrounding buildings including the historic Cosin's Library.

> **阅读辅助**
>
> 杜伦大学占地227.8公顷，其中包括1项联合国教科文组织世界文化遗产，1座古代纪念碑，5个登记在册的一级文物保护建筑物，68个登记在册的二级文物保护建筑物以及44.9公顷的森林。整个学

校分为两个校区：杜伦市校区和斯托克顿的女王校区。杜伦大学的建筑十分特别，它拥有很多世界性的遗产建筑，如达勒姆城堡和科辛图书馆等。

✧ Summary

As a collegiate university, its main functions are divided between the academic departments of the university and 16 colleges. In general, the departments perform research and provide lectures to students, while the colleges are responsible for the domestic arrangements and welfare of undergraduate students, graduate students, post-doctoral researchers and some university staff.

The university is currently ranked 5th to 8th by all the latest league tables of the British universities. "Long established as the leading alternative to Oxford and Cambridge", the university attracts "a largely middle class student body", according to The Times's Good University Guide. Durham has the second highest proportion of privately educated students as well as the best quality of student life in the country, according to the Lloyds Bank rankings. The university was named Sunday Times University of the Year in 2005, having previously been shortlisted for the award in 2004.

The Durham University Library system holds over 1.5 million printed items. The library was founded in January, 1833 at Palace Green by a 160-volume donation by the then Bishop of Durham, William Van Mildert. The library operates four branches: Bill Bryson Library, Education Library, Queen's Campus Library and the Palace Green Library which holds the special and heritage collections. The Bishop Cosin's Library contains medieval **manuscripts**（手稿）and over 5,000 printed books, many early, and the Sudan Archive of the central library was granted Designation Status in 2005 by the Museums, Libraries and Archives Council.

阅读辅助

杜伦大学仍与剑桥大学和牛津大学维持相同的学院制,它的主要职能是由各大院系和16所学院分担着。通常而言,院系负责科研和教学工作,而学院则负责为本科生、硕士研究生、博士研究生以及一些教职工安排住宿及生活福利。长久以来,"作为牛津大学和剑桥大学之外最好的选择",杜伦大学吸引了"大量来自中产阶级和更富有家庭的学生"。杜伦大学在英国大学排行榜上名列前茅,仅次于牛津大学和剑桥大学。杜伦大学图书馆系统藏书超过了150万册。图书馆始建于1833年1月,最早位于杜伦的宫殿草坪上,当时的杜伦教区主教威廉·范·米尔德特捐赠了160卷书。整个图书馆系统包括四个部分,分别是:主图书馆、教育图书馆、女王校区图书馆,以及宫殿草坪图书馆。其中,宫殿草坪图书馆对特殊物品以及文物都有收藏。

6 巴斯大学 University of Bath
——英国大学中规模较小的一所

✧ **History**

The University of Bath can trace its roots to a technical school established in Bristol in 1856, the Bristol Trade School. In 1885 the school became part of the Society of Merchant Venturers and was renamed the Merchant Venturers' Technical College, an institution founded as a school in 1595. Meanwhile, in the neighboring city of Bath, a **pharmaceutical**（药物）school, the Bath School of Pharmacy, was founded in 1907. This became part of the Technical College in 1929. The college came under the control of the Bristol Education Authority in 1949; it was renamed then the Bristol College of Technology, and in 1960 the Bristol College of Science and Technology, when it became one of ten technical colleges under the umbrella of the Ministry of Education. In 1963, the Robbins Committee report paved the way for the college to assume university status as Bath University of Technology. Construction of the purpose-built campus began in 1964, with the first building, now known as 4 South, completed in 1965, and the Royal Charter was granted in 1966. Over the **subsequent**（随后的）decade, new buildings were added as the campus took shape.

阅读辅助

巴斯大学的前身最早可追溯到1856年建立在布里斯托尔的一间技术学校——布里斯托尔贸易学校。1885年，布里斯托尔贸易学校成为商界冒险家学会的一员，并更名为商界冒险家技术学院。与此

> 同时，巴斯药剂学校在1907年建立于毗邻布里斯托尔的巴斯市。到1929年，巴斯药剂学校正式成为商界冒险家技术学院的一部分。商界冒险家技术学院于1949年被纳入布里斯托尔教育部门的监管，并更名为布里斯托尔技术学院。之后在1963年，根据罗宾斯委员会的报告，布里斯托尔科学及技术学院被初定为巴斯技术大学。

◇ Campus

The university's main campus is located on Claverton Down, two kilometers from Bath. The design involved the separation of **vehicular**（车辆的）and pedestrian traffic, with road traffic on the ground floors and pedestrians on a raised central thoroughfare, known as the Parade. Buildings would line the parade and student residences built on tower blocks rise from the central **thoroughfare**（大道）. Such plans were mostly adhered to. At the centre of the campus is the Library and Learning Centre, a facility open round the clock offering computing services, information and research assistance as well as books and journals. A number of outlets are housed around the parade, including restaurants, bars and fast-food cafés, plus three banks, a union shop, and one small general and one oriental supermarket, as well as academic blocks.

Buildings, as in many of the so-called plate glass universities, were constructed in a functional modernist style using concrete, although such designs were later derided for lacking the charm of the Victorian red-brick universities or the ancient and medieval ones. In Bath, there is a particular contrast between the concrete campus and the Georgian style architecture of the World Heritage City of Bath.

> **阅读辅助**
>
> 巴斯大学建校于1966年，是英国典型的"平板玻璃大学"。其现代化设计的校舍与巴斯市中心乔治亚式被列为联合国文化遗产的建筑形成独特的对比。大部分用于教学的建筑都用高架行人路连接，这些建筑物的主入口改为由高一层进入而不是地面进入。

◇ Academics

The university's major academic strengths have been engineering, the physical sciences, mathematics and technology. Today, the university is also strong in management, humanities, architecture and the social sciences. Courses place a strong emphasis on vocational education. According to the latest government assessments, Bath has 15 subjects rated "excellent".

Bath is 8th in the Complete University Guide League table and has 24 out of 28 subjects placed within the top 10 in the UK. In addition, Bath's biosciences, physics, mathematics and statistics all achieve maximum points in the latest Quality Assurance Agency for Higher Education. According to 2014 National Student Survey (NSS), the University of Bath was ranked 1st for student **satisfaction**（满意）out of more than 150 UK higher education institutions.

> **阅读辅助**
>
> 根据2013和2014年的全国学生调查，巴斯大学在学生满意度方面在150所大学中排名第一。巴斯大学主要的学术优势是在工程、物理科学、数学和技术等学科。而今天的巴斯大学也在管理、人文、建筑和社会科学等学科方面极具优势，其课程都非常强调教育的职业性。

7 埃克塞特大学 University of Exeter
——花园式的大学

◇ **History**

The university can trace its origins back to three separate educational institutions that existed in the city of Exeter and in Cornwall in the middle of the nineteenth century. The university was founded and received its Royal Charter in 1955, although its **predecessor**（前任）institutions, the Royal Albert Memorial College and the University College of the South West of England, were established in 1900 and 1922 respectively.

To celebrate the educational and scientific work of Prince Albert, and inspired by the Great Exhibition of 1851, Exeter School of Art in 1855 and the Exeter School of Science in 1863 were founded. In 1838, the Exeter Diocesan Board of Education resolved to found an institution for the education and training of schoolmasters, the first such **initiative**（创举）in England. As a result, a year later, the Exeter Diocesan Training College was created in Cathedral Close, Exeter at the former house of the Archdeacon of Totnes, adjacent to Exeter Cathedral. During the eighteenth and nineteenth centuries, Cornwall was among the most significant metalliferous mining regions in the world. Camborne School of Mines was founded in 1888 to meet the needs of this local industry.

阅读辅助

埃克塞特大学是经几所学府合并而成的。早于1851年，在埃克塞特市举行了一场展览会，这引起了公众对艺术和科学的兴趣，随后在1855年创立了"埃克塞特艺术学校",在1863年成立了"埃克塞特科学学校"。这两所学府于1900年合并成"皇家亚厘毕学院",并于到1922年更名为"西南英格兰大学学院",此学院于1955年获得皇家特许状,升格成为埃克塞特大学。

◆ Summary

The university has three campuses: Streatham, St. Luke's, and Tremough in Cornwall. The university is centered in the city of Exeter, Devon, where it is the principal higher education institution. Streatham is the largest campus containing many of the university's administrative buildings, and is regarded as one of the most beautiful in the country. The Tremough campus is maintained in conjunction with Falmouth University under the Combined Universities in Cornwall initiative.

The university was named The Sunday Times University of the Year in 2013 and was the Times Higher Education University of the Year in 2007. Exeter has maintained a top ten position in the National Student Survey since the survey was launched in 2005. In 2011, it was considered as being one of the top 12 elite universities in the United Kingdom, and has been consistently ranked as one of the top 10 UK universities in recent years. Exeter is a member of the Russell Group of leading research-intensive UK universities. The university is also a member of Universities UK, the European University Association, and the Association of Commonwealth Universities and is an **accredited**(认可的)institution of the Association of MBAs.

阅读辅助

埃克塞特大学由三大校区构成:斯特里萨姆校区、圣路克校区和康沃尔校区。埃克塞特大学位于英国西部城市埃克塞特。埃克塞特是一个治安良好、消费价格合理和绿化率高的城市。该校在近几年英国媒体发布的英国大学排名中上升迅速，由30多名上升至前10名。埃克塞特也是英国的罗素大学集团联盟成员中的研究型大学。

✧ Campus

　　Streatham is the main campus, sitting on a hillside, one side of which looks down across Exeter city centre. The campus has several galleries, including the Bill Douglas Centre for the History of Cinema and Popular Culture. There is a bar called the "Ram" and a bar (previously called the "Ewe") within a nightclub called the Lemon Grove, both run by the Students' Guild. The campus hosts a medical centre, a counseling service, a children's day-care centre, and numerous catering outlets. Many halls of residence and some self-catering **accommodation**（住处）are located on this campus or in the near **vicinity**（邻近）. The Northcott Theatre resides on the campus.

　　St. Luke's Campus is just over a mile from the larger Streatham campus and ten minutes walk from the centre of Exeter. The campus is home to the largest academic school of the university, the Graduate School of Education. It shares the campus with the Department of Sport and Health Sciences. The University of Exeter, Cornwall Campus, is a campus of the University of Exeter at Tremough, in Penryn, Cornwall. The campus is part of the Combined Universities in Cornwall project, and is shared with University College Falmouth.

【阅读辅助】
　　斯特里萨姆校区是该校本部，邻近埃克塞特市中心，其中包括的商学院、法学院等科系均在此校区上课。圣路克校区位于埃克塞特市中心，教育学院及体育学院在此校区上课。康沃尔校区则位于康沃尔郡。

华威大学 University of Warwick
——英国名门大学

达人了解英美

✧ History

The idea for a university in Warwickshire was first mooted shortly after the Second World War, although it would not be founded for a further two decades. A partnership of the city and county councils **ultimately**（最后）provided the impetus for the university to be established on a 400-acre site jointly granted by the two authorities. There was some discussion between local sponsors from both the city and county over whether it should be named after Coventry or Warwickshire. The name "University of Warwick" was adopted, even though the County Town of Warwick itself lies some 8 miles to its southwest and Coventry's city centre is only 3.5 miles northeast of the campus. The establishment of the University of Warwick was given approval by the government in 1961 and received its Royal Charter of Incorporation in 1965. Since then, the university has incorporated the former Coventry College of Education in 1979 and has extended its land holdings by the continuing purchase of adjoining farm land. The university also benefited from a **substantial**（本质）donation from the family of Jack Martin, which enabled the construction of the Warwick Arts Centre.

（英）享誉世界的名牌大学   Section 1-1

> **阅读辅助**
>
> 初建华威大学的想法始于二战之后，虽然该大学并不是在接下来20年就建成的。随后有些赞助人讨论是否应该给这个学校以其所在地命名，但是最后却决定使用华威大学这个名字，虽然它实际上坐落于可爱又美丽的考文垂市郊，离市中心大约三英里的路程。该大学由政府批准最终成立于1961年，之后于1965年获得皇家特许状。

✧ **Summary**

Warwick is primarily based on a 290 hectare campus on the outskirts of Coventry with a satellite campus in Wellesbourne and a London base at the Shard in central London. It is organized into four faculties—Arts, Medicine, Science and Social Sciences—within which there are 32 departments. Warwick has around 23,400 full-time students and 1,390 academic and research staff and had a total income of £481 million in 2013/14, of which £90 million was from research grants and contracts. Warwick Arts Centre, a multi-venue arts complex in the university's main campus, is the largest venue of its kind in the UK outside London.

Warwick consistently ranks in the top ten of all major domestic rankings of British universities and is the only multi-faculty institution aside from Oxford, Cambridge and Imperial to have never been ranked outside of the top ten. It is ranked by QS as the world's third best university under 50 years and as the world's 13th best university based on employer **reputation**（声望）. Warwick is a member of AACSB, the Association of Commonwealth Universities, the Association of MBAs, EQUIS, the European University Association, the M5 Group, the Russell Group and Universities UK. It is the only European member of the Center for Urban Science and Progress, a **collaboration**（合作）with New York University.

> **阅读辅助**
>
> 华威大学的学科分为人文、自然科学、社会科学和医学四大类，有30个院系和50个研究中心，提供120个不同专业的本科学位和超过100个硕士与博士研究生学位。该校现有23,800余名在校生及近5,500名教职人员。华威大学在2008年加入素有英国常春藤之称的罗素大学集团联盟，在国内外的声誉及排名也不容小觑，该校在2014年官方RAE科学研究水准评估中，位居全英第7位。

◇ **Campus**

Warwick is located on the outskirts of Coventry, 5.5 km southwest of the city centre. The university's main site comprises three contiguous campuses, all within walking distance of each other. The original buildings of the campus are in contemporary 1960s architecture, a style chosen in **deliberate**（故意的）contrast to the medieval, classical, or "red brick" character of older British universities. The campus contains all of the main student **amenities**（便利设施）, all but four of the student halls of residence, and the Students' Union.

The Warwick Arts Centre is a multi-venue arts complex situated at the centre of Warwick's main campus. In 2003, Warwick acquired the former headquarters of National Grid plc, which it converted into an administration building renamed University House.

> **阅读辅助**
>
> 华威大学校址位于距英格兰中部城市考文垂市中心西南部约5.5公里处的市郊，学校既有现代化的教学大楼与基础设施，更有景色怡人的湖区和森林。华威学生会是英国最大的学生会之一，此外还有伦敦以外最大规模的艺术中心——华威艺术中心。

9 约克大学 University of York
——风景秀丽的大学

> 达人了解英美

◆ History

The first petition for the establishment of a university in York was presented to James I in 1617. In 1641, a second **petition**（请愿）was drawn up however was not delivered due to the English Civil War in 1642. A third petition was created in 1647 but was rejected by Parliament. In the 1820s, discussions began about the founding of a university in the North, however, this did not come to fruition due to the founding of Durham University in 1832. In 1903, F. J. Munby and the Yorkshire Philosophical Society, amongst others, proposed a "Victoria University of Yorkshire". In 1963, the University opened with 216 undergraduates, 14 postgraduates, and 28 academic and **administrative**（行政的）staff. The University started with six departments: Economics, Education, English, History, Mathematics, Politics.

> 阅读辅助
>
> 约克大学于1963年建校，60年代与华威大学和伦敦大学学院同为新生代大学，但其校史可以追溯到700年前。1617-1642年，人们就不断提出建校的倡议，但是都被各种因素推延了。随着杜兰大学的建立，建校的议案又被提出，最终在1903年终被两个人以约克郡维多利亚大学为名重新被提及。

✧ Summary

In 2012, York joined the Russell Group in recognition of the institution's world-leading research and outstanding teaching. In the 2014, Research Assessment Exercise, York was also named as the 14th best research institution in the United Kingdom. Along with the LSE, York is the only university in the UK to have **displaced**（取代）the University of Oxford to second place in league tables, second only to the University of Cambridge. The university also places among the top 20 in the country, top 50 universities in Europe, and ranked 120th in the world, according to the 2015 QS World University Rankings.

The university attracts a student body with a wide range of backgrounds, including a large number of international students, and a relatively high number of state school students in comparison to other well-ranked universities according to The Times Good University Guide.

> **阅读辅助**
> 约克大学为英国罗素大学集团联盟成员之一，约克大学的教学和科研享誉全世界，教学质量与剑桥大学并列为大学联盟的首位，约克大学在世界都名列前茅。

✧ Campus

At the time, the university consisted of three buildings, principally the historic King's Manor in the city centre and Heslington Hall, which has Tudor foundations and is in the village of Heslington on the edge of York. A year later, work began on purpose-built structures on the Heslington Campus, which now forms the main part of the university.

Situated to the south-east of the city of York, the university campus is **approximately**（大约）200 acres in size, incorporating the York Science Park and the National Science Learning Centre. Its wildlife, campus lakes and greenery are prominent, and the institution also occupies buildings in the city of York. In May, 2007, the university was granted permission to build an extension to its main campus, on arable land just east of the nearby village of Heslington. The second campus, known as Heslington East, opened in 2009 and now hosts three colleges and three departments as well as conference spaces, sports village and a business start-up "incubator".

> **阅读辅助**
>
> 建立之初,大学由3座大楼组成,主要是英王庄园,以及黑斯林顿大厅,一年后,开始拓展了黑斯林顿校区,进而形成今天大学的主要组成部分。高质量的研究型学校,有着雄厚的学术实力,约克大学吸引着全球各地的优秀人才来此进修。

10 兰卡斯特大学 Lancaster University
——最佳研究型的大学

达人了解英美

◆ **History**

After the Second World War, higher education became an important concern of government as it tried to cope with the demands of an expanding population and the advent of a new technological age. Between 1958 and 1961, seven new plate glass universities were announced including Lancaster.

The university was established by Royal Charter in 1964. The charter stipulated that HRH Princess Alexandra of Kent be the first Chancellor. On her departure, she gave approval for a Chancellor's Medal to be awarded for academic merit to the highest-performing undergraduates and postgraduates. Each year, presentations are made to up to five graduates of taught masters' courses, and up to six to the highest-performing undergraduates.

The university accepted its first students in October, 1964 and there were initially 13 professors, 32 additional members of teaching and research staff, 8 library staff and 14 administrators on academic grades. The motto, "patet omnibus veritas", was adopted.

阅读辅助

二战之后，随着人口的扩张和新技术不断涌现，高等教育的发展成为英国政府的重要关注点。兰卡斯特大学就是在这种背景下于1964年获皇家特许状并成立的。兰卡斯特大学是英国平板玻璃大学中的一所。1964年10月该校接收了第一批学生。大学最初有13名教授，32名教学和科研工作人员，8名图书馆工作人员和14名学术管理员。

✧ Campus

The university was initially based in St. Leonard's Gate in the city centre, until moving to a purpose-built 300 acres campus at Bailrigg in 1968.The campus buildings are located on a hilltop, the lower slopes of which are landscaped parkland which includes "Lake Carter" duck pond and the university playing fields. Lake Carter is named after Charles Carter, the first Vice Chancellor of the university, and it was built in the early 1900s. The campus buildings are arranged around a central walkway known as "The Spine", which is connected to a central plaza, named "Alexandra Square" in honors of its first chancellor, Princess Alexandra.

The Bailrigg campus hosts a range of shops and services. Services on campus include Bailrigg post office, Barclays Bank, Santander Bank, a health centre, a pharmacy and a **dental**（牙科的）practice.

> **阅读辅助**
>
> 大学最初建在圣伦纳德门的市中心，之后于1968年将校园迁到了贝尔里格，占地300英亩。主体建筑位于山顶，可以俯瞰山下景观，此外校园里还有"卡特湖"和运动场，还建了一个纪念总理的广场——亚历山德拉广场。校园的配套设施十分完善，提供各种服务。

11 伯明翰大学 University of Birmingham
——英国"红砖大学"之一

达人了解英美

◆ **History**

The University of Birmingham is the oldest red brick university in the United Kingdom. Located in the leafy suburb of Edgbaston just outside Birmingham City Centre, it received its royal charter in 1900 as a successor to Queen's College, Birmingham and Mason Science College. It was largely due to Chamberlain's tireless enthusiasm that the university was granted a Royal Charter by Queen Victoria on 24 March, 1900. The Calthorpe family offered twenty-five acres (10 hectares) of land on the Bournbrook side of their estate in July. The Court of Governors received the Birmingham University Act 1900, which put the Royal Charter into effect on 31 May. Birmingham was therefore **arguably**（可争辩地）the first so-called red brick university, although several other universities claim this title.

阅读辅助

伯明翰大学是一所于1900年创立在英格兰伯明翰市的著名"红砖大学"。该大学的历史可追溯至1825年的伯明翰药理与外科医学院以及后来的梅森理学院。约瑟夫·张伯伦被公认为伯明翰大学的创立者，主要是因为他孜孜矻矻的精神与努力最终促使维多利亚女王于1900年同意颁布皇家特许状，允许成立该大学。

✧ College

Although the earliest beginnings of the university were previously traced back to the Queen's College which is linked to William Sands Cox in his aim of creating a medical school along strictly Christian lines, unlike the London medical schools, further research has now **revealed**（透露）the roots of the Birmingham Medical School in the medical education seminars of Mr. John Tomlinson, the first surgeon to the Birmingham Workhouse Infirmary, and later to the General Hospital. In 1870, the medical school which grew out of the Birmingham Workhouse Infirmary was founded in 1828 but Cox began teaching in December, 1825. Queen Victoria granted her patronage to the Clinical Hospital in Birmingham and allowed it to be styled "The Queen's Hospital". It was the first provincial teaching hospital in England. In 1843, the medical college became known as Queen's College.

Sir Josiah Mason, the Birmingham industrialist and philanthropist, who made his fortune in making key rings, pens, pen nibs and **electroplating**（电镀）, drew up the Foundation Deed for Mason Science College. The college was founded in 1875. It was this institution that would eventually form the nucleus of the University of Birmingham.

> **阅读辅助**
>
> 女王学院由伯明翰首位外科医生在伯明翰济贫院医务所开始，1825年12月进行正式教学。至此，维多利亚女王同意捐献赞助临床教学医院，并特许其改名为女王医院，这也是英格兰第一间地方教学医院，而伯明翰医学院则正式更名为女王学院。约书亚·梅森爵士是伯明翰的实业家与慈善家，靠生产钥匙圈、笔、笔芯、电镀致富。1870年，他起草了梅森理学院的创立契约，并于1875年创立梅森理学院，该机构最后成为伯明翰大学的核心。

✧ Campus

The main campus of the university occupies a site some 3 miles southwest of Birmingham city centre, in Edgbaston. It is arranged around Joseph Chamberlain Memorial Clock Tower, a grand **campanile**（钟楼）which commemorates the university's first chancellor, Joseph Chamberlain. The university's Selly Oak campus is a short distance to the south of the main campus. It was the home of a **federation**（联邦）of nine colleges, known as Selly Oak Colleges, mainly focused on theology, social work, and teacher training. The Victorian neo-gothic Mason College building in Birmingham city centre housed Birmingham University's Faculties of Arts and Law for over 50 years after the founding of the university in 1900.

The University of Birmingham was ranked 11th in the UK and 64th in the world by QS World University Rankings. The student population includes around 19,000 undergraduate and 9,000 postgraduate students, which is the 11th largest in the UK. The annual income of the institution for 2010–2011 was £470.7 million, with an **expenditure**（经费）of £443.7 million.

The university is home to the Barber Institute of Fine Arts, housing works by Van Gogh, Picasso and Monet, the Lapworth Museum of Geology, the Cadbury Research Library, home to the Mingana Collections of Middle Eastern **manuscripts**（草稿）and the Chamberlain Collections, and the Joseph Chamberlain Memorial Clock Tower, which is a prominent landmark visible from many parts of the city.

（英）享誉世界的名牌大学 **Section 1-1**

> **阅读辅助**
>
> 　　主校区位于伯明翰市爱居巴斯顿区，距伯明翰市中心西南3公里，这块地1900年由卡索洛普勋爵赠给新成立的伯明翰大学。赛利橡树校区位于主校区南方大约2.5公里处，前身是九所学校联盟，主要致力于神学、社会工作以及师资培训。维多利亚时代哥德复兴式建筑的梅森学院校区坐落于伯明翰市中心。这里原本是艺术与法律学院的所在地，1959-1961年爱居巴斯顿校区各个新馆建成后，这两个学院都迁移到现在的主校区。该校在2014年QS世界大学排名中，位列全英第11名，伯明翰大学拥有巴柏美术馆，馆藏有文森·梵高、巴勃罗·毕加索、克洛德·莫内等大师的作品。

12 爱丁堡大学 University of Edinburgh
——英国第四大难以申请的大学

达人了解英美

◇ **History**

The University of Edinburgh, founded in 1582, is the sixth-oldest university in the English-speaking world and one of Scotland's ancient universities. The university is deeply **embedded**（嵌入）in the fabric of the city, with many of the buildings in the historic Old Town belonging to the university.

Founded by the Edinburgh Town Council, the university began life as a College of Law using part of a legacy left by Bishop Robert Reid of St. Magnus Cathedral, Orkney. Through efforts by the Town Council and Ministers of the City, the institution broadened in scope and became formally established as a university by a Royal Charter, granted by James VI in 1582 after the **petitioning**（请求）of the Council. This was an unusual move at the time, as most universities were established through Papal bulls. Known as the "Tounis College", it was renamed King James's College in 1617. Instruction began in 1583 under the charge of a young St. Andrews graduate, Robert Rollock.

It was the fourth Scottish university in a period when the much more populous and richer England had only two. By the 18th century, Edinburgh was a leading centre of the European Enlightenment.

> **阅读辅助**
>
> 爱丁堡大学是一所创建于1582年的公立研究型大学，它是苏格兰的第四所也是整个英语世界的第六所大学。爱丁堡大学的建立归功于圣马格努斯大教堂的主教罗伯特·里德，他在1558年去世后将其财产遗留下来作为大学最初的创建基金，并由爱丁堡镇议会付诸实施，最终在多方努力下于1582年由詹姆斯六世颁发皇家特许状，成立爱丁堡大学。

✧ Colleges

The College of Humanities and Social Science is the largest of the three Colleges in the University of Edinburgh. It has 11 schools, 16,300 students and 1,460 staff. An advantage of its size is the very wide range of subjects and research **specialism**（专长）. The College of Medicine and Veterinary Medicine has a long history as one of the best medical institutions in the world. All of the work was rated at international level and 40% at the highest, "world-leading" level. In the sixteenth century science was taught as "natural philosophy". The seventeenth century saw the institution of the University Chairs of Mathematics and Botany, followed the next century by Chairs of Natural History, Astronomy, Chemistry and Agriculture. During the eighteenth century, the University was a key contributor to the Scottish Enlightenment and it educated many of the most **notable**（显要的）scientists of the time.

The QS World University Rankings 2013 and 2014 ranked the University of Edinburgh 17th in the world. The University of Edinburgh is a member of the Russell Group of research-led British universities and, along with Oxford and Cambridge, one of several British universities to be a member of both the Coimbra Group and the LERU.

> **阅读辅助**
>
> 爱丁堡大学并非像牛津剑桥那样是学院制大学。爱丁堡大学的三大学院分别为：人文和社会科学学院、医学及兽医学院和科学及工程学院、人文和社会科学学院，是规模最大、研究领域最广的学院，它悠久历史、崇高声誉和光荣传统吸引了国内外众多优秀的学生和学者。在四百多年的历史中，它培养了许多影响世界文明发展进程的人物。爱大医学院始建于1726年，是世界著名的医学教育中心之一，在此求学或执教过的世界著名医学家为数众多。科学和工程学院在十八世纪的苏格兰启蒙运动、工业革命及日后的世界发展进程中都起到了不可或缺的引领作用，培养出了众多享誉全国乃至全球的顶尖科学家，包括6个诺贝尔物理学奖和2个诺贝尔化学奖的获得者。
>
> 爱丁堡大学排名为世界第17、全英第5。它是唯一的同时身为罗素大学集团联盟、科英布拉集团及欧洲研究型大学联盟成员的苏格兰大学。

◇ Influence

The university played an important role in leading Edinburgh to its reputation as a chief **intellectual**（智力的）centre during the Age of Enlightenment, and helped give the city the nickname of the Athens of the North. Alumni of the university include some of the major figures of modern history, including the physicist , naturalist, philosopher, mathematician, surgeon, first president of Tanzania , and a host of famous authors. Associated people include 20 Nobel Prize winners, 2 Turing Award winners, 1 Abel Prize winner, 1 Fields Medal winner, 1 Pulitzer Prize winner, 3 Prime Ministers of the United Kingdom, 2 currently-sitting UK Supreme Court Justices, and several Olympic gold medalists. It continues to have links to the British Royal Family, having had the Duke of Edinburgh as its Chancellor from 1953 to 2010 and Princess Anne since 2011.

阅读辅助

爱丁堡大学在欧洲启蒙时代就具有相当重要的领导地位,这使得爱丁堡市成为了当时的启蒙中心之一,享有"北方雅典"之盛名。爱丁堡大学著名的毕业生包括自然学家、物理学家、哲学家、数学家还有著名的作家。爱丁堡大学共有20名诺贝尔奖获奖人,一名阿贝尔奖获奖人。爱大与英国皇室保有良好关系,菲利普亲王在1953到2010年担任校监,2011年至今则由长公主安妮公主担任。

读书笔记

Section 1-2　（美）享誉世界的名牌大学

美国是当今最发达的资本主义国家之一，也是世界上最年轻的国家之一。只用几百年的时间就创造出如此辉煌成绩，从根本上来说要算精英般的教育了。"常春藤盟校"可能是美国最被外人熟知的一面，那是顶尖名校的代名词，也是美国最为光彩的明信片。

1 哈佛大学 *Harvard University*
——美国思想源泉的诞生地

达人了解英美

✧ History

Established originally by the Massachusetts legislature and soon thereafter named for John Harvard , Harvard is the United States' oldest institution of higher learning, and the Harvard Corporation is its first chartered corporation. Although never formally **affiliated**（附属的）with any denomination, the early college primarily trained Congregationalist and Unitarian clergy. Its curriculum and student body were gradually **secularized**（改作俗用）during the 18th century, and by the 19th century, Harvard had emerged as the central cultural establishment among Boston elites. Following the American Civil War, President Charles W. Eliot's long tenure transformed the college and affiliated professional schools into a modern research university. Harvard was a founding member of the Association of American Universities in 1900. James Bryant Conant led the university through the Great Depression and World War II and began to reform the curriculum and liberalize admissions after the war. The undergraduate college became **coeducational**（男女合校的）after its 1977 merger with Radcliffe College.

阅读辅助

哈佛于1636年由当地的殖民地立法机关立案成立，迄今为全美历史最悠久的高等学府，并拥有北美最古老的校董委员会。最初称之为"新学院"，为了感谢一名年轻的牧师约翰·哈佛所作出的捐赠而改名为"哈佛学院"。

✧ Campus

The University is organized into eleven separate academic units—ten faculties and the Radcliffe Institute for Advanced Study—with campuses throughout the Boston **metropolitan**（大主教区）area: its 209-acre main campus is centered on Harvard Yard in Cambridge, approximately 3 miles northwest of Boston; the business school and athletics facilities, including Harvard Stadium, are located across the Charles River in the Allston neighborhood of Boston and the medical, **dental**（牙科的）, and public health schools are in the Longwood Medical Area. Harvard has the largest financial endowment of any academic institution in the world, standing at $32.3 billion as of June, 2013.

Harvard is a large, highly residential research university. The nominal cost of attendance is high, but the university's large **endowment**（捐赠）allows it to offer generous financial aid packages. It operates several arts, cultural, and scientific museums, **alongside**（在……旁边）the Harvard Library, which is the world's largest academic and private library system, comprising 79 individual libraries with over 18 million volumes.

> 阅读辅助
>
> 哈佛大学目前共有十所学院及一所高等研究院。这些单位遍布邻近各区，学校的研究生课程较为多元化，而本科教育则主要集中在文理学范畴。

✧ Notable Alumni

It has many **eminent**（杰出的）alumni. Eight U.S. presidents and several foreign heads of state have been graduates. It is also the alma of 62 living billionaires and 335 Rhodes Scholars, both the most in the country. To date, some 150 Nobel laureates have been affiliated as students, faculty, or staff.

> **阅读辅助**
>
> 　　哈佛有众多知名人士。此校校友包括8名美国总统及多名多国领袖与政治要员。哈佛培养了62名富豪企业家及335位罗德学者,人数均为全美最多。

（美）享誉世界的名牌大学　　Section 1-2

2　耶鲁大学 Yale University
——未来领袖人物的实验室

达人了解英美

◇ History

Yale University is a private Ivy League research university in New Haven, Connecticut. Founded in 1701 as the "Collegiate School" by a group of Congregationalist ministers and chartered by the Colony of Connecticut, the university is the third-oldest institution of higher education in the United States. In 1718, the school was renamed "Yale College" in recognition of a gift from Elihu Yale, a governor of the British East India Company. Established to train Connecticut ministers in theology and **sacred**（神圣的）languages, by 1777 the school's curriculum began to incorporate humanities and sciences. During the 19th century, Yale gradually incorporated graduate and professional instruction, awarding the first Ph.D. in the United States in 1861 and organizing as a university in 1887.

阅读辅助

耶鲁始创于1701年，为全美第三古老的高等学府，最初称之为"大学学院"，旨在为殖民地培养新一代的神职人员及领导者。该学院后来为了感谢不列颠东印度公司总裁伊利胡·耶鲁的捐助而改名为"耶鲁学院"。

◇ Campus

Yale is organized into twelve constituent schools: the original

45

undergraduate college, the Graduate School of Arts & Sciences, and ten professional schools. While the university is governed by the Yale Corporation, each school's faculty oversees its curriculum and degree programs. Yale College undergraduates follow a liberal arts curriculum with departmental majors and are organized into a system of residential colleges. Almost all faculties teach undergraduate courses, more than 2,000 of which are offered annually.

In addition to a central campus in downtown New Haven, the university owns athletic facilities in Western New Haven, including the Yale Bowl, a campus in West Haven, Connecticut, and forest and nature preserves throughout New England. The University's assets include an **endowment**（捐款）valued at $23.9 billion as of September 27, 2014. The Yale University Library, serving all twelve schools, holds more than 15 million volumes and is the third-largest academic library in the United States. Students compete inter-collegiately as the Yale Bulldogs in the NCAA Division I Ivy League.

> **阅读辅助**
>
> 耶鲁大学现有15个学术学院及12所住宿院，提供不同的本科及研究生课程和配套设施。该校很重视本科教育，目前大部分的学士课程均由教授亲自任教。耶鲁尤以法学见长，其法学院长期以来也是全美最难入读的。

◇ Notable Alumni

Yale has graduated many notable alumni, including five U.S. Presidents, 19 U.S. Supreme Court Justices, 13 living billionaires, and many foreign heads of state. In addition, Yale has graduated hundreds of members of Congress and many high-level U.S. diplomats, including former U.S. Secretary of State Hillary Clinton and current Secretary of State John

Kerry. Fifty-two Nobel laureates have been affiliated with the university as students, faculty, or staff, and 230 Rhodes Scholars graduated from the university.

> **阅读辅助**
> 耶鲁已经培养了5名美国总统及19名美国联邦最高法院大法官，另有52名诺贝尔奖得主现在或曾经在耶鲁学习或工作。

3 普林斯顿大学 Princeton University
——充满朝气的圣学天堂

达人了解英美

◇ **History**

Princeton University is a private Ivy League research university in Princeton, New Jersey. Founded in 1746 in Elizabeth as the College of New Jersey, Princeton was the fourth chartered institution of higher education in the American colonies and thus one of the nine Colonial Colleges established before the American Revolution. The institution moved to Newark in 1747, then to the current site nine years later, where it was **renamed**（改名）Princeton University in 1896. The present-day College of New Jersey in nearby Ewing Township, New Jersey, is an unrelated institution. Princeton had close ties to the Presbyterian Church, but has never been affiliated with any denomination and today **imposes**（征收）no religious requirements on its students.

阅读辅助

普林斯顿历史悠久。它成立于1746年，是九所在美国革命前成立的殖民地学院之一，同时也是美国第四古老的高等教育机构。它在1747年迁移至纽瓦克，最终在1756年搬到了现在的普林斯顿，并于1896年正式改名为"普林斯顿大学"。

◇ **Campus**

Princeton provides undergraduate and graduate instruction in the humanities, social sciences, natural sciences, and engineering. It offers professional degrees through the Woodrow Wilson School of Public and International Affairs, the School of Engineering and Applied Science, the School of Architecture and the Bendheim Center for Finance. The University has ties with the Institute for Advanced Study, Princeton Theological Seminary, and the Westminster Choir College of Rider University.

The main campus sits on about 500 acres in Princeton. In 2011, the main campus was named by Travel Leisure as one of the most beautiful in the United States. The James Forrestal Campus is split between nearby Plainsboro and South Brunswick. The University also owns some property in West Windsor Township. The campuses are situated about one hour from both New York City and Philadelphia.

A group of 20th-century **sculptures**（雕塑）scattered throughout the campus forms the Putnam Collection of Sculpture. It includes works by Alexander Calder, Jacob Epstein, Henry Moore, Isamu Noguchi, and Pablo Picasso. Richard Serra's The Hedgehog and The Fox is located between Peyton and Fine halls next to Princeton Stadium and the Lewis Library.

> 阅读辅助
>
> 普林斯顿提供各种有关人文、自然科学、社会科学及工程学的本科及研究生课程，该校并没有设立医学院、法学院、神学院及商学院。

◇ Notable Alumni

By endowment per student, Princeton is the wealthiest school in the United States. Princeton has been associated with 37 Nobel laureates, 17 National Medal of Science winners, two Abel Prize winners, eight Fields Medalists, nine Turing Award laureates, three National Humanities Medal recipients and 204 Rhodes Scholars.

> **阅读辅助**
>
> 　　至今，已经有37名诺贝尔得奖者、17名美国国家科学奖章得主，8名菲尔兹奖得主，9名图灵奖得主及3名美国国家人文奖章夺得人曾经或现在为普林斯顿大学的毕业生或教职员。

4　哥伦比亚大学 Columbia University
——匠心独运的帝王学院

达人了解英美

◆ **History**

The university was founded in 1754 as King's College by a royal charter of George II of Great Britain. After the American Revolutionary War, King's College briefly became a state entity, and was renamed Columbia College in 1784. The university now operates under a 1787 charter that places the institution under a private board of **trustees**（受托者）, and in 1896 it was further renamed Columbia University. That same year, the university's campus was moved from Madison Avenue to its current location in Morningside Heights, where it occupies more than six city blocks, or 32 acres.

It is the oldest institution of higher learning in the State of New York, the fifth oldest in the United States, and one of the country's nine Colonial Colleges founded before the American Revolution. Today the university operates Columbia Global Centers overseas in Amman, Beijing, Istanbul, Paris, Mumbai, Rio de Janeiro, Santiago and Nairobi.

阅读辅助

　　哥伦比亚大学最初于1754年以国王学院之名，根据英王乔治二世颁布的《王室特许状》成立。美国独立战争之后，国王学院短暂成为了纽约州下辖的一个实体，并在1784年被重命名为哥伦比亚学院。

✧ Campus

The university **encompasses**（包含）twenty schools and is affiliated with numerous institutions, including Teachers College, Barnard College, and the Union Theological Seminary, with joint undergraduate programs available through the Jewish Theological Seminary of America as well as the Juilliard School.

The majority of Columbia's graduate and undergraduate studies are conducted in Morningside Heights on Seth Low's late-19th century vision of a university campus where all disciplines could be taught in one location. The campus was designed along Beaux-Arts principles by architects McKim, Mead and White. Columbia's main campus occupies more than six city blocks, or 32 acres, in Morningside Heights, New York City, a neighborhood that contains a number of academic institutions. The university owns over 7,800 apartments in Morningside Heights, housing faculty, graduate students and staff. Almost two dozen undergraduate **dormitories**（宿舍）are located on campus or in Morningside Heights. Columbia University has an **extensive**（大量的）underground tunnel system more than a century old, with the oldest portions predating the present campus.

阅读辅助

校园占地六个街区，共32英亩。学校本部拥有十七个学院，并且下辖许多教育机构，包括教师学院、巴纳德学院、协和神学院以及美洲犹太教神学院。

✧ Notable Alumni

Columbia annually administers the Pulitzer Prize. 101 Nobel Prize laureates have been affiliated with the university as students, faculty, or staff. Columbia is one of the fourteen founding members of the Association of American Universities, and was the first school in the United States to grant the M.D. degree. Notable alumni and former students of the university and its predecessor, King's College, include five Founding Fathers of the United States, nine Justices of the United States Supreme Court, 43 Nobel Prize laureates, 20 living billionaires, 29 Academy Award winners and 29 heads of state, including three United States Presidents.

> **阅读辅助**
>
> 哥伦比亚大学是每年一度的普利策奖的颁发机构,一百零一位学校现在或曾经的学生或者教职工是诺贝尔奖获得者。哥伦比亚大学是美国大学协会的十四个创始会员之一,并且是美国第一个授予药学博士的学校。

5 达特茅斯学院 Dartmouth College
——全美无线化做得最好的高校

达人了解英美

◆ History

Dartmouth was founded by Eleazar Wheelock, a Puritan minister from Columbia, Connecticut, who had previously sought to establish a school to train Native Americans as missionaries. Wheelock's **ostensible**（假装的）inspiration for such an establishment resulted from his relationship with Mohegan Indian Samson Occom. Wheelock founded Moor's Indian Charity School in 1755. The Charity School proved somewhat successful, but additional funding was necessary to continue school's operations, and Wheelock sought the help of friends to raise money. With these funds, they established a trust to help Wheelock. The head of the trust was a Methodist named William Legge, 2nd Earl of Dartmouth. Although the fund provided Wheelock ample financial support for the Charity School, Wheelock had trouble recruiting Indians to the institution, primarily because its location was far from tribal territories. In seeking to expand the school into a college, Wheelock relocated it to Hanover, in the Province of New Hampshire Dartmouth emerged **onto**（在……之上）the national academic stage at the turn of the 20th century. Prior to this period, the college had **clung**（贴近）to traditional methods of instruction and was relatively poorly funded.

> **阅读辅助**
>
> 依利扎·维洛克牧师当初成立这个学校的目的是为了培养当地印第安部落的年轻人和年轻白人。1819年，新罕布什尔州的行政官员设立了对学院单独管理的机构，并且要把它的校名改为达特茅斯大学，但学院的董事在弗兰西斯·布朗院长的领导下，坚持了原来宪章的有效性。

✧ Campus

It consists of a liberal arts college, the Geisel School of Medicine, the Thayer School of Engineering and the Tuck School of Business, as well as 19 graduate programs in the arts and sciences. Incorporated as the "Trustees of Dartmouth College", it is one of the nine Colonial Colleges founded before the American Revolution. With an undergraduate enrollment of 4,276 and a total student enrollment of 6,342, Dartmouth is the smallest university in the Ivy League.

Dartmouth's somewhat-isolated **rural**（田园的）269-acre campus is in the Upper Valley region of New Hampshire. Participation in athletics and the school's Greek system is strong. Dartmouth's 34 varsity sports teams compete in the Ivy League conference of the NCAA Division I. Students are well known for preserving a variety of strong campus traditions.

A notable feature of the Dartmouth campus is its many trees, particularly American elms. Unfortunately, like American **elms**（榆树）throughout the United States, the elm trees at Dartmouth have been affected by Dutch elm disease and damaged by storms and other environmental conditions. However, because the college is committed to maintaining the campus **aesthetic**（审美的）, the trees are well cared-for, and new plantings replace diseased or damaged trees that must be removed. Dartmouth's graduate community newsletter reported in October, 2014 that there are still approximately 200 elm trees on campus, making it the most common species at Dartmouth.

> 阅读辅助
>
> 达特茅斯学院除拥有文学艺术类的本科课程外，还拥有医学院，工程学院，商学院以及18个自然科学和人文社会科学方面的研究生项目。基于此一现状，按照美国的通行标准，达特茅斯学院被称之为"大学"似乎更为合适。

◇ Notable Alumni

Dartmouth's alumni are known for their **devotion**（献身）to the college. Most start by giving to the Senior Class Gift. According to a 2008 article in The Wall Street Journal, Dartmouth graduates also earn higher median salaries at least 10 years after graduation than alumni of any other American university **surveyed**（调查）. By 2008, Dartmouth had graduated 238 classes of students and has over 60,000 living alumni in a variety of fields.

> 阅读辅助
>
> 该学院的著名毕业生有美国政治家，企业家和文学家，为世界各行各业培养大量的优秀人才。

6 康奈尔大学 Cornell University
——真正意义的全民大学

达人了解英美

◇ **History**

Cornell University was founded on April 27, 1865, as the result of a New York State (NYS) Senate bill that named the university as the state's land-grant institution. Senator Ezra Cornell offered his farm in Ithaca, New York as a site and $500,000 of his personal fortune as an initial endowment. Fellow senator and experienced educator Andrew Dickson White agreed to be the first president. During the next three years, White oversaw the construction of the initial two buildings and traveled around the globe to attract students and faculty. The university was **inaugurated**（开幕）on October 7, 1868, and 412 men were enrolled the next day. Cornell continued to be a technological innovator applying its research to its own campus as well as to **outreach**（拓广）efforts. Cornell has had active alumni since its earliest classes and was one of the first universities to include alumni-elected representatives on its Board of Trustees.

Cornell expanded significantly, particularly since World War II, with its student population in Ithaca growing to its current count of about 20,000 students. The faculty also expanded, and by the century's end, the university had about 3,000 faculty members. The school also increased its breadth of course offerings.

> **阅读辅助**
>
> 康奈尔大学由埃兹拉·康奈尔和安德鲁·迪克森·怀特于1865年建立，为八个常春藤盟校中唯一一所在美国独立战争后创办的成员。康奈尔大学男女同校，不论信仰和种族皆可入学。自学校成立伊始，其创始人就期待将康大办成一所全科型的新式大学，教授内容从文学名著至自然科学，自理论研究扩及实际应用，无所不包。

✧ Campus

The university is broadly organized into seven undergraduate colleges and seven graduate divisions at its main Ithaca campus, with each college and division defining its own admission standards and academic programs in near autonomy. The university also administers two satellite medical campuses, one in New York City and one in Education City, Qatar. Cornell is one of three private land-grant universities. Of its seven undergraduate colleges, three are state-supported **statutory**（法定的）or contract colleges, including its agricultural and veterinary colleges. As a land-grant college, it operates a cooperative extension outreach program in every county of New York and receives annual funding from the State of New York for certain educational missions. The Cornell University Ithaca Campus comprises 745 acres, but in actuality, is much larger due to the Cornell Plantations (more than 4,300 acres) as well as the numerous university owned lands in New York.

> **阅读辅助**
>
> 康奈尔大学主校区位于纽约州伊萨卡。校园内约260座主要建筑大致分为三个院子：人文、工程、农业，另外还有一个科学实验室建筑群和体育建筑群。康奈尔大学第一幢建筑物是建于1868年的莫里尔楼。

✧ Notable Alumni

Since its founding, Cornell has been a co-educational, non-sectarian institution where admission is offered **irrespective**（不考虑的）of religion or race. Cornell counts more than 245,000 living alumni, 34 Marshall Scholars, 29 Rhodes Scholars and 44 Nobel laureates as affiliated with the university. The student body consists of nearly 14,000 undergraduate and 7,000 graduate students from all 50 American states and 122 countries.

> **阅读辅助**
>
> 目前康奈尔的校友逾240万名，先后有超过44位师生获颁诺贝尔奖。科学研究是康奈尔的兴学方针，在2004年7月至2005年6月之间的财政年度中，共有5.613亿美元被应用于各项领域的研究。

7 麻省理工学院 MIT
——全球高科技人才的摇篮

达人了解英美

◆ **History**

Founded in 1861 in response to the increasing industrialization of the United States, MIT adopted a **European polytechnic**（理工专科学校）university model and stressed laboratory instruction in applied science and engineering. In 1859, a proposal was submitted to the Massachusetts General Court to use newly filled lands in Back Bay, Boston for a "Conservatory of Art and Science", but the proposal failed. A proposal by William Barton Rogers for a charter for the incorporation of the Massachusetts Institute of Technology was signed by the governor of Massachusetts on April 10, 1861. Two days after the charter was issued, the first battle of the Civil War broke out. After a long delay through the war years, MIT's first classes were held in the Mercantile Building in Boston in 1865. The new institute had a mission that matched the **intent**（打算）of the 1862 Morrill Land-Grant Colleges Act to fund institutions "to promote the liberal and practical education of the industrial classes", and was a land-grant school. In 1866, the proceeds from land sales went toward new buildings in the Back Bay.

In 1916, MIT moved to a **spacious**（广阔的）new campus largely consisting of filled land on a mile-long tract along the Cambridge side of the Charles River. In January 1920, the donor was revealed to be the industrialist George Eastman of Rochester, New York, who had invented methods of film production and processing, and founded Eastman Kodak.

Between 1912 and 1920, Eastman **donated**（捐献）$20 million in cash and Kodak stock to MIT.

> **阅读辅助**
>
> 美国麻省理工学院于1861年由一位著名的自然科学家威廉·巴顿·罗杰斯创立。他希望能够创建一个自由的学院来适应快速发展的美国。由于南北战争爆发，直到1865年麻省理工学院才迎来了第一批学生。在大萧条时期，麻省理工学院曾一度被认为会同哈佛大学合并，但在该校学生的抗议之下，这一计划被迫取消了。1916年，麻省理工学院从波士顿迁往剑桥。

✧ Campus

MIT, with five schools and one college which contain a total of 32 departments, is traditionally known for research and education in the physical sciences and engineering, and more recently in biology, economics, linguistics, and management as well. The "Engineers" **sponsor**（赞助商）31 sports, most teams of which compete in the NCAA Division III's New England Women's and Men's Athletic Conference; the Division I rowing programs compete as part of the EARC and EAWRC.

Researchers worked on computers, radar, and inertial guidance during World War II and the Cold War. Post-war defense research contributed to the rapid expansion of the faculty and campus under James Killian. The current 168-acre campus opened in 1916 and extends over 1 mile along the northern bank of the Charles River basin.

> **阅读辅助**
>
> 麻省理工学院共有6所学院，从原本只有物理科学及工程学发展到生物科学以至于经济金融、管理学及语言学等领域。麻省理工学院的学者在二次世界大战及冷战期间致力于研究旋风计算机、雷达及惯性导航系统，为美国国家的高科技发展贡献良多。

◇ Notable Alumni

MIT is often cited as among the world's top universities. As of 2014, 81 Nobel laureates, 52 National Medal of Science recipients, 45 Rhodes Scholars, 38 MacArthur Fellows, and 2 Fields Medalists have been affiliated with MIT. MIT has a strong entrepreneurial culture and the **aggregated**（合计的）revenues of companies founded by MIT alumni would rank as the eleventh-largest economy in the world.

> **阅读辅助**
>
> 有81名诺贝尔得奖者、52名美国国家科学奖章获奖人、45名罗德学者及38位麦克阿瑟奖得主现在或曾经在麻省理工学院学习或工作。

8 斯坦福大学 Stanford University
——象征21世纪科技精神的名校

达人了解英美

◆ **History**

Stanford was founded in 1885 by Leland Stanford, former governor of and U.S. senator from California and leading railroad tycoon, and his wife, Jane Lathrop Stanford, in memory of their only child, Leland Stanford, Jr., who had died of typhoid fever at age 15 the previous year. Stanford was opened on October 1, 1891 as a coeducational and non-denominational institution. Tuition was free until 1920. The university struggled financially after Leland Stanford's 1893 death and after much of the campus was damaged by the 1906 San Francisco earthquake. Following World War II, Provost Frederick Terman supported faculty and graduates' entrepreneurialism to build **self-sufficient**（自给自足的）local industry in what would later be known as Silicon Valley. By 1970, Stanford was home to a linear accelerator, and was one of the original four ARPANET nodes.

阅读辅助

大学于1885年由时任加州参议员及州长的铁路大亨利兰·斯坦福和他的妻子简·莱思罗普·斯坦福创办。这是为了纪念他们因伤寒而于16岁生日前夕去世的儿子。该校为男女合校及宗教自由的学校，在1920年前所有学费全免。二次世界大战后，时任学校教务长的弗雷德里克·特曼全力支持校友与教职员的企业精神，希望能建立自给自足的本地工业，这也是现今硅谷的源流。

✧ Campus

Stanford is located in northern Silicon Valley near Palo Alto, California. The University's academic departments are organized into seven schools, with several other holdings, such as laboratories and nature reserves, located outside the main campus. Its 8,180-acre campus is one of the largest in the United States. The University is also one of the top fund raising institutions in the country, becoming the first school to raise more than a billion dollars in a year.

Contemporary campus landmarks include the Main Quad and Memorial Church, the Cantor Center for Visual Arts and art gallery, the Stanford Mausoleum and the Angel of Grief, Hoover Tower, the Rodin sculpture garden, the Papua New Guinea Sculpture Garden, the Arizona Cactus Garden, the Stanford University Arboretum, Green Library and the Dish. Frank Lloyd Wright's 1937 Hanna–Honeycomb House and the 1919 Lou Henry Hoover House are both listed on the National Historic Register.

> **阅读辅助**
>
> 学校的校园位于硅谷的西北方，邻近帕罗奥图。校方的各个学术部门被归入七所学术学院内，而包括生物保育区及加速实验室在内的其他资产则设于主校区之外。此校为最富有的教育机构之一，并为第一所在一年内获得超过十亿美元捐款升幅的大学。

✧ Notable Alumni

Stanford faculty and alumni have founded many companies including Google, Hewlett-Packard, Nike, Sun Microsystems, and Yahoo!, and companies founded by Stanford alumni generate more than $2.7 trillion in annual revenue, **equivalent**（相当于）to the 10th-largest economy in the world. Fifty-nine Nobel laureates have been affiliated with the university, and it is the alma mater of 30 living billionaires and 17 astronauts. Stanford has produced a total of 18 Turing Award laureates, the highest in the world for any one institution. It is also one of the leading producers of members of the United States Congress.

> **阅读辅助**
>
> 斯坦福培养了不少著名人士。其校友涵盖30名富豪企业家及17名太空员,亦为培养最多美国国会成员的院校之一。斯坦福校友创办了众多著名的公司机构。

9 布朗大学 Brown University
——美国学术界精英的伊甸园

达人了解英美

◇ History

Brown was founded in 1764—the third college in New England and the seventh in Colonial America. Brown was the first Ivy League school to accept students from all religious affiliations, a **testament**（遗嘱）to the spirit of openness that still typifies Brown today. Originally located in Warren, Rhode Island, and called the College of Rhode Island, Brown moved to its current spot on College Hill overlooking Providencein 1770 and was renamed in 1804 in recognition of a $5,000 gift from Nicholas Brown, a prominent Providence businessman and alumnus, Class of 1786.

Women were first admitted to Brown in 1891. The Women's College was later renamed Pembroke College in Brown University before merging with Brown College, the men's undergraduate school, in 1971. The northern section of campus where the women's school was situated is known today as the Pembroke Campus. Undergraduate education changed **dramatically**（戏剧性地）in 1970 with the introduction of what became known as the Brown Curriculum.

阅读辅助

悠久历史展示布朗大学这一高等学府的神圣气势。如同殖民地时期建立的大多数大学一样，布朗大学建立之初也蒙上了一层较浓的宗教色彩，以训练和培养神职人员为主要任务，兼管培养人文、语言和逻辑学科方面的人才。但由于布朗大学地处宗教思想比较开朗

> 的地方，所以，布朗大学相对而言没有完全受教会控制，而是较早地给世俗力量以相当大的发言权。因此，布朗大学先于其他许多大学开设了自然科学方面的课程。

✧ Campus

Brown is the largest institutional landowner in Providence, with **properties**（属性）on College Hill and in the Jewelry District. The College Hill campus was built contemporarily with the eighteenth- and nineteenth-century precincts that surround it, so that University buildings blend with the architectural fabric of the city. The only indicator of "campus" is a brick and wrought-iron fence on Prospect, George, and Waterman streets, enclosing the College Green and Front Green. The character of Brown's urban campus is, then, European organic rather than American landscaped.

Brown's main campus is located in the College Hill Historic District in the city of Providence, the third largest city inNew England. The University's neighborhood is a federally listed architectural district with a **dense**（密集的）concentration of ancient buildings. On the western edge of the campus, Benefit Street contains "one of the finest cohesive collections of restored seventeenth- and eighteenth-century architecture in the United States".

> **阅读辅助**
>
> 该校最大的特征之一就是小而精，布朗大学堪称小型的研究型大学，布朗大学不论是在学术上还是在非学术方面，特别强调和崇尚自由。其本科生课程也因此备受美国高等教育界人士的推崇。在这里，学生都被当作成人平等对待，他们可以自主选择自己感兴趣的专业和课程。

✧ **Notable Alumni**

Brown University is home to many **prominent**（显著的）alumni, known as Brunonians, including current president of the World Bank Jim Yong Kim and Chair of the Federal Reserve Janet Yellen. While considered a small research university, Brown has been affiliated with 7 Nobel laureates as students, faculty, or staff. It has been associated with 54 Rhodes Scholars, five National Humanities Medalists, 10 National Medal of Science laureates, and is a leading producer of Fulbright Scholarsand **startup**（启动）companies.

> 阅读辅助
>
> 布朗大学好像与总统的儿女特别有缘，最受他们欢迎，美联储主席珍妮特·耶伦于1967年以优等生成绩获布朗大学经济学士学位。

Section 2-1 （英）叹为观止的地标建筑

古老的一切，处处积淀着文化底蕴，凝聚着古老风俗的气息，在这片土地上，让人回想的东西太多了……英国和欧洲其他国家一样，以拥有大量具有历史文化遗产价值的地标性建筑而自豪。那么这些建筑里哪一个价值最高呢？

1 伊丽莎白塔 Elizabeth tower
——英国古典文化的代表

达人了解英美

◇ Elizabeth Tower

The tower is officially known as the Elizabeth Tower, renamed as such to celebrate the Diamond Jubilee of Elizabeth II, named in tribute to Queen Elizabeth II in her Diamond Jubilee year, more popularly known as Big Ben,was raised as a part of Charles Barry's design for a new palace, after the old Palace of Westminster was largely destroyed by fire on the night of 16 October 1834. The new Parliament（议会）was built in a Neo-gothic style. Although Barry was the chief architect（建筑师）of the Palace, he turned to Augustus Pugin for the design of the clock tower, which resembles（类似于）earlier Pugin designs, including one for Scarisbrick Hall.

阅读辅助

2009年6月1日，钟楼举行了庆祝启用150周年的活动。2012年6月26日，英国政府宣布为庆祝伊丽莎白二世登基60周年，将大本钟所在的钟楼正式改名为伊丽莎白塔。

◇ Structure

The tower is designed in Pugin's celebrated Gothic Revivalstyle, and is 315 feet high. The bottom 200 feet of the tower's structure consists of **brickwork**（砖砌的建筑物）with sand colored Anston limestone cladding. The remainder of the tower's height is a framed spire of cast iron. The tower is founded on a 50 feet square raft, made of 10 feet thick **concrete**（用混凝土修筑）, at a depth of 13 feet below ground level. The four clock dials are 180 feet above ground. The interior volume of the tower is 164,200 cubic feet.

> **阅读辅助**
>
> 钟楼坐落在英国伦敦泰晤士河畔，是伦敦的标志之一。于1858年4月10日建成，高315英尺，是世界第三高的钟楼。外墙上有四面巨大的钟表朝向东南西北四个方向，分针有14英尺长，国会开会期间，钟面会发出光芒。伊丽莎白塔直径7米，重13.5吨，是英国最大的钟，每15分钟敲响一次。

◆ Nickname

The origin of the nickname Big Ben is the subject of some debate. The nickname was applied first to the Great Bell; it may have been named after Sir Benjamin Hall, who oversaw the **installation**（安装）of the Great Bell, or after boxing's English Heavyweight Champion Benjamin Caunt. Big Ben was often used, by extension, to refer to the clock, the tower and the bell **collectively**（共同地）, although the nickname is not universally accepted as referring to the clock and tower. Some authors of works about the tower, clock and bell **sidestep**（台阶）the issue by using the words Big Ben first in the title, then going on to **clarify**（阐明）that the subject of the book is the clock and tower as well as the bell.

> **阅读辅助**
>
> 伊丽莎白塔原名大本钟。大本钟的命名来源众说纷纭，有一种说法称大本钟的名字是来自于本杰明·豪尔爵士，他负责修建了威斯敏斯特宫。而现在的伊丽莎白塔则是钟和塔的一种昵称。

✧ **Significance**

The clock has become a symbol of the United Kingdom, particularly in the visual media. When a television or film-maker wishes to indicate a **generic**（一般的）location in the country, a popular way to do so is to show an image of the tower, often with a red double-decker bus orblack cab in the **foreground**（前景）. The sound of the clock **chiming**（打钟报时）has also been used this way in audio media, but as the Westminster Quarters are heard from other clocks and other devices, the unique nature of this sound has been considerably **diluted**（无力的）. Big Ben is a focus of New Year celebrations in the United Kingdom, with radio and TV stations tuning to its chimes to welcome the start of the New Year.

阅读辅助

在英国，伊丽莎白塔是人们庆祝新年的重要地方，收音机和电视都会播出它的钟声来迎接新一年的开始。而伊丽莎白塔的钟声今天仍会用于所有独立电视新闻频道新闻快报的新闻预告，及威斯敏斯特宫大本钟的钟面图。

2 伦敦眼 London Eye
——飞翔在伦敦上空的"胶囊"

达人了解英美

◆ **Structure**

The entire structure is 135 meters tall and the wheel has a diameter of 120 meters. When **erected**(竖立)in 1999 it was the world's tallest Ferris wheel. Its height was **surpassed**(超过)by the 160 m Star of Nanchangin 2006, the 165 m Singapore Flyer in 2008, and the 167.6 m High Roller in 2014. Supported by an A-frame on one side only, unlike the taller Nanchang and Singapore wheels, the Eye is described by its operators as "the world's tallest **cantilevered**(悬臂式的)observation wheel". It is currently Europe's tallest Ferris wheel, and offered the highest public viewing point in London until it was superseded by the 245-metre observation deck on the 72nd floor of The Shard, which opened to the public on 1 February 2013.It is the most popular paid tourist attraction in the United Kingdom with over 3.5 million visitors annually,and has made many **appearances**(外观)in popular culture.

阅读辅助

它于1999年年底开启,总高度135米,屹立于伦敦泰晤士河南畔的兰贝斯区,面向坐拥国会大楼与伊丽莎白塔的西敏市。伦敦眼被视为"世界上最高的悬臂式观光轮"。是目前欧洲最高的摩天轮,可以提供伦敦的最佳观看位置,直到245米的碎片大厦取而代之。但是它仍是英国最受欢迎的旅游观光景点,而且还代表着伦敦的流行文化。

✧ **Passenger capsules**

The wheel's 32 sealed and air-conditioned **ovoidal**（椭圆形）passenger capsules, designed and supplied by Poma, are attached to the external circumference of the wheel and **rotated**（旋转的）by electric motors. Each of the 10-tonne **capsules**（太空舱）represents one of the London Boroughs, and holds up to 25 people, who are free to walk around inside the capsule, though seating is provided. It does not usually stop to take on passengers; the rotation rate is slow enough to allow passengers to walk on and off the moving capsules at ground level. It is, however, stopped to allow disabled or elderly passengers time to embark and **disembark**（使……上岸）safely.

> **阅读辅助**
>
> 伦敦眼共有32个乘坐舱，全部设有空调并不能打开窗。每个乘坐舱可载客约25名，回转速度约为每秒0.26米，即一圈需时30分钟。缓慢的回转速度，让摩天轮不停驶也能让乘客自由上下乘坐舱，不过老人、残疾人士等如有需要也可作暂时停止旋转。

3 白金汉宫 *Buckingham Palace*
——全球最昂贵的豪宅

达人了解英美

✧ History

Located in the City of Westminster, the palace is often at the centre of state occasions and royal hospitality. It has been a focus for the British people at times of national **rejoicing**（庆祝）.

Originally known as Buckingham House, the building which forms the core of today's palace was a large townhouse built for the Duke of Buckingham in 1703 on a site which had been in private ownership for at least 150 years. It was subsequently **acquired**（取得）by King George III in 1761 as a private residence for Queen Charlotte and was known as "The Queen's House". During the 19th century it was enlarged, principally by **architects**（建筑师）John Nash and Edward Blore, who formed three wings around a central courtyard. Buckingham Palace finally became the official royal palace of the British monarch on the **accession**（就职）of Queen Victoria in 1837. The last major structural additions were made in the late 19th and early 20th centuries, including the East front, which contains the well-known balcony on which the royal family traditionally **congregates**（聚集）to greet crowds outside. However, the palace chapel was destroyed by a German bomb during World War II; the Queen's was built on the site and opened to the public in 1962 to exhibit works of art from the Royal Collection.

The original early 19th-century interior designs, many of which still survive, included **widespread**（广泛的）use of brightly colored scagliola and blue and pink lapis, on the advice of Sir Charles Long. King Edward VII oversaw a partial **redecoration**（再装饰）in a Belle Époque cream and gold color scheme. Many smaller reception rooms are furnished in the Chinese **regency**（摄政）style with furniture and fittings brought from the Royal Pavilion at Brighton and from Carlton House. The Buckingham Palace Garden is the largest private garden in London.

> **阅读辅助**
>
> 1703年至1705年，白金汉和诺曼比公爵约翰·谢菲尔德在此兴建了一处大型镇厅建筑"白金汉屋"，成为了今天的主体建筑，1761年，乔治三世获得该府邸，并作为一处私人寝宫。此后宫殿的扩建工程持续超过了75年，主要由建筑师约翰·纳西和爱德华·布罗尔主持，为中央庭院构筑了三侧建筑。1837年，维多利亚女王登基后，白金汉宫成为英王正式宫寝。19世纪末20世纪初，宫殿公共立面修建，形成延续至今天白金汉宫形象。二战期间，宫殿礼拜堂遭一枚德国炸弹袭击而毁；在其址上建立的女王画廊于1962年向公众开放，展示皇家收藏品。现在的白金汉宫对外开放参观，每天清晨都会进行著名的禁卫军交接典礼，成为英国王室文化的一大景观。

◆ Interior

The Palace measures 108 meters by 120 meters, is 24 meters high and contains over 77,000 m^2 of floor space. The principal rooms of the palace are contained on the piano nobile behind the west-facing garden façade at the rear of the palace. The centre of this **ornate**（华丽的）suite of state rooms is the Music Room, its large bow the **dominant**（占优势的）feature of the façade. Flanking the Music Room are the Blue and the White Drawing Rooms. At the centre of the suite, serving as a corridor to link the state rooms, is the Picture Gallery, which is top-lit and 55 yards long. The Gallery is hung with numerous works including some by Rembrandt, van

Dyck, Rubens and Vermeer; other rooms leading from the Picture Gallery are the Throne Room and the Green Drawing Room. The Green Drawing Room serves as a huge **anteroom**（前厅）to the Throne Room, and is part of the ceremonial route to the throne from the Guard Room at the top of the Grand Staircase. The Guard Room contains white marble statues of Queen Victoria and Prince Albert, in Roman **costume**（装束）, set in a **tribune**（护民官）lined with tapestries. These very formal rooms are used only for ceremonial and official entertaining, but are open to the public every summer.

> **阅读辅助**
>
> 王宫西侧为宫内正房，其中最大的是皇室舞厅，建于1850年，专为维多利亚女王修建。厅内悬挂有巨型水晶吊灯。蓝色客厅被视为宫内最雅致的房间，摆有为拿破仑一世制作的指挥桌。拿氏失败后，法国路易十八将桌子赠送给当时英摄政王乔治四世。白色客厅用白、金两色装饰而成，室内有精致的家具和豪华的地毯，大多是英、法工匠的艺术品。御座室内挂有水晶吊灯，四周墙壁顶端绘有15世纪玫瑰战争的情景。正中的御座是当今女王1953年加冕时和王夫爱丁堡公爵使用的，室内还保存了维多利亚女王的加冕御座和乔治四世加冕时用的四张大座椅。

◆ Garden & the Royal Mews

At the rear of the palace is the large and park-like garden, which together with its lake is the largest private garden in London. Here the Queen hosts her annual garden parties each summer, and also holds large functions to celebrate royal milestones, such as jubilees. It covers 40 acres, and includes a helicopter landing area, a lake, and a tennis court.

Adjacent to the palace is the Royal Mews, also designed by Nash, where the royal carriages, including the Gold State Coach, are housed. This rococo gilt coach, designed by Sir William Chambers in 1760, has painted panels by G. B. Cipriani. It was first used for the State Opening of Parliament by George III in 1762 and has been used by the monarch for every coronation since George IV. It was last used for the Golden Jubilee of Elizabeth II.Also housed in the mews are the carriage horses used in royal ceremonial **processions**（列队行进）.

> **阅读辅助**
>
> 　　白金汉宫建筑外立面装修材料为巴斯石灰岩。内部装修则以人造大理石及青金石为主。正面广场围以铸铁栅栏，为皇家卫队换岗仪式的场所。广场外为手持权杖、塑造为天使形象的维多利亚女王雕像。白金汉宫的附属建筑包括皇家画廊、皇家马厩和花园。

4 伦敦塔桥 *Tower Bridge*
——拥有"伦敦正门"之美称

达人了解英美

◆ **History**

In the second half of the 19th century, increased commercial development in the East End of London led to a requirement for a new river crossing **downstream**（下游的）of London Bridge. A traditional fixed bridge could not be built because it would cut off access by tall-masted ships to the port **facilities**（设备）in the Pool, between London Bridge and the Tower of London.

Jones' engineer, Sir John Wolfe Barry, devised the idea of a bascule bridgewith two bridge towers built on piers. The central span was split into two equal **bascules**（活动结构）or leaves, which could be raised to allow river traffic to pass. The two side-spans were **suspension**（悬浮）bridges, with the suspension rods **anchored**（抛锚）both at the abutments and through rods contained within the bridge's upper walkways.

The bridge was officially opened on 30 June 1894 by The Prince of Wales , and his wife, The Princess of Wales. The bridge connected Iron Gate, on the north bank of the river, with Horselydown Lane, on the south – now known as Tower Bridge Approach and Tower Bridge Road, respectively.

> **阅读辅助**
>
> 　　19世纪下半叶，随着伦敦经济的发展城市东部越来越紧要地需要一座横跨泰晤士河的桥梁。但这座桥不能是传统的桥，因为当时的码头位于伦敦桥和伦敦塔之间，假如新桥太低的话船就无法开到码头了。于是在1870年开凿了位于泰晤士河河床下的伦敦塔地铁被通车启用，这是一条利用索道方式载运旅客渡河的古老地铁系统，但它依然无法完全取代修筑一座新桥的需要。

✧ Structure

The bridge consists of two bridge towers tied together at the upper level by two **horizontal**（水平的）walkways, designed to withstand the horizontal forces exerted by the suspended sections of the bridge on the landward sides of the towers. The **vertical**（垂直线）components of the forces in the suspended sections and the vertical reactions of the two walkways are carried by the two **robust**（强健的）towers. The **bascule**（竖旋桥活动桁架）pivots and operating machinery are housed in the base of each tower. The bridge's present color scheme dates from 1977, when it was painted red, white and blue for Queen Elizabeth II'sSilver Jubilee. Originally it was painted a mid greenish-blue color.

> **阅读辅助**
>
> 　　琼斯的设计是一座244米长的开启桥，桥有两个桥塔，每个塔高65米。桥的中部长61米，分为两扇，每扇可以竖起到83度来让河道交通通过。而这两扇桥段各重上千吨，它们的轴位于它们的重心上来减小它们起升时所需要的力，它们可以在一分钟内升起。

✧ Mistaken identify

Tower Bridge is often mistaken for London Bridge, the next bridge upstream. A popular urban legend is that in 1968, Robert P. McCulloch, the purchaser of the old London Bridge that was later shipped to Lake Havasu City, Arizona, believed that he was in fact buying Tower Bridge. This was denied by McCulloch himself and has been debunked by Ivan Luckin, the vendor of the bridge.

阅读辅助

伦敦塔桥有时被误称为伦敦桥（London Bridge），其实真正的伦敦桥是另一座完全不同的桥梁，位于伦敦塔桥的上游。有个都市传说，在1968年Robert P. McCulloch买下古老的伦敦桥，之后运到了亚利桑那州的哈瓦苏湖城，但事实上这只是个传说。

5 国会大厦 Palace of Westminster
——英国政治的中心舞台

达人了解英美

◆ **History**

Its name, which derives from the neighboring Westminster Abbey, may refer to either of two structures: the Old Palace, a **medieval**（中世纪的）building complex that was destroyed by fire in 1834, and its replacement, the New Palace that stands today. For ceremonial purposes, the palace retains its original style and status as a royal residence and is the property of the Crown.

The first royal palace was built on the site in the eleventh century, and Westminster was the primary residence of the Kings of England until a fire destroyed much of the complex in 1512. After that, it served as the home of the Parliament of England, which had been meeting there since the thirteenth century, and also as the seat of the Royal Courts of Justice, based in and around Westminster Hall. In 1834, an even greater fire ravaged（毁坏）the heavily rebuilt Houses of Parliament, and the only medieval structures of significance to survive were Westminster Hall, the Cloisters of St Stephen's, the Chapel of St Mary Undercroft, and the Jewel Tower.

阅读辅助

中世纪时期，由于威斯敏斯特宫处在泰晤士河畔的独特位置，已然成为一处战略要地。威斯敏斯特宫在中世纪是王室的主要居住地。后来的议会，也就是皇家委员会设于威斯敏斯特厅。尽管今天的宫殿基本上在19世纪重修而来，但依然保留了初建时的许多历史遗迹，如威斯敏斯特厅，今天用作重大的公共典仪，如国葬前的停灵等。在1834年发生的火灾几乎将威斯敏斯特宫完全烧毁，所以今天的宫殿是于1830年代开始由建筑师查尔斯·巴里爵士和他的助手A.W.普金设计完成，并在此后进行了30余年的施工。

✧ Structure

The subsequent competition for the reconstruction of the Palace was won by the architect Charles Barry, whose design was for new buildings in the Perpendicular style. The remains of the Old Palace were **incorporated**（合并的）into its much larger replacement, which contains over 1,100 rooms organized **symmetrically**（平衡地）around two series of courtyards. Part of the New Palace's area of 3.24 hectares was reclaimed from the Thames, which is the setting of its principal 266-metre façade, called the River Front. Barry was assisted by Augustus W. N. Pugin, a leading authority on Gothic architecture and style, who provided designs for the decorations and furnishings of the Palace. Construction started in 1840 and lasted for thirty years, suffering great delays and cost **overruns**（泛滥成灾）, as well as the death of both leading architects; works for the interior decoration continued **intermittently**（间歇地）well into the twentieth century. Major conservation work has been carried out since, to reverse the effects of London's air pollution, and extensive repairs took place after the Second World War, including the reconstruction of the Commons Chamber following its bombing in 1941.

阅读辅助

　　威斯敏斯特宫是哥特复兴式建筑的代表作之一，该建筑包括约1,100个独立房间、100座楼梯和4.8公里长的走廊。大厦分为四层，首层有办公室、餐厅和雅座间。二层为宫殿主要厅室，如议会厅、议会休息室和图书厅。该建筑从1840开始兴建，历经30载，中间经历延时和预算超支，以及主建筑师的去世等等一系列的问题。最近期的维护修整是在二战之后，并重建了1941年被轰炸的下议院。

◇ Rules and traditions

The Palace has accumulated many rules and traditions over the centuries. Smoking has not been allowed in the chamber of the House of Commons since the 17th century. As a result, Members may take snuff instead and the doorkeepers still keep a snuff-box for this purpose. Members may not eat or drink in the chamber; the exception to this rule is the Chancellor of the **Exchequer**（财政部）, who may have an alcoholic beverage while delivering the Budget statement.Hats must not be worn and Members may not wear military decorations or **insignia**（徽章）. Members are not allowed to have their hands in their pockets.

Animals are not allowed to enter the Palace of Westminster, with the exception of guide dogs for the blind. Sniffer dogs and police horses are also allowed on the grounds. Speeches may not be read out during debate in the House of Commons, although notes may be referred to. Similarly, the reading of newspapers is not allowed. Visual aids are discouraged in the chamber. Applause is also not normally allowed in the Commons.

阅读辅助

威斯敏斯特宫在几个世纪以来，制定并形成了一系列规定和传统。17世纪后，在上下两院厅室内禁止吸烟，结果议员们用鼻烟取而代之，看门人也为此保留有鼻烟匣子。进厅必须脱帽，军装的配饰不被允许穿戴，官职证章等也不必佩戴，双手不可插兜。所有的动物也不允许进入威斯敏斯特宫，只有导盲犬例外；在辩论时是不能演讲的，同样，阅读报章也不被许可。同时厅室内的视觉辅助也会被劝阻。上下院内鼓掌通常也是没有必要的。

6 威斯敏斯特教堂 *Westminster Abby*
——不简单的宗教场所

达人了解英美

◇ **History**

Between 1042 and 1052 King Edward the Confessor began rebuilding St. Peter's Abbey to provide himself with a royal burial church. It was the first church in England built in the Norman Romanesque style. It was not completed until around 1090 but was **consecrated**（神圣的）on 28 December 1065, only a week before Edward's death on 5 January 1066. A week later he was buried in the church, and nine years later his wife Edith was buried **alongside**（在……旁边）him. His successor, Harold II, was probably crowned in the abbey, although the first documented **coronation**（加冕礼）is that of William the Conqueror later the same year. Construction of the present church was begun in 1245 by Henry III who selected the site for his burial.

The abbey is a Royal Peculiar and between 1540 and 1556 had the status of a **cathedral**（大教堂）; the building is no longer an abbey nor cathedral however, having instead the status since 1560 of a "Royal Peculiar" – a church responsible directly to the Sovereign. According to a tradition first reported by Sulcard in about 1080, a church was founded at the site in the 7th century, at the time of Mellitus, a Bishop of London. Construction of the present church began in 1245, on the orders of Henry III. Since 1066, when Harold Godwinson and William the Conqueror were crowned, the coronations of English and British monarchs have been held here. Since 1100, there have been at least 16 royal weddings at the abbey.

Two were of reigning monarchs, although before 1919 there had been none for some 500 years.

> **阅读辅助**
>
> 传说中威斯敏斯特教堂在 Saberht 国王时期就已经建成,最初建在泰晤士河中的一个小岛上。1045年至1065年间按照忏悔者爱德华的命令重建威斯敏斯特教堂。威斯敏斯特教堂最早是为本笃会教士而建的,于1065年12月28日完成。在1245－1517年间威斯敏斯特教堂再次重建,第一阶段的重建工作由亨利三世组织,但是大部分的工作是在理查三世时期完成的。

✧ Coronations

Since the coronations in 1066 of both King Harold and William the Conqueror, coronations of English and British monarchs were held in the Abbey. Henry III was unable to be crowned in London when he first came to the throne because the French prince Louis had taken control of the city, and so the king was crowned in Gloucester Cathedral. This **coronation**（加冕礼）was deemed by the Pope to be improper, and a further coronation was held in the Abbey on 17 May 1220. The Archbishop of Canterbury is the traditional cleric in the coronation ceremony. King Edward's Chair, the throne on which English and British **sovereigns**（君主）have been seated at the moment of coronation, is housed within the Abbey and has been used at every coronation since 1308. From 1301 to 1996, the chair also housed the Stone of Scone upon which the kings of Scots are crowned. Although the Stone is now kept in Scotland, in Edinburgh Castle, at future coronations it is intended that the Stone will be returned to St Edward's Chair for use during the coronation ceremony.

（英）叹为观止的地标建筑　Section 2-1

> **阅读辅助**
>
> 1066年，哈罗德二世在此加冕，他是第一个在此加冕的国王。同一年的圣诞节，征服者威廉也在此加冕，从此之后一般的英国君主都在威斯敏斯特教堂加冕。绝大多数的英国君王都由坎特伯雷大主教加冕，只有少数几个君王例外。

✧ Museum

The Westminster Abbey Museum is located in the 11th-century vaulted **undercroft**（地下室）beneath the former monks' dormitory in Westminster Abbey. This is one of the oldest areas of the Abbey, dating back almost to the foundation of the Norman church by Edward the Confessor in 1065. This space has been used as a museum since 1908.

The exhibits include a collection of royal and other funeral **effigies**（雕像）, together with other treasures, including some panels of mediaeval glass, 12th-century sculpture **fragments**（碎片）, Mary II's coronation chair and replicas of the coronation **regalia**（王权）, and historic effigies of Edward III, Henry VII and his queen, Elizabeth of York, Charles II, William III, Mary II and Queen Anne. A recent addition to the exhibition is the late 13th-century Westminster Retable, England's oldest **altarpiece**（祭坛的装饰品）, which was most probably designed for the high altar of the abbey. Although it has been damaged in past centuries, the panel has been expertly cleaned and conserved.

> **阅读辅助**
>
> 威斯敏斯特教堂内还有大量馆藏，加冕用品以及勋章等庆典用品都收藏于此。还有英国宫廷收集的关于历史、艺术、科学等各个方面的资料，如1500年以来富于戏剧性的历史记录都保存于此。人们在赞叹威斯敏斯特教堂建筑艺术的同时，还可以从中了解到英国的历史。

7 哈罗德百货公司 *Harrods*
——英国的百年老店

达人了解英美

◇ **History**

　　Harrods founder Charles Henry Harrod first established his business in 1824, aged 25. The business was located south of the River Thames in Southwark. The premises were located at 228 Borough High Street. He ran this business, variously listed as a draper, mercer and a haberdasher, certainly until 1831. During 1825 the business was listed as 'Harrod and Wicking, Linen Drapers, Retail', but this partnership was dissolved at the end of that year. His first grocery business appears to be as 'Harrod & Co.Grocers' at 163 Upper Whitecross Street, Clerkenwell, E.C.1., in 1832. In 1834 in London's East End, he established a **wholesale**（大规模的）grocery in Stepney, at 4, Cable Street, with a special interest in tea. In 1849, to escape the vice of the inner city and to capitalise on trade to the Great Exhibition of 1851 in nearby Hyde Park, Harrod took over a small shop in the district of Brompton, on the site of the current store. Harrods rapidly expanded, acquired the **adjoining**（毗连的）buildings, and employed one hundred people by 1880.

阅读辅助

　　哈洛德百货在1834年于伦敦的East End，创立者是查尔斯·亨利·哈洛德，当时他对茶相当有兴趣，因而在Stepney成立了一批发商。1849年，为了远离城市中心的脏乱，并把握住1851年在海德公园举办的万国工业博览会所带来的商机，哈洛德便顶下骑士桥附近的一个小商店，也就是现今百货公司所在的位置。此后哈洛德百货迅速地扩张，并收购相邻的建筑，雇用了100位的员工。

◇ Products

The shop's 330 departments offer a wide range of products and services. Products on offer include clothing for women, men, children and infants, electronics, jewellery, sporting gear, bridal **trousseau**（妆奁）, pets and pet accessories, toys, food and drink, health and beauty items, packaged gifts, stationery, house wares, home appliances, furniture, and much more. A representative sample of shop services includes 32 restaurants, serving everything from high tea to tapas to pub food tohaute cuisine; a personal shopping-assistance programme known as "By Appointment"; a watch repair service; a tailor; a dispensing **pharmacy**（药房）; a beauty spa and salon; a barbers shop; Harrods Financial Services; Harrods Bank; Ella Jade Bathroom Planning and Design Service; private events planning and catering; food delivery; a wine steward; bespoke picnic hampers and gift boxes; bespoke cakes; bespoke **fragrance**（香味）formulations; and Bespoke Arcadesmachines.

阅读辅助

哈洛德百货的330个部门提供了多元化的产品和服务。产品包括服饰（男女装、童装、婴儿装）、电器、珠宝、运动器材、结婚礼服、宠物和周边产品、玩具、饮食、健康美容产品、礼品、文具、家居用品、家电、家具等等。百货内服务设施包括：28间餐厅、预约式的个人购物协助、钟表修复、服装订制、药妆部、美容spa和沙龙、理发厅、哈洛德金融服务、哈洛德银行、私人活动据点、食物递送、个人蛋糕订制、个人香水调配等等。

◆ Memorials

Since the deaths of Diana, Princess of Wales, and Dodi Fayed, Mohamed Al-Fayed's son, two memorials commissioned by Al-Fayed have been erected inside Harrods to the couple. The first, located at the base of the Egyptian Escalator, was **unveiled**（原形毕露）on 12 April 1998, consisting of photographs of the two behind a pyramid-shaped display that holds a wine glass **smudged**（弄脏）with lipstick from Diana's last dinner as well as what is described as an engagement ring Dodi purchased the day before they died.

The second memorial, unveiled in 2005 and located by the **escalator**（电动扶梯）at door three is entitled "Innocent Victims", a bronze statue of the two dancing on a beach beneath the wings of an **albatross**（信天翁）, a bird said to symbolize the "Holy Spirit". The sculpture was created by William Mitchell, a close friend of Al-Fayed and artistic design advisor to Harrods for 40 years. Al-Fayed said he wanted to keep the pair's "spirit alive" through the statue.

阅读辅助

自戴安娜王妃和多迪·法耶兹去世后，Mohamed Al Fayed在百货内设立两个纪念碑以纪念这对情侣。第一座纪念碑在1998年4月12日落成，纪念碑上有：两人的照片、有戴安娜王妃唇印的酒杯、多迪在去世前一天买的订婚戒指。第二座纪念碑在2005年完成，摆设在第三道门旁带有埃及风格的手扶梯旁，为一铜雕像，称做"无辜的受害者"。

圣保罗大教堂 St.Paul's Cathedral
——世界著名的宗教圣地

达人了解英美

✧ History

Its dedication to Paul the Apostle dates back to the original church on this site, founded in AD 604. The fourth St. Paul's, generally referred to as Old St. Paul's, was begun by the Normans after the 1087 fire. A further fire in 1136 disrupted the work, and the new cathedral was not consecrated until 1240. During the period of construction, the style of architecture had changed from Romanesque to Gothic and this was reflected in the pointed arches and larger windows of the upper parts and East End of the building. The Gothic ribbed vault was constructed, like that of York Minster, of wood rather than stone, which affected the **ultimate**（基本原则）fate of the building. By the 16th century the building was starting to decay. Under Henry VIII and Edward VI, the Dissolution of the Monasteries and Chantries Acts led to the destruction of interior **ornamentation**（装饰物）and the **cloisters**（隐居地）, charnels, crypts, chapels, shrines, chantries and other buildings in St. Paul's Church yard. The present church, dating from the late 17th century, was designed in the English Baroque style by Sir Christopher Wren. Its construction, completed within Wren's lifetime, was part of a major rebuilding programme which took place in the city after the Great Fire of London.

> **阅读辅助**
>
> 圣保罗大教堂最早在604年建立，第四个圣保罗大教堂，一般称为旧圣保罗教堂，在1087年由诺曼人大规模修建，之后经多次毁坏、重建。期间由罗马式到哥特式的建筑风格不断转变，直到16世纪建筑开始腐朽，亨利八世和爱德华六世开始再次整改人教堂各区域的建筑，而现在的教堂是由英国著名设计大师和建筑家克托弗．雷恩爵士在17世纪末完成这伦敦最伟大的教堂设计，整整花了45年的心血。

◆ Structure

The cathedral is one of the most famous and most recognizable sights of London, with its dome, framed by the **spires**（尖顶）of Wren's City churches, dominating the skyline for 300 years. At 365 feet high, it was the tallest building in London from 1710 to 1962, and its dome is also among the highest in the world. In terms of area, St. Paul's is the second largest church building in the United Kingdom after Liverpool Cathedral.

> **阅读辅助**
>
> 圣保罗大教堂是伦敦的宗教中心，建筑为华丽的巴洛克风格，是世界第二大圆顶教堂，17世纪末建成。教堂是文艺复兴风格，覆有巨大穹顶，高约111米，宽约74米，纵深约157米，穹顶直径达34米。这座宏伟建筑设计完美，内部静谧安详，是建筑大师莱恩最优秀的作品。

◆ Services

St. Paul's Cathedral is a busy church with three or four services every day, including Matins, Eucharist and Evening Prayer or Evensong. In addition, the Cathedral has many special services associated with the City of London, its corporation, **guilds**（公会）and institutions.

(英) 叹为观止的地标建筑　　Section 2-1

St. Paul's Cathedral occupies a significant place in the national identity of the English population. It is the central subject of much promotional material, as well as postcard images of the dome standing tall, surrounded by the smoke and fire of the Blitz. Important services held at St. Paul's have included the funerals of Lord Nelson, the Duke of Wellington, Sir Winston Churchill and Margaret Thatcher; Jubilee celebrations for Queen Victoria; peace services marking the end of the First and Second World Wars; the wedding of Charles, Prince of Wales, and Lady Diana Spencer, the launch of the Festival of Britain and the thanksgiving services for the Golden Jubilee, the 80th Birthday and the Diamond Jubilee of Elizabeth II. St. Paul's Cathedral is a busy working church, with hourly prayer and daily services.

阅读辅助

圣保罗大教堂是一所繁忙的教堂，每天都会有晨祷，圣餐，晚上祈祷或晚祷。查尔斯王子和戴安娜王妃的婚礼就是在圣保罗大教堂举行。而且圣保罗大教堂在英国文化处于举足轻重的地位，无论是国家宣传片，明信片都会以该建筑作为标识。此外这里还举行很多知名人士的葬礼如纳尔逊勋爵，威灵顿公爵，温斯顿·丘吉尔爵士和玛格丽特·撒切尔；还有很多庆典如伊丽莎白二世登基50周年，80岁生日，伊丽莎白二世的钻石禧年。

9 大英博物馆 *British Museum*
——古代文明的汇聚地

达人了解英美

◆ **History**

The British Museum was established in 1753, largely based on the collections of the physician and scientist Sir Hans Sloane. The museum first opened to the public on 15 January 1759 in Montagu House in Bloomsbury, on the site of the current museum building. Its expansion over the following two and a half centuries was largely a result of an expanding British colonial **footprint**（足迹）and has resulted in the creation of several branch institutions, the first being the British Museum in South Kensington in 1881. Some objects in the collection, most notably the Elgin Marbles from the Parthenon, are the objects of **controversy**（辩论）and of calls for **restitution**（归还）to their countries of origin.

阅读辅助

大英博物馆的渊源最早可追溯到1753年，是当时的一位著名收藏家汉斯·斯隆爵士，在1753年他去世后遗留下来的个人藏品71000件，还有大批植物标本及书籍、手稿，并根据他的遗嘱，将所有藏品都捐赠给国家。通过公众募款筹集建筑博物馆的资金后，才有了大英博物馆，最终在1759年成立并对公众开放。

◆ **Building**

The Greek Revival façade facing Great Russell Street is a characteristic building of Sir Robert Smirke, with 44 columns in the Ionic 45 ft high, closely based on those of the temple of Athena Polias at Priene in Asia Minor. The pedimentover the main entrance is decorated by **sculptures**（雕像）by Sir Richard Westmacott depicting The Progress of Civilization, consisting of fifteen **allegorical**（寓言的）figures, installed in 1852. The construction commenced around the courtyard with the East Wing in 1823–1828, followed by the North Wing in 1833–1838, which originally housed among other galleries a reading room, now the Wellcome Gallery.

> **阅读辅助**
>
> 该馆的主体建筑在伦敦的布隆斯伯里区，核心建筑占地约56000平方米。博物馆正门的两旁，各有8根又粗又高的罗马式圆柱，大中庭位于英国国家博物馆中心，于2000年12月建成开放，是欧洲最大的有顶广场。现有建筑为19世纪中叶所建，共有100多个陈列室，面积六七万平方米，共藏有展品400多万件。

◆ Departments I

The British Museum houses the world's largest and most comprehensive collection of Egyptian **antiquities**（古文明）outside the Egyptian Museum in Cairo. A collection of immense importance for its range and quality, it includes objects of all periods from virtually every site of importance in Egypt and the Sudan. Together, they **illustrate**（阐明）every aspect of the cultures of theNile Valley, from the PredynasticNeolithic period through to the Coptic times, a time-span over 11,000 years.

The British Museum has one of the world's largest and most comprehensive collections of antiquities from the Classical world, with over 100,000 objects. These mostly range in date from the beginning of the Greek Bronze Age to the establishment of Christianity as the official religion of the Roman Empire, with the Edict of Milan under the reign of the Roman Emperor Constantine I in 313 AD.

✧ Departments II

With a collection numbering some 330,000 works, the British Museum possesses the world's largest and most important collection of Mesopotamian antiquities outside Iraq. The collections represent the civilizations of the ancient Near East and its **adjacent**（邻近的）areas. These cover Mesopotamia, Persia, the Arabian Peninsula, Anatolia, the Caucasus, parts of Central Asia, Syria, Palestine and Phoenician settlements in the western Mediterranean from the **prehistoric**（史前的）period and include objects from the beginning of Islam in the 7th century.

The scope of the Department of Asia is extremely broad; its collections of over 75,000 objects cover the material culture of the whole Asian continent and from the Neolithic up to the present day. Until recently, this department concentrated on collecting Oriental antiquities from urban or semi-urban societies across the Asian continent.

The British Museum houses one of the world's most comprehensive collections of Ethnographic material from Africa, Oceania and the Americas, representing the cultures of **indigenous**（本土的）peoples throughout the world. Over 350,000 objects spanning thousands of years tells the history of mankind from three major continents and many rich and **diverse**（多种多样的）cultures; the collecting of modern **artifacts**（史前古器物）is ongoing.

阅读辅助

开馆以后的200多年间，继续收集了英国本国及埃及、巴比伦、希腊、罗马、印度、中国等古老国家的文物。古埃及艺术品是英国国家博物馆最富盛名的收藏。英国国家博物馆里最引人注目的要数东方艺术文物馆。该馆有来自中国、日本、印度及其他东南亚国家的文物十多万件。

10 伦敦碎片大厦 *The Shard*
——欧洲第一高楼

达人了解英美

◆ Background

In 1998, London-based entrepreneur Irvine Sellar and his then partners decided to redevelop the 1970s-era Southwark Towers following a UK government white paper encouraging the development of tall buildings at major transport hubs. The Shard's construction began in March 2009; it was topped out on 30 March 2012 and **inaugurated**（开幕）on 5 July 2012. Practical completion was achieved in November 2012. The tower's privately operated observation deck, The View from The Shard, was opened to the public on 1 February 2013.

It was designed by the Italian architect Renzo Piano and replaced Southwark Towers, a 24-storey office block built on the site in 1975. The Shard was developed by Sellar Property on **behalf**（利益）of LBQ Ltd and is jointly owned by Sellar Property and the State of Qatar.

> **阅读辅助**
>
> 碎片大厦由曾担任巴黎的蓬皮杜艺术中心设计的意大利建筑师伦佐·皮亚诺负责设计。大厦在经济不景气的时候开幕，开幕之时一个单位都未售出。从1998年伦敦的企业家决定从简70年代的南华克区塔这个主意开始到2013年正式对众人开放，历时10多年。

◆ Design

Renzo Piano, the project's architect, designed the Shard as a spire-like sculpture emerging from the River Thames. He was inspired by the railway lines next to the site, the London **spires depicted**（描画）by the 18th-century Venetian painter Canaletto, and the masts of sailing ships. Piano's design met criticism from English Heritage, who claimed the building would be "a shard of glass through the heart of historic London", giving the building its name, The Shard. Piano considered the **slender**（苗条的）, spire-like form of the tower a positive addition to the London skyline, recalling the church steeples featured in historic **engravings**（雕刻）of the city, and believed that its presence would be far more delicate than opponents of the project alleged. He proposed a **sophisticated**（久经世故的）use of glazing, with expressive façades of angled glass panes intended to reflect sunlight and the sky above, so that the appearance of the building will change according to the weather and seasons.

> 阅读辅助
>
> 碎片大厦的整体形态是下宽上窄，最后顶部的塔尖渐渐消失在空中，就像16世纪的小尖塔或高桅横帆船的桅杆。建筑的形式以伦敦具有历史性的尖顶和桅杆为基础而设计。这一设计灵感来自于18世纪威尼斯画家卡纳莱托。另外钢琴的设计满足对英国的印象，另外它的名字"碎片"也是有来历的"一个玻璃碎片贯穿历史悠久的轮动"决定这一名字。

◆ Building

Standing 309.6768 meters high, the Shard is currently the tallest building in the European Union. It is also the second-tallest free-standing structure in the United Kingdom, after the concrete tower at the Emley Moor transmitting station. The glass-clad **pyramidal**（金字塔形的）tower has 72 **habitable**（可居住的）floors, with a viewing gallery and open-air observation deck on the 72nd floor, at a height of 244.3 meters.

The Shard is the second-tallest free-standing structure in the United Kingdom, after the 330-metre concrete transmission tower at Emley Moor. Another planned London skyscraper, the Pinnacle, was originally proposed to rival the height of the Shard, but was **reduced**（缩减的）to a height of 287.9 meters because of concerns from the Civil Aviation Authority.

阅读辅助

碎片大厦高达1017英尺，是全欧洲第二高的大厦，586,509平方英尺的建筑所包含了办公空间，居住公寓。另外它还包含了一个15层楼高的公共观景廊。

Section 2-2　（美）叹为观止的地标建筑

美国，一个现代化、多元化、摩登的发达国家。历史在这个国家留下了纪念式的痕迹 ---- 建筑，每一个建筑物都注入建造时代的精神和人文，都代表了一个时代的风向标。所以说每个建筑就是一本传奇性的历史书一点都不错，当你想要真正去了解美国时，你需要仔细阅读书中所倾注的情感和文化。

1 白宫 *White House*
——美国政府的代名词

达人了解英美

◇ **History**

The house was designed by Irish-born James Hoban and built between 1792 and 1800 of white-painted Aquia Creek **sandstone**（砂岩）in the Neoclassical style. When Thomas Jefferson moved into the house in 1801, he expanded the building outward, creating two **colonnades**（柱廊）that were meant to conceal stables and storage. In 1814, during the War of 1812, the mansion was set **ablaze**（闪耀的）by the British Army in the Burning of Washington, destroying the interior and charring much of the exterior. Reconstruction began almost immediately, and President James Monroe moved into the partially reconstructed Executive Residence in October 1817. Construction continued with the addition of the South Portico in 1824 and the North in 1829.

Because of crowding within the executive mansion itself, President Theodore Roosevelt had all work offices **relocated**（迁移）to the newly constructed West Wing in 1901. Eight years later, President William Howard Taft expanded the West Wing and created the first Oval Office which was eventually moved as the section was expanded. The third-floor attic was converted to living quarters in 1927 by **augmenting**（使扩张）the existing hip roof with long shed dormers. A newly constructed East Wing was used as a reception area for social events; Jefferson's colonnades connected the new wings. East Wing alterations were completed in 1946, creating additional office space. By 1948, the house's load-bearing exterior walls and internal wood beams were found to be close to failure. Under Harry S. Truman, the interior rooms were completely **dismantled**（拆除）and a new internal load-bearing steel frame constructed inside the walls. Once this work was completed, the interior rooms were rebuilt.

> **阅读辅助**
>
> 　　1790年12月，在华盛顿哥伦比亚特区寻址后，根据一项国会动议，建造白宫。乔治•华盛顿总统亲自协助城市规划师皮埃尔•查尔斯•朗方选址。这幢大楼最初称作"总统宫"或"总统府"。 直到1811年才首次出现公众因为它漆成白色的石制外墙而称之为"白宫"的记载。1800年11月1日，约翰•亚当斯成为首位入住白宫的总统。

◆ **Construction**

Today, the White House Complex includes the Executive Residence, West Wing, East Wing, the Eisenhower Executive Office Building—the former State Department, which now houses offices for the President's staff and the Vice President—and Blair House, a guest residence.

The Executive Residence is made up of six stories—the Ground Floor, State Floor, Second Floor, and Third Floor, as well as a two-story basement. The term White House is often used as a **metonym**（转喻）for the Executive Office of the President of the United States and for the president's administration and advisers in general. The property is a National Heritage Site owned by the National Park Service and is part of the President's Park. In 2007, it was ranked second on the American Institute of Architects list of "America's Favorite Architecture".

> **阅读辅助**
>
> 　　如今一组总统建筑构成了白宫建筑群，包括作为主居住区的中央建筑和东西两个侧翼。白宫总管每天协调管理着日常生活事务。白宫在1960年12月19日已确认为一处国家历史地标。

2 帝国大厦 Empire State Building
——美国经济复苏的象征

达人了解英美

◇ **History**

The site of the Empire State Building was first developed as the John Thompson Farm in the late 18th century. Beginning in the late 19th century, the block was occupied by the Waldorf-Astoria Hotel, **frequented**（经常光顾）by The Four Hundred, the social elite of New York. The Empire State Building was designed by William F. Lamb from the architectural firm Shreve, Lamb and Harmon.

Excavation of the site began on January 22, 1930, and construction on the building itself started symbolically on March 17—St. Patrick's Day—per Al Smith's influence as Empire State, Inc. president. The project involved 3,400 workers, mostly immigrants from Europe, along with hundreds of Mohawk iron workers, many from the Kahnawake reserve near Montreal. According to official accounts, five workers died during the construction.

The construction was part of an intense competition in New York for the title of "world's tallest building". Two other projects fighting for the title, 40 Wall Street and the Chrysler Building, were still under construction when work began on the Empire State Building.

阅读辅助

帝国大厦是由设计师威廉·F. 兰博负责建筑的主要设计。1930年项目开始动工，大厦于同年3月17日开始建筑。项目涉及了3400名工人的劳动，工人主要是欧洲移民。根据官方统计，施工过程中共有5名工人身亡。

✧ Height records and comparisons

Its name is derived from the nickname for New York, the Empire State. It stood as the world's tallest building for nearly 40 years, from its completion in early 1931 until the topping out of the original World Trade Center's North Tower in late 1970. Following the September 11 attacks in 2001, the Empire State Building was again the tallest building in New York, until One World Trade Center reached a greater height on April 30, 2012. The Empire State Building is currently the fourth-tallest completed **skyscraper**（摩天大楼）in the United States (after the One World Trade Center, the Willis Tower and Trump International Hotel and Tower, both in Chicago), and the 25th-tallest in the world (the tallest now is Burj Khalifa, located in Dubai). It is also the fifth-tallest **freestanding**（独立的）structure in the Americas.

> 阅读辅助
>
> 帝国大厦为纽约市以至美国最著名的地标和旅游景点之一，为美国及美洲第4高，世界上第25高的摩天大楼，也是保持世界最高建筑地位最久的摩天大楼。

✧ Influence

The Empire State Building is generally thought of as an American cultural icon. It is designed in the **distinctive**（与众不同的）Art Decostyle and has been named as one of the Seven Wonders of the Modern World by the American Society of Civil Engineers. The building and its street floor interior are designated landmarks of the New York City Landmarks Preservation Commission, and confirmed by the New York City Board of Estimate. It was designated as a National Historic Landmark in 1986. In 2007, it was ranked number one on the AIA's List of America's Favorite Architecture.

阅读辅助

帝国大厦被美国土木工程师学会评价为现代世界七大工程奇迹之一,纽约地标委员会选其为纽约市地标。

世贸中心 *World Trade Center*
——美国人心中永远的伤痛

达人了解英美

◇ Original Building

The original World Trade Center featured landmark twin towers, which opened on April 4, 1973, and were destroyed in the September 11 attacks of 2001, along with 7 World Trade Center. The other buildings in the complex were severely damaged by the collapse of the twin towers, and their ruins were eventually **demolished**（被拆毁的）.

At the time of their completion, the "Twin Towers" — the original 1 World Trade Center, at 1,368 feet; and 2 World Trade Center — were the tallest buildings in the world. The other buildings in the complex included the Marriott World Trade Center, 4 WTC, 5 WTC, 6 WTC, and 7 WTC. All these buildings were built between 1975 and 1985, with a construction cost of $400 million. The complex was located in New York City's Financial District and **contained**（包含的）13,400,000 square feet of office space.

The World Trade Center experienced a fire on February 13, 1975, a bombing on February 26, 1993, and a robbery on January 14, 1998. In 1998, the Port Authority decided to **privatize**（使私有化）the World Trade Center, leasing the buildings to a private company to manage, and awarded the lease to Silverstein Properties in July 2001.

阅读辅助

原来的建筑群是山崎实于1960年代初设计的，于1973年7月完工。整个建筑群位于纽约内市金融区的中心，这两座最高楼合称为"世贸双子星大楼"。

✧ Destruction

On the morning of September 11, 2001, Al-Qaeda-affiliated **hijackers**（劫持者）flew two Boeing 767 jets into the complex, beginning with the North Tower at 8:46 a.m. then the South Tower at 9:03 a.m., in a coordinated act of terrorism. After burning for 56 minutes, the South Tower collapsed at 9:59 a.m.. 29 minutes later, the North Tower collapsed. The attacks on the World Trade Center killed 2,753 people. Falling debris from the towers, combined with fires that the debris initiated in several surrounding buildings, led to the partial or complete collapse of all the other buildings in the complex and caused **catastrophic**（灾难性）damage to ten other large structures in the surrounding area (including the World Financial Center); three buildings in the World Trade Center complex collapsed due to fire-induced structural failure, and when the North Tower collapsed, **debris**（杂物）fell on the nearby 7 WTC, damaging it and starting fires so that it eventually collapsed. The process of cleaning up and recovery at the World Trade Center site took eight months.

> **阅读辅助**
>
> 9·11委员会官方报告称2001年9月11日晨，在一次有组织的恐怖袭击事件中，基地组织成员劫持两架波音767分别撞入世界贸易中心的南北两楼。在燃烧56分钟后南楼（2号楼）倒塌。半小时后北楼（1号楼）也倒塌。这次袭击共造成2753人死亡。

✧ New Building

After years of delay and **controversy**（争论），reconstruction at the World Trade Center site is now underway. The new complex includes One World Trade Center (formerly known as the Freedom Tower), 7 World Trade Center, three other high-rise office buildings, a museum and memorial, and a transportation hub similar in size to Grand Central Terminal. The

(美) 叹为观止的地标建筑　　Section 2-2

One World Trade Center was completed on August 30, 2012, and the final component of its spire installed on May 10, 2013. The Four World Trade Center is on track for completion and occupancy by 2014. The 9·11 memorial is complete, and the museum opened on May 21, 2014. Three World Trade Center and the Transportation Hub are also making progress, and are set to be finished by around late 2017 and late 2015, respectively. Two World Trade Center's full construction was placed on hold in the early 2010s, until **tenants**（租户）are found.

阅读辅助

　　经过多年的延迟和争论世界贸易中心原址的重建已经开始。清理和修复工作首先进行了八个月，2002年一座新的7号楼在主世界贸易中心原址的北面动工。2014年11月为止仅世界贸易中心一号大楼、世界贸易中心四号大楼及世界贸易中心七号大楼已重建完成，其它三座计划于2020年前完成。

4 林肯纪念堂 Lincoln Memorial
——美国永恒的塑像

达人了解英美

◇ **History**

The first public memorial to Abraham Lincoln in Washington, D.C., was a statue by Lot Flannery erected in front of the District of Columbia City Hall in 1868, three years after Lincoln's assassination. Demands for a fitting national memorial had been voiced since the time of Lincoln's death. In 1867, Congress passed the first of many bills incorporating a commission to erect a **monument**（纪念碑）for the sixteenth president. The matter lay dormant until the start of the 20th century, when, under the leadership of SenatorShelby M. Cullom of Illinois, six separate bills were introduced in Congress for the incorporation of a new memorial commission.

There were questions regarding the commission's plan. Many thought that architect Henry Bacon's Greek temple design was far too ostentatious for a man of Lincoln's humble character. Instead they proposed a simple log cabin shrine. The site too did not go **unopposed**（不反对的）. In 1914, a dedication ceremony was conducted and the following month the actual construction began. Work progressed steadily according to schedule. Despite these changes, the Memorial was finished on schedule.

阅读辅助

林肯遇刺后两年的1867年3月，美国国会通过了兴建纪念堂的法案。1913年由建筑师亨利·培根提出设计方案，1915年，于林肯的生日（2月12日）动土兴建，1922年5月30日竣工。

◆ **Construction**

The exterior of the Memorial echoes a classic Greek temple and features Yule marble from Colorado. The structure measures 189.7 by 118.5 feet and is 99 feet tall. It is surrounded by a **peristyle**（列柱廊）of 36 fluted Doric columns, one for each of the 36 states in the Union at the time of Lincoln's death, and two columns in-antis at the entrance behind the colonnade. The columns stand 44 feet tall with a base diameter of 7.5 feet. Each column is built from 12 drums including the capital. The columns, like the exterior walls and facades, are inclined slightly toward the building's interior. This is to compensate for perspective distortions which would otherwise make the memorial appear to **bulge**（膨胀）out at the top when compared with the bottom, a common feature of Ancient Greek architecture. Above the colonnade, inscribed on the frieze, are the names of the 36 states in the Union at the time of Lincoln's death and the dates in which they entered the Union. Their names are separated by double wreath medallions in bas-relief. The cornice is composed of a carved **scroll**（卷轴）regularly interspersed with projecting lions' heads and ornamented with palmetto cresting along the upper edge. Above this on the attic frieze are inscribed the names of the 48 states present at the time of the Memorial's dedication. A bit higher is a garland joined by ribbons and palm leaves, supported by the wings of eagles.

The building is in the form of a Greek Doric temple and contains a large seated **sculpture**（雕塑）of Abraham Lincoln and inscriptions of two well-known speeches by Lincoln, The Gettysburg Address and his Second Inaugural Address. The memorial has been the site of many famous speeches, including Martin Luther King's "I Have a Dream" speech, delivered on August 28, 1963, during the rally at the end of the March on Washington for Jobs and Freedom.

> 阅读辅助
>
> 整座建筑呈长方形，长约58米，宽约36米，高约25米。是一座仿古希腊巴特农神庙式的大理石构建的古典建筑。36根白色的大理石圆形廊柱环绕着纪念堂，象征林肯任总统时所拥有的36个州。每个廊柱的横楣上分别刻有这些州的州名。

✧ Statue

Lying between the north and south chambers is the central hall containing the **solitary**（隐士）figure of Lincoln sitting in contemplation. The statue was carved by the Piccirilli Brothers under the supervision of the sculptor, Daniel Chester French, and took four years to complete.

The statue rests upon an **oblong**（椭圆形）pedestal of Tennessee marble, Lincoln's arms rest on representations of Romanfasces, a **subtle**（微妙的）touch that associates the statue with the Augustan (and imperial) theme (obelisk and funerary monuments) of the Washington Mall. The statue is discretely bordered by two pilasters, one on each side. Between these pilasters and above Lincoln's head stands the engraved **epitaph**（墓志铭）, composed by Royal Cortissoz, shown in the box to the left.

> 阅读辅助
>
> 进入纪念堂，迎面正中是一座大理石制林肯坐像，像高5.8米，由雕塑家丹尼尔·彻斯特·法兰屈设计雕刻。坐像左侧墙壁上，镌刻着林肯连任总统时的演说辞；右侧，则刻着著名的盖茨堡演说。周围还装饰着有关解放黑奴、南北统一，以及象征正义与不朽、博爱与慈善的壁画。

金门大桥 The Golden Gate Bridge
——进入古稀之年的大桥

达人了解英美

◆ History

Before the bridge was built, the only practical short route between San Francisco and what is now Marin County was by boat across a section of San Francisco Bay. Many wanted to build a bridge to connect San Francisco to Marin County. San Francisco was the largest American city still served primarily by ferry boats. Because it did not have a **permanent**（永久的）link with communities around the bay, the city's growth rate was below the national average.

Although the idea of a bridge spanning the Golden Gate was not new, the proposal that eventually took hold was made in a 1916 San Francisco Bulletin article by former engineering student James Wilkins. Strauss was chief engineer in charge of overall design and construction of the bridge project. Strauss' initial design proposal was unacceptable from a visual standpoint. The final graceful **suspension**（暂停）design was conceived and championed by New York's Manhattan Bridge designer Leon Moisseiff.

Construction began on January 5, 1933. The project cost more than $35 million, completing ahead of schedule and under budget. The project was finished and opened May 27, 1937. It was completed $1.3 million under budget.

> **阅读辅助**
>
> 金门大桥的最初的构想来源于桥梁工程师约瑟夫·斯特劳斯。这座桥的其他主要设计者包括决定其艺术造型和颜色的艾尔文·莫罗、合作进行复杂的数学推算的工程师查尔斯·埃里斯、桥梁设计师里昂·莫伊塞弗。大桥于1933年1月5日开始施工，1937年4月完工，同年5月27日对外开放。

✧ Symbol

The Golden Gate Bridge is a suspension bridge spanning the Golden Gate strait, the mile-wide, three-mile-long channel between San Francisco Bay and the Pacific Ocean. The structure links the U.S. city of San Francisco, on the northern tip of the San Francisco Peninsula, to Marin County, bridging both U.S. Route 101 and California State Route 1 across the strait. The bridge is one of the most internationally recognized symbols of San Francisco, California, and the United States. It has been declared one of the Wonders of the Modern World by the American Society of Civil Engineers.

> **阅读辅助**
>
> 金门大桥是世界著名大桥之一，被誉为20世纪桥梁工程的一项奇迹，也被认为是旧金山的象征。建成时曾是世界上跨距最大的悬索桥，金门大桥拥有世界第四高的桥塔。

✧ Visiting the Bridge

The bridge is popular with pedestrians and bicyclists, and was built with walkways on either side of the six vehicle traffic lanes. Initially, they were separated from the traffic lanes by only a metal curb, but railings between the walkways and the traffic lanes were added in 2003, primarily as a measure to prevent bicyclists from falling into the roadway.

Bus service across the bridge is provided by two public transportation agencies: San Francisco Muni and Golden Gate Transit. Muni offers Saturday and Sunday service on the 76X Marin Headlands Express bus line, and Golden Gate Transit runs numerous bus lines throughout the week.

A visitor center and gift shop, dubbed the "Bridge Pavilion", is located on the San Francisco side of the bridge, **adjacent**（邻近的）to the southeast parking lot. It opened in 2012, in time for the bridge's 75th anniversary celebration. A cafe, outdoor exhibits, and restroom facilities are located nearby.

> 阅读辅助
>
> 来到金门大桥参观的人，可以利用自行车和巴士两种交通方式，另外，大桥还有礼品商店为客人提供大桥建成75周年的纪念品。

6 拉什莫尔山 Mount Rushmore
——被全球人"玩坏"了的圣山

达人了解英美

◆ **History**

Originally known to the Lakota Sioux as Six Grandfathers, the mountain was renamed after Charles E. Rushmore, a prominent New York lawyer, during an expedition in 1885. At first, the project of carving Rushmore was undertaken to increase tourism in the Black Hills region of South Dakota. After long negotiations involving a **Congressional delegation**（代表团）and President Calvin Coolidge, the project received Congressional approval. The carving started in 1927, and ended in 1941 with no **fatalities**（灾祸）.

As Six Grandfathers, the mountain was part of the route that Lakota leader Black Elk took in a spiritual journey that **culminated**（达到高潮）at Harney Peak. It was named Mount Rushmore during a prospecting expedition by Charles Rushmore, David Swanzey, and Bill Challis. Historian Doane Robinson conceived the idea for Mount Rushmore in 1923 to promote tourism in South Dakota. In 1924, Robinson **persuaded**（劝说）sculptor Gutzon Borglum to travel to the Black Hills region to ensure the carving could be accomplished. Borglum had been involved in **sculpting**（雕刻）the Confederate Memorial Carving, a massive bas-relief memorial to Confederate leaders on Stone Mountain in Georgia, but was in disagreement with the officials there. Between October 4, 1927, and October 31, 1941, Gutzon Borglum and 400 workers sculpted the **colossal**（庞大的）60 foot high carvings of U.S. presidents George Washington, Thomas Jefferson, Theodore Roosevelt, and Abraham Lincoln to represent the first 130 years of American history.

(美)叹为观止的地标建筑 **Section 2-2**

> **阅读辅助**
>
> 1885年,美国纽约的著名律师查尔斯•E. 拉什莫尔将其在南达科他州布拉克山所拥有的矿山附近的一座花岗岩山以其姓氏命名为"拉什莫尔山",这就是拉什莫尔山名字的来由。数十年后拉什莫尔山国家纪念公园的建造计划正式启动。在拉什莫尔山上建造雕塑初衷是为了吸引更多的人们前来布拉克山地区旅游。

✧ **In culture**

Because of its fame as a monument, Mount Rushmore has been depicted in multiple places in popular culture. It is often depicted as a cover for a secret location; shown with faces removed, modified, or added; or **parodied**(拙劣模仿). The memorial was also famously used as the location of the climactic chase scene in Alfred Hitchcock's 1959 movie North by Northwest. On August 11, 1952, the U.S. Post Office issued the Mount Rushmore Memorial **commemorative**(纪念的)stamp on the 25th anniversary of the **dedication**(尽心尽力)of the Mt. Rushmore National Memorial in the Black Hills of South Dakota.

> **阅读辅助**
>
> 由于拉什莫尔山以其壮观的总统头像雕刻闻名于世,流行媒介常常会在恶搞时将四位总统换成其他人物或角色。由于拉什莫尔山是一个极具历史意义的地理标志,在许多动作片和小说的故事中,它常常会被作为某一方势力基地的所在。

7 自由女神像 *Statue of Liberty*
——美利坚民族和美法人民友谊的象征

达人了解英美

✧ **History**

Due to the troubled political situation in France, work on the statue did not commence until the early 1870s. In 1875, Laboulaye proposed that the French finance the statue and the Americans provide the site and build the pedestal. Bartholdi completed the head and the torch-bearing arm before the statue was fully designed, and these pieces were exhibited for publicity at international expositions. The statue was constructed in France, shipped overseas in crates, and assembled on the completed pedestal on what was then called Bedloe's Island. The statue's completion was marked by New York's first ticker-tape parade and a dedication ceremony presided over by President Grover Cleveland.

The statue was administered by the United States Lighthouse Board until 1901 and then by the Department of War; since 1933 it has been maintained by the National Park Service. The statue was closed for **renovation**（修理）for much of 1938. In the early 1980s, it was found to have **deteriorated**（恶化的）to such an extent that a major restoration was required. While the statue was closed from 1984 to 1986, the **torch**（火把）and a large part of the internal structure were replaced.

> **阅读辅助**
>
> 法国人认为法国和美国人民应该共同制作美国独立的纪念品。这一想法可能是为了纪念南北战争以北军胜利、奴隶制寿终正寝结束。但由于当时法国在政治形势上陷入困境，因此塑像的建造工作一直到19世纪70年代初才展开。塑像完成之际，纽约举行了历史上的首次纸带游行，美国总统格罗弗·克利夫兰主持了落成仪式。

✧ Significance

The statue is of a robed female figure representing Libertas, the Roman goddess, who bears a torch and a **tabula**（书板）ansata upon which is inscribed the date of the American Declaration of Independence, July 4, 1776. A broken chain lies at her feet. The statue is an icon of freedom and of the United States: a welcoming signal to immigrants arriving from abroad.

Bartholdi was inspired by French law professor and politician, who is said to have **commented**（注释）in 1865 that any monument raised to American independence would properly be a joint project of the French and American peoples. He may have been minded to honor the Union victory in the American Civil War and the end of slavery.

> **阅读辅助**
>
> 这座塑像主要由一位身穿长袍的女性人物构成，代表罗马神话中的自主神，她右手高举火炬、左手的册子上写有美国独立宣言的签署日期，脚下还有断裂的锁链。这座塑像是自由和美国的象征，是对外来移民的欢迎信号。

✧ Tourism

The statue is situated in Upper New York Bay on Liberty Island south of Ellis Island, which together comprise the Statue of Liberty National Monument. No charge is made for entrance to the national monument, but there is a cost for the ferry service that all visitors must use, as private boats may not dock at the island. A **concession**（特许）was granted in 2007 to Statue Cruises to operate the transportation and ticketing facilities, replacing Circle Line, which had operated the service since 1953.

> 阅读辅助
>
> 自由女神像坐落在上纽约湾的自由岛，位于埃利斯岛以南。自由女神像国家纪念区的入口不收门票，但游客上岛必须搭乘收费的轮渡服务，因为私人船只不能在岛上停泊。

8 纽约中央车站 Grand Central Terminal
——见证了岁月流逝的大中央火车站

达人了解英美

◆ History

Three buildings serving essentially the same function have stood on this site. The original large and imposing scale was intended by the New York Central Railroad to enhance competition and compare favorably in the public eye with the **archrival**（对手赛）Pennsylvania Railroad and smaller lines. The station was designed by John B. Snook and opened in October 1871. The headhouse building containing passenger service areas and railroad offices was an "L" shape with a short leg running east-west on 42nd Street and a long leg running north-south on Vanderbilt Avenue.

Between 1899 and 1900, the head house was essentially **demolished**（拆卸）. It was expanded from three to six stories with an entirely new façade, on plans by railroad architect Bradford Gilbert. The train shed was kept. The tracks that **previously**（预先）continued south of 42nd Street were removed and the train yard reconfigured in an effort to reduce congestion and turn-around time for trains. The reconstructed building was renamed Grand Central Station.

Between 1903 and 1913, the entire building was torn down in phases and replaced by the current Grand Central Terminal, which was designed by the architectural firms of Reed and Stem and Warren and Wetmore, who entered an agreement to act as the associated architects of Grand Central Terminal in February 1904.

> **阅读辅助**
>
> 大中央车站由美国铁路大王出资建造，于1913年正式启用并取代了之前的旧站。自车站落成后，车站附近的公园大道上如雨后春笋般出现了许多饭店、办公大楼及豪宅，也因此使这里成为全曼哈顿岛地价最高的地区。

❖ Layout

The tracks are numbered according to their location in the terminal building. The upper-level tracks are numbered 11 to 42 east to west. The lower level has 27 tracks, numbered 100 to 126, east to west; currently, only tracks 102–112, and 114–116 are used for passenger service.

Grand Central has restaurants, such as the Oyster Bar and various fast food outlets surrounding the Dining Concourse on the level below the Main Concourse, as well as delis, bakeries, newsstands, a **gourmet**（食客）and fresh food market, an annex of the New York Transit Museum, and more than 40 retail stores.

The Main Concourse is the center of Grand Central. The space is **cavernous**（洞穴状的）and usually filled with bustling crowds. The large American flag was hung in Grand Central Terminal a few days after the September 11 attacks on the World Trade Center. The Main Concourse has an **elaborately**（苦心经营地）decorated astronomical ceiling, conceived in 1912 by Warren with his friend.

The terminal has 44 platforms, the most in any railway station in the world; 67 tracks are in regular passenger use. The upper level has 42 tracks overall. The lower level is smaller, having only 27 tracks, but is also circled by several balloon loops.

Section 2-2 (美)叹为观止的地标建筑

> **阅读辅助**
>
> 中央大厅位于车站的正中央,经常挤满人潮,售票亭和询问处就设在此处。9·11恐怖攻击事件之后,大厅上挂了一幅美国国旗。大厅里的星空穹庐原画于1912年,由法国艺术家创作。用餐大厅位于中央大厅的下面。这里有很多高级餐馆和速食店。

✧ In Popular Culture

Grand Central Terminal has been used in numerous novels and film and TV productions over the years. Kyle McCarthy, who handles production at Grand Central Terminal for MTA Metro-North Railroad, "Grand Central is one of the **quintessential**(精萃的) New York places. Whether filmmakers need an establishing shot of arriving in New York or transportation scenes, the restored landmark building is visually **appealing**(吸引人的) and authentic."

> **阅读辅助**
>
> 中央车站经常会出现在小说电影和电影中,作为背景地点而闻名于世。

123

联合国总部大厦 The United Nations Headquarters
——世界上唯一的一块"国际领土"

达人了解英美

◇ **History**

The property was originally a **slaughter**(屠杀)house before the donation took place. While the United Nations had dreamed of constructing an independent city for its new world capital, multiple obstacles soon forced the Organization to downsize their plans. Thus, it was a given that the Secretariat would be housed in a tall office tower. During daily meetings from February to June 1947, the collaborative team produced at least 45 designs and variations. Rather than hold a competition for the design of the facilities for the headquarters, the UN decided to commission a multinational team of leading architects to collaborate on the design.

After much discussion, Harrison, who coordinated the meetings, determined that a design based on Niemeyer's project 32 and Le Corbusier's project 23 would be developed for the final project.

It consisted of a large block containing both the Assembly Hall and the Council Chambers near the centre of the site with the Secretariat tower emerging as a slab from the south. Niemeyer's plan was closer to that actually constructed, with a distinctive General Assembly building, a long low **horizontal**(水平线)block housing the other meeting rooms, and a tall tower for the Secretariat. The complex as built, however, repositioned Niemeyer's General Assembly building to the north of this **tripartite**(三重的)composition. This plan included a public plaza as well.

> **阅读辅助**
>
> 因为毗邻东河快车道和东河的缘故，有必要将之建成高层建筑。建筑团队在50个提案中选出尼梅耶的32号提案以及柯布西耶的23号提案，其中前者将分别用于联合国大会和秘书处的建筑分开为两座，而后者则只包括一个囊括一切机构的建筑。

◆ Significance

The United Nations has three additional, **subsidiary**（附属机构）, regional headquarters, or headquarters districts. These were opened in Geneva in 1946, Vienna in 1980, and Nairobi in 2011. These adjunct offices help represent UN interests, facilitate diplomatic activities, and enjoy certain extraterritorial privileges, but only the main headquarters in New York contains the seats of the principal organs of the UN, including the General Assembly and Security Council. All fifteen of the United Nations' specialized are located outside New York at these other headquarters or in other cities.

Although it is situated in New York City, the land occupied by the United Nations Headquarters and the spaces of buildings that it rents are under the sole administration of the United Nations and not the US government. They are technically **extraterritorial**（域外）through a treaty agreement with the U.S. government. However, in exchange for local police, fire **protection**（防卫）and other services, the United Nations agrees to acknowledge most local, state, and federal laws.

> **阅读辅助**
>
> 联合国总部大楼是联合国总部的所在地，位于美国纽约市曼哈顿区东侧，这块领土的所有权已经不属于美国以及任何一国，而是世界上唯一的一块"国际领土"。用来处理国际日常事务。

✧ Construction

The United Nations Headquarters complex was constructed in stages with the core complex completed between 1948 and 1952. The Headquarters occupies a site beside the East River, on between 17 and 18 acres of land **purchased**（已购买）from the foremost New York real estate developer of the time, William Zeckendorf, Sr. Nelson Rockefeller arranged this purchase, after an initial offer to locate it on the Rockefeller family estate of Kykuit was rejected as being too isolated from Manhattan. The US$8.5 million purchase was then funded by his father, John D. Rockefeller, Jr., who donated it to the city. Wallace Harrison, the personal architectural adviser for the Rockefeller family, and a prominent corporate architect, served as the Director of Planning for the United Nations Headquarters. His firm, Harrison and Abramovitz, oversaw the execution of the design.

> **阅读辅助**
>
> 此大楼于1949年和1950年间兴建，土地购自于当时的纽约房地产家威廉·杰肯多夫，面积阔达17英亩。之后，纳尔逊·洛克菲勒便协助新的土地的购买，其父小约翰·戴维森·洛克菲勒则捐助了850万美元协助兴建大楼。

Section 3-1 （英）流连忘返的旅游胜地

英国是世界上第一个工业化国家，是一个具有多元文化和开放思想的社会。这个美丽的国家，文物古迹比比皆是，自然风景秀丽，旅游资源丰富。许多城市，如"万城之花"伦敦，"北方雅典"爱丁堡，大学城牛津、剑桥，古色古香的约克城，莎翁故乡斯特拉特福，都是享有世界声誉的旅游名城，让我们背上背包出发吧。

1 巨石阵 *Stonehenge*
——怪异的史前文明遗址

达人了解英美

◇ **History**

One of the most famous sites in the world, Stonehenge is the remains of a ring of standing set within **earthworks**（大地艺术品）. It is in the middle of the most dense complex of Neolithic and Bronze **Agemonuments**（遗迹）in England, including several hundred burial.

Archaeologists（考古学家）believe it was built anywhere from 3000 BC to 2000 BC. Radiocarbon dating in 2008 suggested that the first stones were raised between 2400 and 2200 BC, whilst another theory suggests that bluestones may have been raised at the site as early as 3000 BC.

The surrounding circular earth bank and ditch, which **constitute**（构成）the earliest phase of the monument, have been dated to about 3100 BC. The site was added to the UNESCO's list of World in 1986 in a co-listing with Avebury Henge. It is a national legally protected Scheduled Ancient Monument. Stonehenge is owned by the Crown and managed by English, while the surrounding land is owned by the National Trust.

阅读辅助

巨石阵又称索尔兹伯里石环、环状列石、太阳神庙等名，是欧洲著名的史前时代文化神庙遗址，考古碳年代鉴定的结论认定是建于约公元前4000-2000年，属新石器时代末期至青铜时代。1136年巨石阵第一次被人发现，但是此前的历朝历代却未曾记载，所以，巨石阵的年份不可能有公元前2000年那么久远。

✧ Function & Construction

There is little or no direct evidence for the construction techniques used by the Stonehenge builders. Over the years, various authors have suggested that **supernatural**（超自然现象）or anachronistic methods were used, usually **asserting**（声明）that the stones were impossible to move otherwise. However, **conventional**（传统的）techniques, using Neolithic technology as basic as shear legs, have been **demonstrably**（可论证地）effective at moving and placing stones of a similar size. Proposed functions for the site include usage as an **astronomical**（天文的）observatory or as a religious site.

More recently two major new theories have been proposed. They argue that this accounts for the high number of burials in the area and for the evidence of trauma deformity in some of the graves. However, they do **concede**（让步）that the site was probably multifunctional and used for ancestor worship as well.

阅读辅助

几个世纪以来，没有人知道巨石阵的真正用途，人们对这座巨石阵的用途做出了种种猜测。一些人通过考古发掘，发现土堤内侧有多处墓穴，便据此推测它是古代部落酋长的坟墓。而出土的大量兽骨残骸则被怀疑是祭陵用的牺牲品。于是有人判断，巨石阵是祭祖用的祭祀场所。还有结论认为这是一座古代天文台。

温莎古堡 Windsor Castle
——见证老天荒爱情故事之地

达人了解英美

✧ **History**

The original castle was built in the 11th century after the Norman invasion by William the Conqueror. Since the time of Henry I, it has been used by succeeding monarchs and is the longest-occupied palace in Europe. The castle's **lavish**（滥用）, early 19th-century State Apartments are architecturally significant, described by art historian Hugh Roberts as "a superb and **unrivalled**（无与伦比的）sequence of rooms widely regarded as the finest and most complete expression of later Georgian taste". The castle includes the 15th-century St. George's Chapel, considered by historian John Martin Robinson to be "one of the supreme achievements of English Perpendicular Gothic" design. More than 500 people live and work in Windsor Castle.

Originally designed to protect Norman dominance around the outskirts of London, and to oversee a strategically important part of the River Thames, Windsor Castle was built as a **motte**（丛林）and bailey, with three wards surrounding a central mound. Gradually replaced with stone **fortifications**（防御工事）, the castle withstood a **prolonged**（拖延的）siege during the First Barons' War at the start of the 13th century. Henry III built a luxurious royal palace within the castle during the middle of the century, and Edward III went further, rebuilding the palace to produce an even grander set of buildings in what would become "the most expensive secular building project of the entire Middle Ages in England". Edward's core design lasted through the Tudor period, during which Henry VIII and Elizabeth I made increasing use of the castle as a royal court and centre for diplomatic entertainment.

> **阅读辅助**
>
> 城堡的历史也和英国的君主体制有相当密切的关系，跟随着温莎城堡的历史可以追溯到当时统治的英国君主，温莎城堡的历史可以回溯到威廉一世时期。在和平时期时，温莎城堡扩建了许多巨大且华丽的房间；在战争时期，城堡则会加强防卫，这个模式直到现在仍然不变。温莎城堡是英国君主主要的行政官邸，现任的英国女王伊丽莎白二世每年有相当多的时间在温莎城堡度过。

◆ Nowadays

Windsor Castle survived the **tumultuous**（骚乱的）period of the English Civil War, when it was used as a military headquarters for Parliamentary forces and a prison for Charles I. During the Restoration, Charles II rebuilt much of Windsor Castle with the help of architect Hugh May, creating a set of **extravagant**（奢侈的）, Baroque interiors that are still admired. After a period of neglect during the 18th century, George III and George IV **renovated**（革新）and rebuilt Charles II's palace at colossal expense, producing the current design of the State Apartments, full of Rococo, Gothicand Baroque furnishings. Victoria made minor changes to the castle, which became the centre for royal entertainment for much of her reign. Windsor Castle was used as a refuge for the royal family during the bombing campaigns of the Second World War and survived a fire in 1992. It is a popular tourist attraction, a venue for hosting state visits, and the preferred weekend home of Elizabeth II.

> **阅读辅助**
>
> 伊莉莎白一世之后的英王是詹姆士一世与查理一世，他们并没有对城堡进行重大的修建。而城堡则在伊丽莎白二世统治期间作了许多建设，不仅重建与保护城堡的结构，而且也让城堡成为英国主要的旅游景点之一。现任的英国女王伊丽莎白二世每年有相当多的时间在温莎城堡度过，在这里进行许多国家或是私人的娱乐活动。

◇ Architecture

Windsor Castle occupies 13 acres and combines the features of a **fortification**（防御工事）, a palace, and a small town. The present-day castle was created during a sequence of phased building projects, culminating in the reconstruction work after a fire in 1992. It is in essence a Georgian and Victorian design based on a medieval structure, with Gothic features reinvented in a modern style. Since the 14th century, architecture at the castle has attempted to produce a contemporary **reinterpretation**（重新解释）of older fashions and traditions, repeatedly imitating **outmoded**（过时的）or even antiquated styles. As a result, architect Sir William Whitfield has pointed to Windsor Castle's architecture as having "a certain fictive quality", the Picturesque and Gothic design generating "a sense that a theatrical performance is being put on here", despite late 20th century efforts to expose more of the older structures to increase the sense of **authenticity**（真实性）. Although there has been some criticism, the castle's architecture and history lends it a "place amongst the greatest European palaces".

> **阅读辅助**
>
> 城堡的设计随着时间、皇室的喜好、需求与财政而改变与发展。尽管如此，城堡的许多特征仍然混合了古典与现代元素。整个温莎城堡可以分为上区、中区和下区。上区主要有13世纪的法庭、滑铁卢厅和圣乔治厅、女王交谊厅等房间。中区最明显的标志是玫瑰花园围绕的圆塔为主。而下区主要有圣乔治礼拜堂、爱伯特纪念礼拜堂等建筑。

3 唐宁街 *Downing Street*
——世界上出镜率最高的街道

达人了解英美

◆ History

The street was built in the 1680s by Sir George Downing, 1st Baronet, on the site of a **mansion**（大厦）called Hampden House. Downing was a soldier and diplomat who served under Oliver Cromwell and King Charles II, and who invested in properties and acquired considerable wealth. In 1654, he purchased the lease on land east of Saint James's Park, adjacent to the House at the Back, and within walking distance of Parliament. Between 1682 and 1684, Downing built a cul-de-sac of two-storey townhomes complete with coach-houses, stables and views of St. James's Park. The upper end of the Downing Street cul de sac closed off access to St. James's Park, making the street quiet and private. They had several distinguished residents. The Countess of Yarmouth lived at Number 10 between 1688 and 1689, Lord Lansdowne from 1692 to 1696 and the Earl of Grantham from 1699 to 1703.

Downing probably never lived in his townhouses. In 1675 he retired to Cambridge where he died a few months after they were completed. His **portrait**（肖像）hangs in the entrance foyer of the modern Number 10 Downing Street. The houses between Number 10 and Whitehall were taken over by the government and **demolished**（破坏）in 1824 to allow the construction of the Privy Council Office, Board of Trade and Treasury offices. In 1861 the houses on the south side of Downing Street gave way to new purpose-build government offices for the Foreign Office, India Office, Colonial Office, and the Home Office.

> **阅读辅助**
>
> 唐宁街是由乔治·唐宁爵士——第一代男爵所修建，街名亦以他的姓氏命名。唐宁本人是一位军人和外交家，曾先后为奥利弗·克伦威尔和英皇查理二世效力。在后来，查理二世赐一块贴近圣詹姆士公园的土地予唐宁，而那一块土地就是今日的唐宁街。首相、财政大臣和党鞭都居住在街的一边。

✧ Layout

Downing Street in London, England, has for over three hundred years housed the official residences of two of the most senior British Cabinet ministers: the First Lord of the Treasury, an office now **synonymous**（同义的）with that of Prime Minister of the United Kingdom; and the Second Lord of the Treasury, an office held by the Chancellor of the Exchequer. The Prime Minister's official residence is 10 Downing Street; the Chancellor's official residence is next door at Number 11. The Government's Chief Whip has an official residence at Number 12, though the current Chief Whip's residence is at Number 9.

Downing Street is located in Whitehall in central London, a few minutes' walk from the Houses of Parlia ment and a little farther from Buckingham Palace. The street was built in the 1680s by Sir George Downing , on the site of a mansion called Hampden House. The houses on the south side of the street were **demolished**（被拆毁的）in the nineteenth century to make way for government offices, now occupied by the Foreign and Commonwealth Office. "Downing Street" is often used as a metonym for the Government of the United Kingdom.

> **阅读辅助**
>
> 　　唐宁街位于英国首都伦敦的西敏内,在过往200年来,都是重要内阁官员的宅邸,即英国首相,以及兼任第二财政大臣的财政大臣的官邸。唐宁街内最有名的宅邸,非唐宁街10号莫属,它以往是第一财政大臣的官邸,但自从此职与首相合并后,就成为今日的首相官邸。因此,"唐宁街"和"唐宁街10号"是英国首相或首相办公室的代名词;而"唐宁街11号"就代表财相或其办公室。

4 诺森伯兰国家公园 Northumberland National Park
——宛如仙境的国家公园

达人了解英美

◆ Geography

Northumberland National Park is the northernmost national park in England. It covers an area of more than 1030 km² between the Scottish border in the north to just south of Hadrian's Wall. The park lies entirely within Northumberland, covering about a quarter of the county. The park covers several distinct areas. In the north are the Cheviots, a range of hills that mark the border between England and Scotland. Further south, the hills give way to areas of rolling **moorland**（荒野）, some of which have been covered by **forestry**（森林地）plantations to form Kielder Forest. The southernmost part of the park covers the dramatic central section of Hadrian's Wall.

The Northumberland National Park covers a large area of Western Northumberland and borders the English county of Cumbria and the Scottishcounty of The Scottish borders. The national park encompasses much of the Cheviot hills and adjoins the Southern **uplands**（高地）of Scotland, of which the Cheviot hills are sometimes referred to as being a part of. Kielder Forest lies within much of the park and in other areas forms a forest park. Kielder Forest is the largest man-made forest in Europe and **surrounds**（围绕）Kielder Water.

（英）流连忘返的旅游胜地 **Section 3-1**

> **阅读辅助**
>
> 诺森伯兰国家公园是英格兰最北部的国家公园。公园位于诺森伯兰郡境内，面积超过1030平方公里，约占该郡四分之一大，西北面与苏格兰接壤，南面则以哈德良长城为界。

◇ **Site**

The 10,000 year history of the region is explored through the many **archaeological**（考古学的）sites, ranging from prehistoric monuments and Roman remains to Pele towers, constructed as a defense against Border Reivers.

Hadrian's Wall also called the Roman Wall, Picts' Wall, or Vallum Hadriani, was a defensive **fortification**（设防）in the Roman province of Britannia, begun in AD 122 during the rule of emperor Hadrian. It had a stone base and a stone wall. There were milecastles with two **turrets**（炮台）in between.

> **阅读辅助**
>
> 公园内的古迹可上溯到10,000年前，有史前遗迹、罗马人遗迹。哈德良长城的中段坐落于公园的最南部。

5 尼斯湖 Loch Ness
——充满谜团的湖泊

达人了解英美

◆ **Geography**

Loch Ness is a large, deep, freshwater loch in the Scottish Highlands extending for approximately 23 miles southwest of Inverness. Its surface is 52 ft above sea level. It is connected at the southern end by the River Oich and a section of the Caledonian Canal to Loch Oich. At the northern end there is the Bona Narrows which opens out into Loch Dochfour, which feeds the River Ness and a further section of canal to Inverness. It is one of a series of interconnected, murky bodies of water in Scotland; its water visibility is exceptionally low due to a high peat content in the surrounding soil.

Loch Ness is the second largest Scottish loch by surface area at 22 sq mi after Loch Lomond, but due to its great depth, it is the largest by volume. Its deepest point is 755 ft, making it the second deepest loch in Scotland after Loch Morar. It contains more fresh water than all the lakes in England and Wales combined and is the largest body of water on the Great Glen Fault, which runs from Inverness in the north to Fort William in the south.

阅读辅助

尼斯湖是横越苏格兰高地的金狮运河的一部分，该运河连结了大西洋和北海。尼斯湖是苏格兰高地众多相连的湖泊的其中一个，其水质因大量的浮藻和泥炭而非常浑浊，水中的能见度极低，不足两米。而且湖底地形复杂，有很多洞穴。

◇ Monster

Loch Ness is best known for alleged sightings of the cryptozoological（神秘动物学）Loch Ness Monster, also known affectionately as "Nessie". Loch Ness is the alleged home of the Loch Ness Monster, a cryptid, reputedly a large unknown animal. It is similar to other supposed lake monsters in Scotland and elsewhere, though its description varies from one account to the next. Popular interest and belief in the animal's existence has varied since it was first brought to the world's attention in 1933.

阅读辅助

关于水怪的最早记载可追溯到公元565年，爱尔兰传教士圣哥伦伯和他的仆人在湖中游泳，水怪突然向仆人袭来，多亏教士及时相救，仆人才游回岸上，保住性命，自此以后，十多个世纪里，有关水怪出现的消息多达一万多宗。但当时的人们对此并不相信，认为不过是古代的传说或无稽之谈。

6 泰晤士河 *River Thames*
——英国著名的"母亲"河

达人了解英美

◆ **Summary**

The River Thames is a river that flows through southern. With a total length of 236 miles, it is the longest river entirely in England and the second, after the River Severn. While it is best known for flowing through London, the river also flows alongside other towns and cities, including Oxford, Reading, Henley-on-Thames, and Windsor.

Along its course are 45 **navigation**（航行）locks with accompanying weirs. Its **catchment**（流域）area covers a large part of South Eastern and a small part of Western England and the river is fed by 38 named tributaries. The river contains over 80 islands. With its waters varying from freshwater to almost seawater, the Thames supports a variety of wildlife and has a number of adjoining Sites of Special Scientific Interest, with the largest being in the remaining parts of the North Kent Marshes and covering 5,449 hectares.

阅读辅助

泰晤士河是位于南英格兰的一条河流，全长约338公里，流经英格兰的三个郡，是英格兰最长的河流，也是这个英国第二长河，次于354公里的塞文河，同时也是全世界水面交通最繁忙的都市河流，而且还被视作伦敦地标之一。

◆ The active river

The river gives its name to three informal areas: the Thames Valley, a region of England around the river between Oxford and west London; the Thames; and the greatly **overlapping**（盖过）Thames around the tidal Thames to the east of London and including the waterway itself. Thames Valley Police is a formal body that takes its name from the river, covering three counties.

In an alternative name, derived from its long tidal up to Teddington Lock in south west London, the lower reaches of the river are called the Tideway.

> 阅读辅助
>
> 泰晤士流域形成了许多英格兰城市，除去伦敦之外，还有牛津、雷丁和温莎等。泰晤士河的源头据称位处威尔士，绵延到与莱茵河等其他欧洲大陆河流汇合。

◆ Sports

Rowing and sailing clubs are common along the Thames, which is navigable to such vessels. Kayaking and **canoeing**（乘独木舟）also take place. Major annual events include the Henley Royal Regatta and The Boat Race, while the Thames has been used during two Summer Olympic Games. Safe headwaters and reaches are a summer venue for organized swimming, which is prohibited on safety grounds in a stretch centered on Central London. Non-Olympic watersports with a lesser presence include **skiffing**（小帆船）and punting.

> **阅读辅助**
>
> 泰晤士河对英国文化意义也不可忽视。泰晤士河是许多英国水上运动,如牛津剑桥赛艇对抗赛、1908年夏季奥运会划艇赛、1948年夏季奥运会划艇赛的举办地。很多文学作品也是以泰晤士河流域的风物为背景写成的。

✧ Human activity

The marks of human activity, in some cases dating back to Pre-Roman Britain, are visible at various points along the river. These include a variety of structures connected with use of the river, such as navigations, bridges, and watermills, as well as prehistoric burial **mounds** (土丘). A major maritime route is formed for much of its length for shipping and supplies: through the Port of London for international trade, internally along its length and by its connection to the British canal system. The river's position has put it at the centre of many events in British history, leading to it being described by John Burns as "liquid history".

> **阅读辅助**
>
> 有考古证据显示在新石器时代就已经有人类在泰晤士河流域生活了。实际上,泰晤士河河畔有许多古罗马和萨克森人的聚居地,早在1300年代,泰晤士河成为了伦敦的排污河。之后由于伦敦国际地位的提高使得泰晤士河上的贸易频繁起来,到了十八世纪,它已经是大英帝国和世界上最繁忙的河道之一。

7 布莱尼姆宫 Blenheim Palace
——英国园林的经典之作

达人了解英美

◇ History

It is the principal residence of the dukes of Marlborough, and the only non-royal non-episcopal country house in England to hold the title of palace. The palace, one of England's largest houses, was built between 1705 and circa 1722.

The building of the palace was originally intended to be a reward to John Churchill, 1st Duke of Marlborough, from a grateful nation for the duke's military triumphs against the French and Bavarians during the War of the Spanish Succession, **culminating**（达到顶点）in the 1704 Battle of Blenheim. However, soon after its construction began, the palace was to become the subject of political infighting; this led to Marlborough's exile, the fall from power of his duchess, and lasting damage to the reputation of the architect Sir John Vanbrugh.

Designed in the rare, and short-lived, English Baroque style, architectural appreciation of the palace is as divided today as it was in the 1720s. It is unique in its combined usage as a family home, **mausoleum**（陵墓）and national monument. The palace is also notable as the birthplace and ancestral home of Sir Winston Churchill.

> **阅读辅助**
>
> 　　1704年马尔伯勒公爵因取得了布莱尼姆战役的胜利，国王将这座府邸赐给了他。布莱尼姆宫是当时著名的建筑大师约翰·范布勒于1705年至1722年间完成的一项杰作。英国首相温斯顿·丘吉尔就诞生在布莱尼姆宫，他是第八代马尔伯勒公爵的孙子，他继承了这个显赫家族的优良传统，发挥了卓越的军事才能。

❖ Nowadays

　　Following the palace's completion, it became the home of the Churchill, later Spencer-Churchill, family for the next 300 years, and various members of the family have in that period wrought changes, in the interiors, park and gardens. At the end of the 19th century, the palace was saved from ruin by funds gained from the 9th Duke of Marlborough's marriage to American railroad heiress Consuelo Vanderbilt. The exterior of the palace remains in good repair.

　　The palace remains the home of the Dukes of Marlborough, the present **incumbent**（现任者）of the title being Charles James Spencer-Churchill, 12th Duke of Marlborough. Charles James succeeded the Dukedom upon his father's death on 16 October 2014.

> **阅读辅助**
>
> 　　20世纪初，第九代马尔伯勒公爵在这座官邸的东西两侧重新修建了形状规整的花园。第九代公爵请当时最著名的法国园林设计师阿希尔·迪歇纳来重新设计这些花园，迪歇纳曾经设计建造过法国埃松的库朗斯水乡泽国。

◆ **Design**

Vanbrugh planned Blenheim in perspective - that is to be best viewed from a distance. As the site covers some seven acres this is also a necessity. Close to, and square on, the facades can appear **daunting**（使人气馁的）, or weighed down by too much stone and ornamentation.

The plan of the Palace's principal block is a rectangle pierced by two courtyards; these serve as little more than light wells. Contained behind the southern facade are the principal state apartments; on the east side are the suites of private apartments of the Duke and Duchess, and on the west along the entire length of the piano nobile is given a long gallery originally conceived as a picture gallery, but is now the library. The corps de logis is flanked by two further service blocks around square courtyards. The east court contains the kitchens, laundry, and other domestic offices, the west court adjacent to the chapel the stables and indoor riding school. The three blocks together form the "Great Court" designed to overpower the visitor arriving at the palace. Pilasters and pillars abound, while from the roofs, themselves resembling those of a small town, great statues in the Renaissance manner of St. Peter's in Rome gaze down on the visitor below, who is rendered **inconsequential**（不合理的）. Other assorted statuary in the guise of martial **trophies**（战利品）decorate the roofs, most notably Britannia standing atop the entrance pediment in front of two reclining chained French captives sculpted in the style of Michelangelo, and the English lion devouring the French cock, on the lower roofs.

> 阅读辅助
>
> 宏伟的大厅中最令人惊叹的是由詹姆斯·桑希尔于1716年绘制的天花板，长长的拱形走廊一直延伸到大厅的南北两边，这是温布勒的典型之作。在国家餐厅中，桌子与银色的镀金明顿餐具摆放在一起。在格林灵吉本斯制作的大理石门上面，装饰有马尔伯勒公爵作为罗马帝国王子时的有两个头的鹰章。长长的图书馆最初被设计为画廊，这个55米长的房间展示了一些宫殿内最好的粉饰灰泥装饰。

8 锡辛赫斯特 *Sissinghurst*
——见证爱情的玫瑰花园

达人了解英美

◇ Summary

Sissinghurst's history is similar to that of nearby Cranbrook. Iron Age working tools have been found and the village was for centuries a meeting and resting place for people travelling towards the south coast. Sissinghurst is situated with Cranbrook to the south, Goudhurst to the west, Tenterden to the east and Staplehurst to the north. It sits just back from the A229 which goes from Rochester to Hawkhurst.

阅读辅助

锡辛赫斯特堡的历史可以追溯到中古时代，在13世纪的时候这块风景优美的土地就已经成为当地的标志。14世纪时，它以舒适的环境和强大的皇家气派俘获了爱德华一世的心。锡辛赫斯特堡位于英国肯特郡，而肯特郡被称为英国的花园，而锡辛赫斯特堡更是被誉为肯特郡里最美丽的地方。

◇ Castle Garden

Sissinghurst's garden was created in the 1930s by Vita Sackville-West, poet and gardening writer, and her husband Harold Nicolson, author and diplomat. Sackville-West was a writer on the **fringes**（云图条纹）of the Bloomsbury group who found her greatest popularity in the weekly columns she contributed as gardening **correspondent**（代表）of The Observer, which incidentally – for she never touted it – made her own garden famous. The garden itself is designed as a series of "rooms", each with a different character of color and/or theme, divided by high clipped **hedges**（树篱）and pink brick walls.

> **阅读辅助**
>
> 1930年，出身贵族的作家维塔科尔森买下了当时已成为废墟的城堡，之后他们将城堡进行修建，并专注于造园。一方面，与丈夫哈罗德的婚姻持续了终生，两个人三十年的爱和对造园艺术的执着追求的结晶就是这花园。白色花园以白色的玫瑰为中心，只有白色的花和银色的枝叶的花园显得分外妖娆。

9 杜莎夫人蜡像馆 *Madame Tussaud's*
——英国古今名人集合之地

达人了解英美

◇ Background

Marie Tussaud was born as Marie Grosholtz in 1761 in Strasbourg, France. Her mother worked as a housekeeper for Dr. Philippe Curtius in Bern, Switzerland, who was a physician skilled in wax **modeling**（造型）. Curtius taught Tussaud the art of wax modeling. Tussaud created her first wax sculpture, of Voltaire, in 1777. Other famous people she modeled at that time include Jean-Jacques Rousseau and Benjamin Franklin. During the French Revolution she modeled many prominent victims. In her memoirs she claims that she would search through **corpses**（尸体）to find the severed heads of executed citizens, from which she would make death masks. Her death masks were held up as revolutionary flags and paraded through the streets of Paris.

Following the doctor's death in 1794, she **inherited**（继承）his vast collection of wax models and spent the next 33 years travelling around Europe. She married to Francois Tussaud in 1795 lent a new name to the show: Madame Tussaud's. In 1802 she went to London, having accepted an invitation from Paul Philidor, a magic lantern and **phantasmagoria**（魔术幻灯）pioneer, to exhibit her work alongside his show at the Lyceum Theatre, London.

阅读辅助

杜莎夫人原名为玛丽·格劳舒兹，生于法国的斯特拉斯堡，是法国一位杰出的艺术家，以制作蜡像而闻名。她自小随一名医生学习蜡像制作技艺，之后这位医生于1770年在巴黎创办了蜡像馆，在当时吸引了大量观众。而杜莎夫人则在1777年为伏尔泰创作了她的第一尊蜡像，那一段时间她也为其他著名人士制作蜡像，包括卢梭、本杰明·富兰克林等。

◇ Origins

By 1835 Marie had settled down in Baker Street, London, and opened a museum. This part of the exhibition included victims of the French Revolution and newly created figures of murderers and other criminals. The name is often credited to a contributor to Punch in 1845, but Marie appears to have **originated**（起源）it herself, using it in advertising as early as 1843. Other famous people were added to the exhibition, including Horatio Nelson, and Sir Walter Scott. Some of the sculptures done by Marie Tussaud herself still exist.

The gallery originally contained some 400 different figures, but fire damage in 1925, coupled with German bombs in 1941, has rendered most of these older models **defunct**（死者）. The casts themselves have survived, and these can be seen in the museum's history exhibit. By 1883 the restricted space and rising cost of the Baker Street site prompted her grandson to commission the building at its current location on Marylebone Road. The new exhibition galleries were opened on 14 July 1884 and were a great success.

阅读辅助

那位医生去世后，便将他的蜡制品收藏全部转给杜莎夫人。1802年，杜莎夫人到了伦敦，后来英法战争的缘故使她无法回到法国，于是杜莎夫人带着她的蜡制品游遍大不列颠和爱尔兰。1835年，在她74岁高龄时，她在伦敦贝克街建立了第一个永久性展览馆。

10 特拉法尔加广场 *Trafalgar Square*
——观光客的必到之地

达人了解英美

◆ **History**

Trafalgar Square is a public space and tourist attraction in central London, built around the area formerly known as Charing Cross. It is situated in the City of Westminster. From the time of Edward I to the early 19th century, most of the area now occupied by Trafalgar Square was the site of the King's Mews, which stretched north from the position of the original Charing Cross, where the Strand from the City met Whitehall, coming north from Westminster. In the 1820s George IV engaged the architect John Nash to redevelop the area. Nash cleared the square as part of his Charing Cross Improvement Scheme. The present architecture of the square is due to Sir Charles Barry and was completed in 1845.

At its centre is Nelson's Column, which is guarded by four lion **statues**（雕像）at its base. There are a number of commemorative statues and sculptures in the square, while one plinth, left empty since it was built in 1840, The Fourth Plinth, has been host to **contemporary**（同时期的东西）art since 1999. The square is also used for political demonstrations and community gatherings, such as the celebration of New Year's Eve.

阅读辅助

特拉法尔加广场南端是伦敦传统中心点查令十字街,再往南是政府办公区白厅,通向国会大厦,西南是水师提督门,背后是通往白金汉宫的仪仗道林荫路。特拉法尔加广场最突出的标志是南端的纳尔逊纪念柱，它是为纪念著名的特拉法尔加港海战而修建的。为了纪念这位为大英帝国立下不朽功勋的海军上将，每年10月21日，总有许多人到特拉法尔加广场举行悼念仪式。

◇ Name

The name commemorates the Battle of Trafalgar, a British naval victory of the Napoleonic Wars over France and Spain which took place on 21 October 1805 off the coast of Cape Trafalgar, Spain. The original name was to have been "King William the Fourth's Square", but George Ledwell Taylor suggested the name "Trafalgar Square".

阅读辅助

英国海军的传奇人物霍莱伊希奥·纳尔逊海军上将是在西班牙南部的特拉法加海战中战死的。为了彰显纳尔逊的战绩，人们特地在19世纪后期建造了这个广场。

◇ Famous

The square was once famous for its feral pigeons, and feeding them was a popular activity. The desirability of the birds' presence was **contentious**（有异议的）: their droppings disfigured stonework, and the flock, estimated at its peak to be 35,000, was considered a health hazard.

For many years, revellers celebrating the start of a New Year have gathered in the square, despite a lack of civic celebrations being arranged. Victory in Europe Day was 8 May 1945, the date when the Allies during the Second World War celebrated the defeat of Nazi Germany. Trafalgar Square was filled with a crowd wanting to hear the formal announcement by Winston Churchill that the war was over. There has been a Christmas ceremony at Trafalgar Square every year since 1947. A Norway spruce is given by Norway's capital Oslo and presented as London's Christmas tree, as a token of gratitude for Britain's support during World War II. Since its construction, Trafalgar Square has been a venue for political demonstrations, though the authorities have often **attempted**（企图）to ban them.

> **阅读辅助**
>
> 在过去，特拉法尔加广场也因为大群野鸽聚集而闻名，以至于在中文里别称为"鸽子广场"。二百多年来它一直是伦敦乃至全英人民聚集庆祝除夕夜、圣诞节及其他节日，举行政治示威的场地。

Section 3-2　（美）流连忘返的旅游胜地

美国，一个既休闲又忙碌的国家。你既可以在这里领略到大自然鬼斧神工般的杰作，也可以感受到人类创造出的奇迹。在这片自由的土地上充满了人文景观和自然景观的和谐景象，不仅让人们感受到了大自然的赐予，还让人们可以回顾历史给这个国家留下的回忆。

1 时代广场 *Times Square*
——世界的十字路口

达人了解英美

◆ **Background**

Before and after the American Revolution, the area belonged to John Morin Scott, a general of the New York militia, in which he served under George Washington. In the first half of the 19th century, it became one of the prized possessions of John Jacob Astor, who made a second fortune selling off lots to hotels and other real **estate**（财产）concerns as the city rapidly spread uptown. By 1872, the area had become the center of New York's carriage industry. The area not having previously been named, the city authorities called it Longacre Square after Long Acre in London, where the carriage trade in that city was centered and which was also a home to stables. As more profitable commerce and **industrialization**（产业化）of lower Manhattan pushed homes, theaters, and prostitution northward from the Tenderloin District, Long Acre Square became nicknamed the Thieves Lair for its rollicking reputation as a low entertainment district.

In 1904, New York Times publisher Adolph S. Ochs moved the newspaper's operations to a new skyscraper on 42nd Street at Longacre Square, on the site of the former Pabst Hotel, which had existed on the site for less than a decade. Ochs **persuaded**（说服）Mayor George B. McClellan, Jr. to construct a subway station there, and the area was renamed "Times Square" on April 8, 1904. Now known simply as One Times Square, it is famed for the Times Square Ball drop on its roof every New Year's Eve.

（美）流连忘返的旅游胜地　　Section 3-2

> **阅读辅助**
>
> 《纽约时报》发行人将该报的总部迁到第四十二街，当时称为朗埃克广场，自1913年起，《纽约时报》不再于时报广场上的大楼办公，之后那里更成为每年最后一天降球仪式的地点。

◆ Nowadays

As early as 1960, 42nd Street between Seventh and Eighth Avenue, was described by The New York Times as "the 'worst' [block] in town". Times Square in that decade, as depicted in Midnight Cowboy, was gritty, dark and **desperate**（孤注一掷）, and it got worse in the 1970s and 1980s, as did the crime situation in the rest of the city things were worse still.In the 1980s, a commercial building boom began in the western parts of Midtown as part of a long-term development plan developed. In the mid-1990s, Rudolph Giuliani led an effort to clean up the area, an effort that is described by Steve Macekin in Urban Nightmares.

In 1992, the Times Square Alliance, a **coalition**（联盟）of city government and local businesses dedicated to improving the quality of commerce and **cleanliness**（洁净度）in the district, started operations in the area. Times Square now boasts attractions such as ABC's Times Square Studios, where Good Morning America is broadcast live, an elaborate Toys "Я" US store, and competing Hershey's and M&M's stores across the street from each other, as well as multiple multiplex movie theaters. The theatres of Broadway and the huge number of **animated**（有生气的）neon and LED signs have been one of New York's iconic images, as well as a symbol of the intensely urban aspects of Manhattan.

In 2002, New York City's mayor, Rudy Giuliani, gave the oath of office to the city's next mayor, Michael Bloomberg, at Times Square after midnight on January 1 as part of the 2001–2002 New Year's celebration. Approximately 500,000 revelers attended. Times Square is the most

155

visited place globally with 360,000 **pedestrian**（步行者）visitors a day, amounting to over 131 million a year.

> **阅读辅助**
>
> 随着1930年代大萧条到来，广场气氛出现转变。时报广场充斥着色情表演场所、通宵放映性爱映画的电影院。到了1990年代中期，纽约市长开展净化该区的工作，取而代之则是比较高级的商业活动。百老汇上的剧院、大量耀眼的霓虹光管广告、以及电视式的宣传版，已经深入成为象征纽约的标志，反映曼哈顿强烈的都市特性。

✧ Celebration

On December 31, 1907, a ball signifying New Year's Day was first dropped at Times Square, and the Square has held the main New Year's celebration in New York City ever since. On that night, hundreds of thousands of people **congregate**（聚集）to watch the Waterford Crystal ball being lowered on a pole atop the building, marking the start of the New Year.

Times Square is the site of the annual New Year's Eve ball drop. About one million revelers crowd Times Squarefor the New Year's Eve celebrations, more than twice the usual number of visitors the area usually receives daily. However, for the **millennium**（千禧年）celebration on December 31, 1999, published reports stated approximately two million people **overflowed**（溢出）Times Square, making it the largest gathering in Times Square since August 1945 during celebrations marking the end of World War II. Today, Countdown Entertainment and One Times Square handle the New Year's Eve event in **conjunction**（结合）with the Times Square Alliance.

(美)流连忘返的旅游胜地 **Section 3-2**

> **阅读辅助**
>
> 　　1904年12月《纽约时报》选在除夕当天迁入该广场的新大楼,并在午夜施放烟火庆祝,人们第一次在时代广场上举办了新年狂欢活动。百年来,每至辞旧迎新之时,都有超过50万来自全美乃至世界各地的人汇集于此,共度不眠之夜。1999年12月31日有200多万人在此恭迎千禧年的降临。人们第一次在时代广场上举办了新年狂欢活动。

2 科罗拉多大峡谷 Grand Canyon National Park
——切割出来的奇迹

达人了解英美

◆ **History**

The first bill to create Grand Canyon National Park was introduced in 1882 by then-Senator Benjamin Harrison, which would have made Grand Canyon National Park the nation's second, after Yellowstone National Park. Harrison unsuccessfully **reintroduced**（重新）his bill, but he established the Grand Canyon Forest Reserve in 1893.

Grand Canyon National Park was named as an official national park in 1919, but the landmark had been well known to Americans for over thirty years prior. In 1903, President Theodore Roosevelt visited the site and said: "The Grand Canyon fills me with awe. It is beyond comparison—beyond description; absolutely **unparalleled**（无与伦比）through-out the wide world... Let this great wonder of nature remain as it now is. Do nothing to mar its grandeur, **sublimity**（气质高尚）and loveliness. You cannot improve on it. But what you can do is to keep it for your children, your children's children, and all who come after you, as the one great sight which every American should see."Despite Roosevelt's **enthusiasm**（狂热）and his strong interest in preserving land for public use, the Grand Canyon was not immediately designated a national park. In 1979, UNESCO declared the park a World Heritage Site.

> **阅读辅助**
>
> 大峡谷国家公园是1908年美国总统罗斯福所提倡与规划的，初时只叫做国家纪念公园。1919年经过美国国会的法案通过，正式将大峡谷最深、景色最壮丽的一段，成立了大峡谷国家公园。目前大峡谷国家公园是全美最受欢迎的国家公园之一。

✦ Geography

The Grand Canyon, including its **extensive**（广阔）system of tributary canyons, is valued for its combination of size, depth, and exposed layers of colorful rocks dating back to Precambrian times. The canyon itself was created by the incision of the Colorado River and its **tributaries**（支流）after the Colorado Plateau was uplifted, causing the Colorado River system to develop along its present path.

The primary public areas of the park are the North and South Rims of the Grand Canyon itself. The rest of the park is extremely rugged and remote, although many places are accessible by pack trail and **backcountry**（穷乡僻壤）roads. Only the Navajo Bridge near Page connects the rims by road in Arizona; this journey can take around five hours by car. Otherwise, the two rims of the Canyon are connected via the Mike O'Callaghan–Pat Tillman Memorial Bridge and the Hoover Dam.

> **阅读辅助**
>
> 大峡谷峡谷平缓倾斜，岩层显露无遗。在板块活动中沉积岩被抬高上千英尺，从而形成了科罗拉多高原。海拔的升高也导致了科罗拉多河流域降雨量的增加，这些都倾向于加深、扩展干旱环境中的峡谷。

◆ **Development**

The US government had **halted**（蹒跚）development of a 1.6 million acres area including the National Park from 1966 to 2009, during the "Bennett Freeze", because of an ownership dispute between Hopi and Navajo. In 2014, a developer announced plans to build a multimedia complex on the canyon's rim called the Grand Canyon Escalade. On 420 acres there would be shops, an IMAX theater, hotels and an RV park. A gondola would enable easy visits of the canyon floor where a "riverwalk" of "connected walkways, an eatery, a tramway station, a seating area and a wastewater package plant" would be situated. Navajo Nation President Ben Shelly has indicated agreement; the tribe would have to invest $65 million for road, water and communication facilities for the $1 billion complex. One of the developers is Navajo and has cited an 8 to 18 percent share of the gross revenue for the tribe as **incentive**（诱因）.

阅读辅助

美国政府一直都企图为公园增加财政投入，但是由于分歧却未成功。直到2014年，才真正达成协议，发展了公园的设施和改善环境。

3 尼亚加拉大瀑布 *Niagara Falls*
——震撼人心的跨国瀑布

达人了解英美

◆ History

There are differing theories as to the origin of the name of the falls. According to Iroquoian scholar, "Niagara" is derived from the name given to a branch of the locally residing native Neutral Confederacy, who are described as being called the "Niagagarega" people on several late-17th-century French maps of the area. It comes from the name of an Iroquois town called "Ongniaahra", meaning "point of land cut in two". A number of figures have been suggested as first circulating an **eyewitness**（见证人）description of Niagara Falls. A Frenchman visited the area as early as 1604 during his exploration of Canada, and members of his party reported to him the **spectacular**（引人入胜的）waterfalls, which he described in his journals.

During the 18th century, tourism became popular, and by mid-century, it was the area's main industry. After the American Civil War, the New York Central railroad publicized Niagara Falls as a focus of pleasure and honeymoon visits. With increased railroad traffic, in 1886, Leffert Buck replaced Roebling's wood and stone bridge with the predominantly steel bridge that still carries trains over the Niagara River today. The first steel **archway**（拱形门廊）bridge near the falls was completed in 1897.

> **阅读辅助**
>
> 尼亚加拉这一奇迹一直不为西方人所知。直到1678年，一位法国传教士来到这里传教，发现了这一大瀑布把这一胜景介绍给了欧洲人。1625年，欧洲探险者第一个写下了这条大河与瀑布的名字，称其为"Niagara"（尼亚加拉）。但让尼亚加拉瀑布真正声名鹊起的是法国皇帝拿破仑的兄弟。

✧ Nowadays

In 1941 the Niagara Falls Bridge Commission completed the third current crossing in the immediate area of Niagara Falls with the Rainbow Bridge, carrying both pedestrian and vehicular traffic between the two countries and Canadian and U.S. customs for each country. In 1941 the Niagara Falls Bridge Commission completed the third current crossing in the immediate area of Niagara Falls with the Rainbow Bridge, carrying both pedestrian and vehicular traffic between the two countries and Canadian and U.S. customs for each country. Before the late 20th century the northeastern end of the Horseshoe Falls was in the United States, flowing around the Terrapin Rocks, which was once connected to Goat Island by a series of bridges. In 1955 the area between the rocks and Goat Island was filled in, creating Terrapin Point.

> **阅读辅助**
>
> 美加两国一直很重视尼亚加拉瀑布的旅游开发。到19世纪20年代，尼亚加拉瀑布城就已成为旅游胜地。1888年尼亚加拉瀑布公园正式对外开放。

(美)流连忘返的旅游胜地   Section 3-2

✦ Renowned

From largest to smallest, the three waterfalls are the Horseshoe Falls, the American Falls and the Bridal Veil Falls. The Horseshoe Falls lie mostly on the Canadian side and the American Falls entirely on the American side, separated by Goat Island. The smaller Bridal Veil Falls are also located on the American side, separated from the other waterfalls by Luna Island. The international **boundary**（界限）line was originally drawn through Horseshoe Falls in 1819, but the boundary has long been in dispute due to natural **erosion**（腐蚀）and construction.

Located on the Niagara River, which drains Lake Erie into Lake Ontario, the combined falls form the highest flow rate of any waterfall in the world, with a vertical drop of more than 165 feet. Horseshoe Falls is the most powerful waterfall in North America, as measured by **vertical**（垂直）height and also by flow rate. Niagara Falls was formed when glaciers receded at the end of the Wisconsin **glaciation**（冰蚀现象）, and water from the newly formed Great Lakes carved a path through the Niagara Escarpment en route to the Atlantic Ocean.

> 阅读辅助
>
> 尼亚加拉瀑布以美丽的景色，巨大的水利发电能力和极具挑战性的环境保护工程而闻名于世，是非常受游客欢迎的旅游景点。

4 黄石国家公园 Yellowstone National Park
——地球上最独一无二的神奇

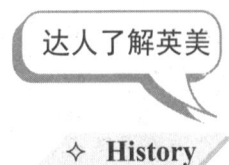

达人了解英美

◇ History

Native Americans have lived in the Yellowstone region for at least 11,000 years. The park is located at the headwaters of the Yellowstone River, from which it takes its historical name. Near the end of the 18th century, French **trappers**（探险者）named the river "Roche Jaune", which is probably a translation of the Hidatsa name. Later, American trappers rendered the French name in English as "Yellow Stone". The region was bypassed during the Lewis and Clark Expedition in the early 19th century. Aside from visits by mountain men during the early-to-mid-19th century, organized exploration did not begin until the late 1860s. The U.S. Army was commissioned to oversee the park just after its establishment. In 1917, administration of the park was transferred to the National Park Service, which had been created the previous year.

阅读辅助

美洲原住民已经在黄石公园地区生活了至少1万1千年，黄石公园因位于黄石河的源头而得名。19世纪早期的刘易斯与克拉克远征也绕过了这一区域。对该地区的有组织的勘探活动直到1860年代末才开始出现。

◆ Describe

Yellowstone National Park spans an area of 3,468.4 square miles, comprising lakes, canyons, rivers and mountain ranges. Yellowstone Lake is one of the largest high-altitude lakes in North America and is centered over the Yellowstone Caldera, the largest supervolcano on the continent. The caldera is considered an active volcano. It has **erupted**（爆发）with tremendous force several times in the last two million years. Half of the world's **geothermal**（地热能）features are in Yellowstone, fueled by this **ongoing**（持续的）volcanism. Lava flows and rocks from volcanic eruptions cover most of the land area of Yellowstone. The park is the centerpiece of the Greater Yellowstone Ecosystem, the largest remaining nearly-intact **ecosystem**（生态系统）in the Earth's northern **temperate**（温带的）zone.

阅读辅助

黄石国家公园占地面积约为8983平方千米，其中包括湖泊、峡谷、河流和山脉。公园内最大的湖泊是位于黄石火山中心的黄石湖，是整个北美地区最大的高海拔湖泊之一。黄石公园也是大黄石生态系统的核心所在，这是北温带地区现存最大且仍然近乎完好的自然生态系统。

◆ Environment

Hundreds of species of **mammals**（哺乳动物）, birds, fish and reptiles have been documented, including several that are either endangered or threatened. The vast forests and grasslands also include unique species of plants. Yellowstone Park is the largest and most famous **megafauna**'s（巨型动物）location in the Continental United States. Grizzly bears, wolves, and free-ranging herds of bison and elk live in the park. The Yellowstone Park bison herd is the oldest and largest public bison herd in the United States. Forest fires occur in the park each year; in the large forest fires of

1988, nearly one third of the park was burnt. Yellowstone has numerous recreational opportunities, including hiking, camping, boating, fishing and sightseeing. Paved roads provide close access to the major geothermal areas as well as some of the lakes and waterfalls. During the winter, visitors often access the park by way of guided tours that use either snow coaches or snowmobiles.

> **阅读辅助**
>
> 公园内有记录的哺乳动物、鸟类、鱼类和爬行动物有数百种之多,其中包括多种濒危或受威胁物种,广袤的森林和草原中同样存有多种独特的植物。黄石公园是美国本土最大和最著名的巨型动物居住地。

5 好莱坞环球影城 Universal Studios Hollywood
——造梦机器的聚集地

达人了解英美

◇ **Past**

Shortly after Music Corporation of America took over Universal Pictures in 1962, accountants suggested a new tour in the studio **commissary**（代表）would increase profits. In 1964, the modern tour was established to include a series of dressing room walk-through; peeks at actual production, and later, staged events. This grew over the years into a full-blown theme park. The narrated tram tour (formerly "GlamorTrams") still runs through the studio's active backlot, but the staged events, stunt demonstrations and high-tech rides overshadow the motion-picture production that once lured fans to Universal Studios Hollywood.

In 1965, the War Lord Tower opened as one of the first attractions in the theme park. This was followed by the opening of the Animal Actors' School Stage in 1970. In 1974, *the Rockslide* staged event was added to the Studio Tour. The following year *The Land of a Thousand Faces* opened on the Upper Lot. In 1979, *the Battle of Galactica* replaced *Rockslide* as a staged event on the Studio Tour.

The Flintstones Show opened, replacing *the Star Trek Adventure*. In 1996, *Jurassic Park: The Ride* opened. In 1997, two shows were replaced: *The Land Before Time Show* replaced *Rocky and Bullwinkle Live*; and *Totally Nickelodeon* replaced *the Flintstones Show*. Just one year after it opened, *the Land Before Time show* was replaced with *Coke Soak*.

> **阅读辅助**
>
> 1962年，美国音乐公司接手环球影业之后，会计师建议在制片厂增加导览可增加利润。在1964年，包括参观更衣化妆间、观察实际拍片过程，以及参与摄影棚录影的导览模式成型。多年后逐渐演变成现在的主题乐园。

◇ Nowadays

In 2000, *the Rugrats Magic Adventure* replaced *Totally Nickelodeon*. In 2001, *the Nickelodeon Blast Zone* opened. Also in 2001, *Animal Planet Live* replaced *the Animal Actors' School Stage*. In 2002 replaced *The Mummy Returns: Chamber of Doom*. The following year, *Fear Factor Live* replaced *Spider-Man Rocks*. In 2007, *Universal's House of Horrors* opened, replacing *Van Helsing: Fortress Dracula*. Both *Lucy: A Tribute and Back to the Future: The Ride* were closed, prior to being replaced in 2008 by the *Simpsons Ride* and *the Universal Story Museum* respectively. Also in 2008, *the Nickelodeon Blast Zone* was rebranded to *the Adventures of Curious George*. In 2009, *Creature from the Black Lagoon: The Musical* replaced *Fear Factor Live* in the Upper Lot.

In 2010, the Special Effects Stages and Backdraft attractions were closed to make way for *Transformers: The Ride* which was announced in 2008. In April 2014, the park announced Springfield: a new dining complex to be built around the existing Simpsons Ride. The new eating locations will feature "signature eateries from Krusty Burger to Luigi's Pizza and Phineas, Q. Butterfat's 5600 Flavors Ice Cream Parlor to iconic watering holes like Moe's Tavern and Duff's Brewery". It is planned to open on March 28, 2015. Universal Studios Hollywood has plans to open *The Wizarding World of Harry Potter* which will feature *the Harry Potter and the Forbidden Journey Ride* sometime in 2016.

(美)流连忘返的旅游胜地 **Section 3-2**

> **阅读辅助**
> 好莱坞环球影城是一个再现电影场景的主题游乐园,其内以多部大制作电影为主题的景点最受欢迎。探索好莱坞最著名的户外场景之一,一窥电影制作幕后的秘密,传奇的影城之旅充满了新鲜刺激。

◇ Layout

Universal Studios Hollywood is split into two areas on different levels, connected by a series of **escalators**(自动扶梯)called the Starway. These areas are known as the Upper lot and Lower lot. As of March 2015, Universal Studios Hollywood contains 7 rides, 4 shows, 2 play areas and a **retrospective**(怀旧的)museum. Each lot features a collection of rides, shows and attractions as well as food, beverage and merchandise shops. Universal Studios has a number of costumed characters roaming the park grounds, representing many different genres. Some are **portrayals**(描绘)of Hollywood icons while others are based on Universal's vast media library.

> **阅读辅助**
> 环球影城好莱坞拆分为两个区域,之间以名为星光大道的多段电扶梯连接。这两个区域通称为上园区和下园区。两区各有许多游乐设施、表演和景点,以及食物、饮料和商品贩售点。环球影城有许多穿着戏服,代表不同类型角色。有些是扮演的好莱坞偶像,而一些角色则是环球影业的象征。

6 大都会博物馆 Metropolitan Museum of Art
——引人入胜艺术的殿堂

达人了解英美

✧ History

The Metropolitan Museum of Art was founded in 1870. The founders included businessmen and financiers, as well as leading artists and thinkers of the day, who wanted to open a museum to bring art and art education to the American people. It opened on February 20, 1872, and was originally located at 681 Fifth Avenue. John Taylor Johnston, a railroad executive whose personal art collection seeded the museum, served as its first president, and the publisher George Palmer Putnam came on board as its founding **superintendent**（负责人）. Under their guidance, the Met's holdings, initially consisting of a Roman stone sarcophagus and 174 mostly European paintings, quickly outgrew the available space.

Between 1879 and 1895, the Museum created and operated a series of educational programs, known as the Metropolitan Museum of Art Schools, intended to provide **vocational**（职业的）training and classes on fine arts.

The museum celebrated its 75th anniversary with a variety of programs, initiatives, and events in 1946, **culminating**（最高的）in the anniversary of the opening of its first exhibition in 1947. The anniversary festivities included speeches, exhibitions, cross-promotions with films and plays, and related displays in Fifth Avenue store windows.

> **阅读辅助**
> 大都会艺术博物馆由一群美国公民于1870年发起构建。当时的发起人包括了商人、理财家、卓越的艺术家与思想家。他们期望博物馆能够给予美国公民有关艺术与艺术教育的熏陶。

◇ Collections

Its permanent collection contains more than two million works, divided among seventeen **curatorial**（馆长的）departments. The main building, located on the eastern edge of Central along Manhattan's Museum Mile, is by area one of the world's largest art galleries. There is also a much smaller second location at The Cloistersin Upper Manhattan that features **medieval**（中世纪的）.

Represented in the permanent collection are works of art from classical antiquity and Ancient Egypt, paintings and sculptures from nearly all the European masters, and an extensive collection of American and modern art. The Met also maintains extensive holdings of African, Asian, Oceanic, Byzantine, and Islamicart. The museum is also home to **encyclopedic**（知识广博的）collections of musical instruments, costumes and accessories, and antique weapons and armor from around the world. Several **notable**（著名的）interiors, ranging from first-century Rome through modern American design, are permanently installed in the Met's galleries.

> **阅读辅助**
> 馆藏超过二百万件艺术品，整个博物馆被划分为十九个馆部。主建筑物通常被简称为"the Met"。 在众多永久艺术收藏品中，包括许多出众的古典艺术品、古埃及艺术品、几乎所有欧洲大师的油画及大量美国视觉艺术和现代艺术作品。博物馆还收藏有大量的非洲、亚洲、大洋洲、拜占庭和伊斯兰艺术品。

7 圣地亚哥海洋世界 SeaWorld San Diego
——人与动物共享的水上乐土

达人了解英美

◆ **History**

SeaWorld was founded in 1964 by four graduates of the University of California, Los Angeles. Although their original idea of an underwater restaurant was not **feasible**（可能的）at the time, the idea was expanded into a 22-acre marine **zoological**（动物学的）park along the shore of Mission Bay in San Diego. After an investment of about $1.5 million, the park opened with 45 employees, several dolphins, sea lions, and two seawater **aquariums**（水族馆）, and hosted more than 400,000 visitors in its first year of operation.

Initially held as a private partnership, SeaWorld offered its stock publicly in 1968 enabling them to expand and open additional parks. The second SeaWorld location, SeaWorld, opened in 1970, followed by SeaWorld Orlando in 1973 and SeaWorld San Antonio. in 1988. The parks were owned and operated by Harcourt Brace Jovanovich between 1976 and 1989, when they were purchased by Anheuser-Busch Companies, Inc.

阅读辅助

圣地亚哥海洋世界由4个加州大学毕业生在1964年建立，原先他们只是想建一间海底餐厅，但是最后却决定在圣地亚哥海岸建一个海洋动物公园。虽然几经转手，但是这个海洋世界越来越好，越来越受欢迎。

✧ Attractions

Bayside Skyride is a 1967 VonRoll type 101 gondola ride located in the northwest corner of the park that travels over Mission bay near the "Cirque De La Mer" lagoon for a 6 minute ride. Journey to Atlantis is a joint flume and rollercoaster. Madagascar Live! Operation: Vacation is an original live musical show features singers, dancers and rock/pop music performed by a live band. The park's popular Bottlenose dolphins are on exhibit here in a multi-pool complex where guests have free access to pet the dolphins. The Sky Tower is a 320-foot Gyro tower that was built in 1969. Sesame Street's Bay of Play is an **interactive**（交互式的）children's play area that opened in 2008 and is based on the long running Sesame Street children's television series. Shipwreck Rapids is a river rapids ride themed to a shipwreck on a **deserted**（荒废的）island. Turtle Reef is attraction housing over 60 sea turtles in an aquarium with a variety of fish and other creatures.

阅读辅助

圣地亚哥的海洋世界是加州最著名的水上主题乐园之一，有多座水族馆，海豚和杀人鲸表演池，企鹅水族馆，触摸池和儿童乐园等。海洋世界有四个主要的海洋动物秀及20个展出项目，其中最有名的秀莫过于杀人鲸招牌秀……在这里你还有与动物亲密互动的机会。

8　大雾山国家公园 *Great Smoky Mountains National Park*
——迷雾中的人间仙境

达人了解英美

◆ **History**

Before the arrival of European settlers, the region was part of the homeland of the Cherokees. Frontiers people began settling the land in the 18th and early 19th century. In 1830 President Andrew Jackson signed the Indian Removal Act, many of the Cherokee left, but some, led by **renegade**（叛徒）warrior Tsali, hid out in the area that is now the Great Smoky Mountains National Park. Some of their descendants now live in the Qualla Boundary to the south of the park.

As white settlers arrived, logging grew as a major industry in the mountains, and a rail line, the Little River Railroad, was constructed in the late-19th Century to **haul**（拖曳）timber out of the remote regions of the area. Cut-and-run-style clear cutting was destroying the natural beauty of the area, so visitors and locals banded together to raise money for preservation of the land. The U.S. National Park Service wanted a park in the eastern United States, but did not have much money to establish one. Then the park was chartered by the United States Congress in 1934 and officially dedicated by President Franklin Delano Roosevelt in 1940. During the Great Depression, the Civilian Conservation Corps, the Works Progress Administration, and other federal organizations made trails, fire **watchtowers**（瞭望塔）, and other **infrastructure**（基础设施）improvements to the park and Smoky Mountains.

> **阅读辅助**
>
> 自十八世纪晚期以来,大雾山很多山凹和峡谷就一直有人居住,但是直到二十世纪伐木工人开始采伐原始木材,这些居民才结束了与世隔绝的生活。Cades Cove 原属切罗基地区,本为印第安人的土地,但在1838年,14000多名切罗基人被迫离开南阿巴拉契亚山脉,该地从此易主。大雾山国家公园历经许多磨难后于1926年宣告建成。

◆ Natural

The majority of rocks in the Great Smoky Mountains National Park are Late **Precambrian**(前寒武纪)rocks that are part of the Ocoee Supergroup. This group consists of metamorphosed sandstones, phyllites, schists, and slate. Early Precambrian rocks are not only the oldest rocks in the park but also the dominant rock type in sites. One of the most visited attractions in the mountains is Cades Cove which is a window or an area where older rocks made out of sandstone surround the valley floor of younger rocks made out of limestone.

The variety of **elevations**(海拔高度), the **abundant**(丰富的)rainfall, and the presence of old growth forests give the park an unusual richness of biota. About 10,000 species of plants and animals are known to live in the park, and estimates as high as an additional 90,000 undocumented species may also be present. Park officials count more than 200 species of birds, 66 species of mammals, 50 species of fish, 39 species of reptiles, and 43 species of amphibians, including many lungless salamanders. The park has a noteworthy black bear population, numbering about 1,500. An experimental re-introduction of elkinto the park began in 2001.

Over 100 species of trees grow in the park. The lower region forests are dominated by deciduous leafy trees. At higher **altitudes**(海拔), deciduous forests give way to coniferous trees like Fraser fir. In addition, the park has over 1,400 flowering plant species and over 4,000 species of non-flowering plants.

> 阅读辅助
>
> 大烟山国家公园以其丰富的物种而闻名。由于大烟山国家公园内的海拔高度变化剧烈，加之降雨量充沛，因而使大烟山公园极富生物多样性。大烟山国家公园号称是美东最后一片广大的原始林。占地2100平方公里。

✧ Attractions

The Great Smoky Mountains National Park is a major tourist attraction in the region. The two main visitors' centers inside the park are Sugarlands Visitors' Center near the Gatlinburg entrance to the park and Oconaluftee Visitor Center near Cherokee, North Carolina at the eastern entrance to the park. These ranger stations provide exhibits on wildlife, geology, and the history of the park. The park has a number of historical attractions. The most well-preserved of these is Cades Cove, a valley with a number of preserved historic buildings including log cabins, barns, and churches. Cades Cove is the single most **frequented**（频繁的）destination in the national park.

> 阅读辅助
>
> 这里不仅自然遗产丰富，同时还拥有悠久的文化历史。许多历史性的建筑依然伫立，97个具有历史意义的建筑集中在5个区域内。

Section 4-1　（英）垂涎欲滴的特色美食

提起英国，你第一时间会想到什么？辉煌灿烂的工业革命、历史悠久的贵族文化、优雅迷人的英国绅士、"戏剧天才"莎士比亚、"学术殿堂"牛津剑桥……相对于这些领域的熠熠生辉，"英伦美食"或多或少有些黯然失色。其实，像传统的全英式早餐、闲适优雅的下午茶、典型的英式烤牛排等等这些英国美食，无论口感还是文化内涵都远远超乎你的想象！

1 哈吉斯 *Haggis*
——苏格兰的"国菜"

达人了解英美

◇ **History**

Haggis is popularly assumed to be of Scottish origin, but there is a lack of historical evidence that could **conclusively**（决定性地）attribute its origins to any one place. The first known written recipes for a dish of the name made with offal and herbs, are, as "hagese", in the verse cookbook Liber Cure Cocorum dating from around 1430 in Lancashire, North West England, and, as "hagws of a schepe" from an English cookbook also of 1430.

Dickson Wright suggests that haggis was invented as a way of cooking quick-spoiling offal near the site of a hunt, without the need to carry along an additional cooking **vessel**（器皿）. The liver and kidneys could be grilled directly over a fire, but this treatment was unsuitable for the stomach, **intestines**（内脏）, or lungs. Chopping up the lungs and stuffing the stomach with them and whatever fillers might have been on hand, then boiling the **assembly**（集合）—probably in a vessel made from the animal's hide—was one way to make sure these parts were not wasted.

阅读辅助

虽然是苏格兰的传统食物，但近年来英格兰和威尔士人相继宣布哈吉斯最早是由他们所发明。目前最早有关哈吉斯的记录是出现于在英格兰的兰开夏郡西北部发现的一本食谱《Liber Cure Cocorum》，大概可以追溯到1430年左右。

✧ Burns Supper

Haggis is traditionally served as part of the Burns supper on or near January 25, the birthday of Scotland's national poet Robert Burns. Burns wrote the poem Address to a Haggis, which starts "Fair fa' your honest, sonsie face, Great chieftain o' the puddin-race!" In Burns's lifetime haggis was a common dish of the poor as it was **nourishing**（滋养）yet very cheap, being made from **leftover**（吃剩的）parts of sheep otherwise thrown away. Scotch whisky is often said to be the traditional **accompaniment**（伴随物）for haggis, though this may simply be because both are traditionally served at a Burns supper.

> **阅读辅助**
>
> 哈吉斯被称为苏格兰"国菜"，一般认为是受到了苏格兰民族诗人罗伯特·伯恩斯创作的 *Address to a Haggis* 一诗的影响。后人为了纪念彭斯，而定于每年1月25日为彭斯之夜，在晚餐时背诵彭斯的《Address to a Haggis》一诗，并享用哈吉斯。

✧ Dishes

A traditional haggis recipe describes haggis as "sheep's 'pluck' (heart, liver and lungs), minced with onion, oatmeal, suet, spices, and salt, mixed with stock, and traditionally encased in the animals stomach and boiled". Ingredients are sheep stomach, heart and lungs of one lamb, lamb, onions, oatmeal, salt, pepper, stock, and water, with optional **ingredients**（作料）dried **coriander**（胡荽）, **cinnamon**（肉桂）, and nutmeg. It can be boiled, baked, or deep fried. Scotch whisky is often said to be the traditional accompaniment for haggis, and adds that lighter-bodied, tannic red wines, such as those made from the Barbera grape, are also suitable, as are strong, powerfully flavored British ales.

Haggis is often served in Scottish fast-food establishments deep fried in batter. Together with chips, this comprises a "haggis supper". A "haggis burger" is a patty of fried haggis served on a bun. A "haggis pakora" is another deep fried variant, available in some Indian restaurants in Scotland. Haggis can be used as an ingredient in other dishes, even pizza, rather than the main part of a dish.

> **阅读辅助**
>
> 　　一道传统的苏格兰菜，它实际上就是羊杂碎。其制法是先将羊的胃掏空，里面塞进剁碎的羊内脏，再加上燕麦、洋葱、羊油、盐、香辣调味料和高汤等，制成袋，水煮约三小时，直到鼓胀为止。如今餐馆通常会把羊的胃袋在上桌前去掉，只留下里面的食物给客人享用。一般会与马铃薯泥和芜菁甘蓝泥以及一杯苏格兰威士忌一起食用，风味独特。

2 炸鱼薯条 Fish and chips
——英国美食的"国粹"

达人了解英美

◇ History

Popular tradition associates the dish with the United Kingdom and Ireland; and fish and chips remains very popular in the UK and in areas colonized by British people in the 19th century, such as Australia, New Zealand and parts of North America. It has also been popular in the Faroe Islands since the time it was introduced during the British **occupation**（占有期）of the Faroe Islands in World War II.

In the United Kingdom, fish and chips became a cheap food popular among the working classes with the rapid development of trawl fishing in the North Sea in the second half of the nineteenth century. In 1860, the first fish and chip shop was opened in London by Jewish **proprietor**（所有者）Joseph Malinwho married together "fish fried in the Jewish fashion" with chips.

阅读辅助

17世纪，英国开始食用土豆。在19世纪，吃油炸鱼在伦敦和英国东南部变得非常普遍。而同时，在英国北部油炸土豆条亦被创造出来。不明何时何地，这两项被配合在一起食用成为我们今天知道的炸鱼薯条。第一间炸鱼薯条店或许是约瑟夫·马林于1860年在伦敦开设的。

✧ **Cooking**

Deep-fried "chips" (slices or pieces of potato) as a dish, may have first appeared in Britain in about the same period: the OED notes as its earliest usage of "chips" in this sense the mention in Dickens' A Tale of Two Cities (published in 1859): "Husky chips of potatoes, fried with some reluctant drops of oil". Fish and chips (sometimes written "fish 'n' chips") is a popular take-away food which originated in the United Kingdom. It consists of deep-fried fish (traditionally cod, haddock or flounder) in batter or breadcrumbs with deep-fried chipped (slab-cut) potatoes.

Traditional frying uses beef dripping or lard; however, vegetable, such as peanut oil (used because of its relatively high smoke point) now **predominate** (在……中占优势). A minority of vendors in the north of England and Scotland and the majority of vendors in Northern Ireland still use dripping or lard, as it imparts a different flavor to the dish, but it has the side effect of making the fried chips unsuitable for **vegetarians**(素食者) and for adherents of certain faiths.

阅读辅助

炸鱼薯条源自英国，是英国最受欢迎的外带食品。在19世纪，吃炸鱼在伦敦和英国东南部变得普遍。英国北部常用牛油来炸鱼，而南方则多用植物油，讲究的店家用的是花生油。做法是将去了鱼刺的鱼，切成片后裹上湿面团，然后油炸，同时配以炸薯条。

✧ **Cultural Impact**

The long-standing Roman Catholic tradition of not eating meat on Fridays, especially during Lent, and of substituting fish for other types of meat on that day continues to influence habits even in predominantly Protestant, Anglican, semi-secular and secular societies. Friday night remains a traditional occasion for eating fish-and-chips; and many cafeterias and similar establishments, while varying their menus on other days of the week, **habitually**（日常地）offer fish and chips every Friday.

> 阅读辅助
>
> 罗马天主教为了纪念耶稣受难，在星期五守小斋，不许吃恒温的动物肉，而以海鲜代之。大多英国圣公会信众也保有这一传统，直到今天依然在影响半世俗的与世俗的社会。周五晚上光顾炸鱼薯条店依旧是英国社会传统的一部分，许多餐饮场所亦有特别菜单，也会提供炸鱼薯条这道菜。

3 鳗鱼冻 Jellied eels
——黑暗料理的奇葩

达人了解英美

◇ **History**

The eel was a cheap, **nutritious**（有营养的）and readily available food source for the people of London; European eels were once so common in the Thames that nets were set as far upriver as London itself, and eels became a staple for London's poor. The earliest known eel, pie and mash houses opened in London in the 18th century, and the oldest surviving shop, M Manze, has been open since 1902. At the end of the Second World War there were around a hundred eel, pie and mash houses in London; in 1995 there were eighty seven. The water quality of the Thames has improved since the 1960s and is now suitable for decolonization by eels. The Environment Agency supports a Thames **fishery**（渔业）, allowing nets as far upriver as Tower Bridge.

阅读辅助

这道菜价格便宜而且营养丰富容易准备，因为鳝鱼在泰晤士河中曾是很常见的，故而受到穷人们的喜爱。第一家出售鳝鱼冻的餐厅开张于18世纪，现存最老的鳝鱼冻餐厅则是1902年开业的 M Manze。第二次世界大战之后，伦敦出现了数百家出售鳝鱼冻的餐厅，称作 Eel Pie & Mash Houses。1960年代之后，泰晤士河水质量得到改善，一度减少的鳝鱼又开始增多了。

◇ Cooking

The dish is traditionally prepared using the freshwater eels native to Britain. Typically, the eels are chopped (shucked) into rounds and boiled in water and vinegar, to make a fish stock, with nutmeg and lemon juice before being allowed to cool. The eel is a naturally **gelatinous**（胶状的）fish so the cooking process releases proteins, like collagen, into the liquid which solidify on cooling to form a jelly, though gelatin may be added in order to aid this process. Recipes for jellied eels are individual to particular London pie and mash shops, and also street sellers; however, traditional recipes for **authentic**（真实的）Victorian jellied eels all have common ingredients and cooking methods. What alters is the choice of herbs and spices used to flavor the dish. Jellied eels are often sold with pie and mash—another traditional East End food—and eaten with chilli vinegar or with malt vinegar and white pepper.

> **阅读辅助**
>
> 传统上，这道菜使用的是伦敦当地的欧洲鳗鲡。鳝鱼切片后放入锅中，加醋煮熟后，在冷却前加入肉豆蔻和柠檬汁。在煮鳝鱼时，鱼体内的胶质会使得汤逐渐凝稠，有时也会加入些许明胶。从伦敦高档餐厅到街边小摊都会有这道菜的身影，鳝鱼冻有时会与另一道伦敦名菜牛肉馅饼和土豆泥一起被食用，或许再加上辣椒醋。

◇ Outside the U.K.

Italy has a similar dish known simply as Anguilla (literally, eel), which is eaten with balsamic rather than chilli vinegar. In Denmark the dish is known as ål i gele, in France as aspic d'anguille, and in Germany as Aal in Aspik; all terms mean jellied eel. The Basque Country is famous for a wormlike dish known as txitxardin in Basque, or angulas in Spanish. These are baby eels, or elvers, which are usually prepared in olive oil, garlic, and peppers.

> **阅读辅助**
>
> 意大利也有同样的菜，一般叫做"anguilla"（字面意思即鳝鱼），使用意大利香醋调味。法国人称这道菜为"aspic d'anguille"，德国人称之为"Aal in Aspik"，都是"鳝鱼冻"的意思。巴斯克地区有一道菜叫做"txitxardin"，西班牙其他地区亦称"angulas"，是由幼鳗做成的。

4 苏格兰蛋 *Scotch Eggs*
——三百年历史的苏格兰美食

达人了解英美

✧ Origin

The London department store Fortnum & Mason claims to have invented Scotch eggs in 1738, but they may have been inspired by the Moghul dish nargisi kofta ("Narcissus meatballs"). The earliest printed recipe appears in the 1809 edition of Mrs. Rundell's *A New System of Domestic Cookery*. Mrs. Rundell—and later 19th-century authors—served them hot, with **gravy**（肉汁）.

阅读辅助

苏格兰蛋，据说是英国一间有三百年历史的 Fortnum & Mason 百货公司在1738年所发明的食物，这个菜可能是灵感来自于莫卧儿菜的水仙肉丸。最早的配方出现在1809年的朗德尔太太烹调菜肴的一种升级做法。

✧ Serving

Scotch eggs are a common picnic food. In the United Kingdom packaged Scotch eggs are commonly available in supermarkets, corner shops and **motorway**（高速公路）service stations. Miniature versions are also widely available, sold as "savoury eggs" "picnic eggs" "party eggs" "snack eggs" "egg bites" or similar. These contain chopped egg or a quail's egg, rather than a whole chicken egg, and sometimes contain **mayonnaise**

（蛋黄酱）or chopped bacon. In the United States, many "British-style" pubs and eateries serve Scotch eggs, usually served hot with dipping sauces such as ranch dressing, hot sauce, or hot mustard sauce. At the Minnesota State Fair Scotch eggs are served on a stick. Scotch eggs are available at most Renaissance Festivals from Maryland to Texas. In the Netherlands and Belgium, Scotch eggs may also be called vogelnestje ("little bird's nest") because they contain an egg or eierbal ("eggball").

阅读辅助

苏格兰蛋经常会出现在野餐的食物中，另外在英国的超市，商店和高速公路服务站都可以买到。此外还有迷你版的，被称为"咸鸡蛋""野餐蛋""聚会蛋"等等。有时候里面可以是碎了的鸡蛋或者是鹌鹑蛋，而不一定是整个鸡蛋。甚至有时只是蛋黄酱或者是切碎了的培根。在美国的很多英式酒吧或者餐馆里的苏格兰蛋，通常是趁着热蘸着沙拉酱、辣椒酱、芥末酱吃。在明尼苏达州的苏格兰蛋是用一根竹签串着的。这种蛋经常还会出现在复活节的餐桌上。

5 皮夹克土豆 *Jacket Potato*
——英国特有的土豆吃法

达人了解英美

◆ **Variations**

A baked potato is sometimes called a jacket potato in the United Kingdom. The baked potato has been popular in the UK for many years. In the mid-19th century, jacket potatoes were sold on the streets by hawkers during the autumn and winter months. In London, it was estimated that some 10 tons of baked potatoes were sold each day by this method. Common jacket potato fillings (or "toppings") in the United Kingdom include cheese and beans, tuna mayonnaise, chili con carne and chicken and bacon. Baked potatoes are often eaten on Guy Fawkes Night; traditionally they were often baked in the glowing **embers**（余烬）of a bonfire. As part of the upsurge for more healthy fast food, the baked potato has again taken to the streets of the UK both in mobile units and restaurants. The fast-food chain Spudulike specializes in baked potatoes.

阅读辅助

烤马铃薯在英国已有二百多年历史,十八世纪中叶,街头小贩常会于秋冬时节售卖烤马铃薯。在伦敦,每天更可售出数以十吨计的烤马铃薯。烤马铃薯是烟火节的传统食品,通常在大篝火上烤。由于健康快餐的热潮,烤马铃薯再次常见于英国街头,在Big Ben'Mobile Oven之类的流动摊档和餐厅都可以看到它的身影,Spud U Like多年来售卖如焗豆、辣肉酱、印度鸡、大虾冷盘、鲔鱼、凉拌卷心菜和干酪等不同配料的烤马铃薯。

✧ Cooking

A baked potato, also known as a jacket potato when given additional fillings such as cheese, ham, or chicken, is the edible result of baking a potato. When well cooked, a baked potato has a **fluffy**（松软的）interior, but a crispy skin. Potatoes can be baked in a convection oven, a microwave oven, on a grill, or on/in an open fire. Some restaurants use special ovens designed specifically to cook large numbers of potatoes, then keep them warm and ready for service. Prior to cooking, the potato needs to be **scrubbed**（揉搓）clean, with eyes and surface blemishes removed, and possibly basted with oil or butter and/or salt. Pricking the potato with a fork or knife allows steam to escape during the cooking process. Potatoes cooked in a microwave without **pricking**（刺痛感）the skin might explode due to built up internal pressure from **unvented**（未放气的）steam. It takes between one and two hours to bake a potato in a conventional oven. Microwaving takes from six to ten minutes depending on the power, but does not generally produce a **crisp**（脆的）skin.

> 阅读辅助
>
> 烤土豆是将土豆带皮烤制，常加以奶酪、火腿、鸡肉等作为馅料一起烤制。烤制后的土豆表皮焦脆，馅料香浓。制作烤土豆时可用传统烤箱，也可使用微波炉或烧烤器具制作，一般烤炉制作需要一到两个小时，而用微波炉仅需6～10分钟，但用微波制作的烤土豆一般制作不出娇脆的外皮。

✧ Healthy

When well cooked, a baked potato has a fluffy interior and a crisp skin. It may be served with fillings and **condiments**（调味品）such as butter, cheese or ham. Once a potato has been baked, some people discard the skin and eat only the softer and moister interior, while others enjoy the taste and texture of the crisp skin. Potatoes baked in their skins may lose between 20 to 40% of their vitamin C content because heating in air is slow and vitamin **inactivation**（失活）can continue for a long time. Small potatoes bake more quickly than large ones and therefore retain more of their vitamin C. Despite the popular misconception that potatoes are **fattening**（养肥）, baked potatoes can be used as part of a healthy diet.

> **阅读辅助**
>
> 从营养角度讲，在吃烤土豆的时候应该连皮一起食用，因土豆皮下表层含有丰富的维生素及微量元素。马铃薯还是低热量、低脂肪食物，既满足人体所需的营养，又可减少食量。

6 烤豆子 Baked beans
——英式早餐不可缺少的一道菜

达人了解英美

◇ **History**

The beans presently used to make baked beans are all native to North America and were introduced to Italy in 1528 and to France by 1547. The dish of baked beans is commonly described as having a savory-sweet flavor and a brownish or reddish **tinted**（着色的）white bean once baked, stewed, canned or otherwise cooked. According to alternative traditions, sailors brought cassoulet from the south of France or northern France and the Channel Islands where bean stews were popular. Most probably, a number of regional bean recipes coalesced and cross-fertilized in North America and **ultimately**（基本上）gave rise to the baked bean culinary tradition familiar today. In the UK, the term baked bean usually refers to tinned beans in a tomato sauce. They were originally imported from American companies, first sold in the UK in 1886 in the upmarket Fortnum & Mason store in London as an expensive foreign **delicacy**（佳肴）.

阅读辅助

用来做焗豆的豆子原产于北美地区，在16世纪被引入意大利和法国。无论是烤、煮、做罐头，还是其他烹饪方法，焗豆类菜肴通常带有鲜和甜的口味，汤汁呈棕色或红色，豆子内是白色。今天流行的焗豆食谱最有可能在北美产生，各地不同的豆类食谱在北美碰撞融合，最终形成一种大多数人都能接受的味道。在英国"baked beans"一词几乎无一例外指罐装茄汁豆。许多人认为现代英式早餐必须包括焗豆，或焗豆拌吐司。1886年，海因茨焗豆第一次在英国出现，被高档百货商店Fortnum & Mason作为高价进口商品销售。

◆ **Health**

In 2002 the British Dietetic Association allowed manufacturers of canned baked beans to advertise the product as contributing to the recommended daily consumption of five – six vegetables per person. This concession was criticized by heart specialists who pointed to the high levels of sugar and salt in the product. However, it has been proven that **consumption**（消费）of baked beans does indeed lower total cholesterol levels and low-density lipoprotein **cholesterol**（胆固醇）, even in normo-cholesterolaemic individuals. Some manufacturers produce a "healthy" version of the product with reduced levels of sugar and salt.

> 阅读辅助
>
> 2002年，英国饮食协会允许焗豆生产商把该产品宣传为健康食品，因为它可以纳入每人每日吃5-6份蔬菜的范畴。这种做法受到心脏内科专家指责，因为焗豆是高盐高糖食品。然而研究证明，食用焗豆的确能降低体内总胆固醇和低密度脂蛋白胆固醇。即使是胆固醇正常的个体身上也能看出这种影响。一些厂家生产的焗豆是低糖和低盐的健康型。

◆ **Influence**

Baked beans is a dish containing beans, sometimes baked but, despite the name, usually stewed, in asauce. Most commercial canned baked beans are made from haricot beans, also known as navy beans – a variety of Phaseolus vulgaris in a sauce. In Ireland and the United Kingdom, a tomato and sugar sauce is most commonly used, and they are commonly eaten on toast or as part of a full English breakfast. In the United Kingdom, tomato sauce is most commonly used. In the U.S., Boston baked beans use pork and a sauce of molasses and are so popular the city has become known as Bean town. Maine and Quebec-style beans often use maple **syrup**（糖浆）.

In the United Kingdom, the term baked beans refers almost exclusively to canned beans in a tomato sauce. Some people regard baked beans as integral part of the modern Full English Breakfast. As the top selling brand of baked beans, historically the H. J. Heinz Company has become synonymous with them, although the growing popularity of other brands has reduced this. Heinz Beans were first sold in the UK in the up market Fortnum & Mason store in London as an exotic import at a high price. Although they are now a staple food, and arguably a **downmarket**（面向低收入阶层）one, the store continues the tradition of selling Heinz Beans among its more expensive wares.

> **阅读辅助**
>
> 烤豆子这道菜肴虽名字中有个烤字，但其烹饪方法多为焖制，是将豆子放入酱汁中焖制而成。多数罐装烤豆是用扁豆制成，人们也称这种罐装豆为"海军豆"。在英国人们习惯用西红柿酱做这道菜，而在美国的波士顿人们喜欢用猪肉和糖蜜酱一起烹饪，由于美国人的这种烹饪方法很受欢迎，所以人们命名波士顿为"豆子城镇"。在英国 baked beans 常指罐装的番茄酱扁豆，在罐装烤豆中 Heinz Beans 为最知名品牌。烤豆子是英国人很喜欢的一种菜肴，一些人把烤豆子作为全英式早餐的一部分。

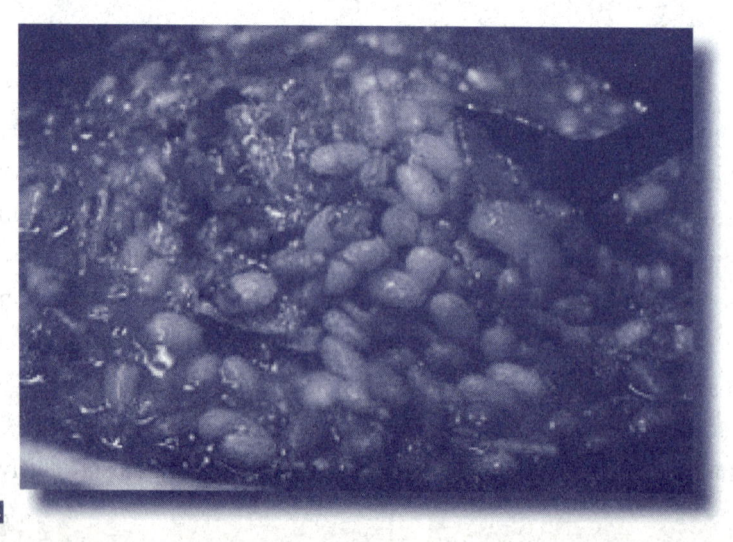

7 血肠 Black Pudding
——人类最早自制的菜肴

达人了解英美

◆ **Savoury**

Black pudding can be eaten cold, as it is cooked in production, but is often **grilled**(烤的), fried, baked or boiled in its skin. It was occasionally flavored with **pennyroyal**(薄荷油), differing from continental European versions in its relatively limited range of ingredients and reliance on oatmeal and barley instead of onions or **chitterlings**(猪肠) to absorb and be mixed with the blood.

In the United Kingdom, black pudding is considered a delicacy in the Black Country and the West Midlands, Stornoway and the North West, especially in Lancashire (in towns such as Bury), where it is traditionally boiled and served with malt vinegar out of paper wrapping. The Stornoway black pudding, made on the Western Isles of Scotland, has been granted Protected Geographical Indicator of Origin status. Black puddings are also served sliced and fried or grilled as part of a traditional full breakfast in much of the UK and Ireland, a tradition that followed British and Irish emigrants around the world.

阅读辅助

血肠可以冷吃或者煮熟食用,通常的吃法是烤或者炸。偶尔里面还会加入一些薄荷油,在不同的国家里面除了猪血以外会混合燕麦或者大麦,还有会加入洋葱。在英国(特别是英格兰),血肠切片是英式早餐常见食物。血肠被切为矮圆柱体,主色调为黑色,故被英国人称为"黑布丁"(Black Pudding)。

✧ Cooking

Unsurprisingly, buying and cooking ready-prepared black puddings is much easier than making your own. Ready-made puddings are already cooked, so they just need a gentle re-heating (gentle is the key word, as they tend to crumble very easily). Slice them thickly and gently grill them, or heat them in the oven or lightly fry.

Black pudding is a breakfast favorite, but it's a **versatile**（万能的）ingredient for brunch, lunch and dinner, too. A wild mushroom sauce complements the crumbly texture and intensely rich taste of black pudding very well, as does a whisky, onion and cream sauce. Grilled black pudding and cherry tomatoes served with potato **scones**（司康饼）is also a good combination, the richness of the pudding contrasting with the tang of tomatoes.

> 阅读辅助
>
> 购买现成的血肠要比自己制作要方便，之后你只需要加热，把它切成厚片然后用微波炉或者平底锅煎炸或者炒。血肠是人们在早餐最喜欢吃到的食物，用野生的蘑菇酱会让血肠更加平添美味，再配上威士忌，洋葱和奶油酱。烤血肠和樱桃酱配上烤土豆饼也是不错的组合。

8 康沃尔馅饼 *Cornish pasty*
——英国传统的矿工食品

达人了解英美

◆ **History**

Other early references to pasties include a 13th-century charter which was granted by Henry III (1207–1272) to the town of Great Yarmouth. The town is bound to send to the sheriffs of Norwich every year one hundred **herrings**（鲱鱼）, baked in twenty four pasties, which the sheriffs are to deliver to the lord of the manor of East Carlton who is then to convey them to the King. Around the same time, 13th century chronicler Matthew Paris wrote of the monks of St Albans Abbey "according to their custom, lived upon pasties of flesh-meat". A total of 5,500 venison pasties were served at the installation feast of George Neville, **archbishop**（大主教）of York and chancellor of England in 1465.

In contrast to its earlier place amongst the wealthy, during the 17th and 18th centuries the pasty became popular with working people in Cornwall, where tin miners and others adopted it due to its unique shape, forming a complete meal that could be carried easily and eaten without cutlery. In a mine the pasty's dense, folded pastry could stay warm for several hours, and if it did get cold it could easily be warmed on a shovel over a candle. Side-crimped pasties gave rise to the suggestion that the miner might have eaten the **pasty**（馅饼）holding the thick edge of pastry, which was later discarded, thereby ensuring that his dirty fingers did not touch food or his mouth. However, many old photographs show that pasties were wrapped in bags made of paper or muslin and were eaten from end-to-end; according to the earliest Cornish recipe book, published in 1929, this is "the true Cornish way" to eat a pasty. Another theory suggests that pasties were marked at one end with an initial and then eaten from the other end so that if not finished in one go, they could easily be **reclaimed**（回收利用）by their owners.

> **阅读辅助**
>
> 康沃尔馅饼有个传说，是在13世纪亨利三世的时候，人们会每年送24个馅饼给地方官，通过他转送给国王。还有人说这种馅饼是来自于圣奥尔本斯修道院的僧侣，根据他们的习俗制作这种馅饼。其实康沃尔馅饼是英国传统的矿工食品，有着穷人食品的典型特征。这东西还是英国矿工拿来给矮人上供的供品，传统上英国人认为矮人也在他们的矿井里活动，而且有时候你还能"听到"他们的声音。不过实际上这个习俗很可能是这么来的：康沃尔地区的矿山主要出产的是锡，锡矿往往是热液，因此里面有可能含有同样热液成的砒霜。所以干完活手上也肯定被污染了，所以要把拿过的那一块留下来，省得吃了中毒。

◇ Recipes

The recipe for a Cornish pasty, as defined by its protected status, includes diced or minced beef, onion, potato and swede in rough chunks along with some "light peppery" seasoning. The cut of beef used is generally skirt steak. Swede is sometimes called turnip in Cornwall but the recipe requires use of actualswede, not turnip. Pasty ingredients are usually seasoned with salt and pepper, depending on individual taste. The use of carrot in a traditional Cornish pasty is frowned upon, though it does appear regularly in recipes. The type of pastry used is not defined, as long as it is golden in color and will not crack during the cooking or cooling, although modern pasties almost always use a **shortcrust**（酥皮糕点）pastry.

(英)垂涎欲滴的特色美食 **Section 4-1**

> **阅读辅助**
>
> 传统的康沃尔馅饼,是用小块牛肉、土豆块、青甘蓝、洋葱和一些清淡的调料做馅,然后包成字母"D"的形状烤制。您能品尝到各种不同的馅饼,但只有在康沃尔郡制作出的馅饼,才叫做康沃尔馅饼。

9 约克郡布丁 *Yorkshire Pudding*
——英国人周日晚餐的重要组成部分

达人了解英美

◇ History

The origin of the Yorkshire pudding is not known but there is no special association with the county of Yorkshire. An early recipe appeared in William Kenrick's The Whole Duty of a Womanin 1737. When wheat flour began to come into common use for making cakes and puddings, cooks in the north of England devised a means of making use of the fat that dropped into the dripping pan to cook a batter pudding while the meat roasted in the oven. Similar instructions were published in 1747 in *The Art of Cookery made Plain and Easy* by Hannah Glasse under the title of *Yorkshire pudding*. It was she who re-invented and renamed the original version, called Dripping Pudding, which had been cooked in England for centuries, although these puddings were much flatter than the **puffy**（松脆的） versions known today. The English celebrity cook Fanny Cradock is reported to have said "The English have never had a cuisine. Even Yorkshire pudding comes from Burgundy [in France]." The Yorkshire pudding is meant to rise.

阅读辅助

约克郡布丁的起源不确定是与约克郡有关，早期的配方是来自一个名叫肯里克女士的烹调。当开始用小麦粉用来制作蛋糕和布丁时，在英格兰北部的厨师设计了一款特殊的方式将面粉制成糊状，进行烤制。这个名字原本是在1747年发布，原先只是叫"水滴布丁"，这种布丁以这个名字一直存在了几个世纪，但是据另一名知情人说，其实约克郡布丁的起源是来自法国的勃艮第地区。

✧ Cooking

Yorkshire pudding is an English side dish made from batter consisting of eggs, flour, and milk. The dish is sometimes served with beef and gravy and is a staple of the traditional British Sunday roast. It may also be served as a dessert. Yorkshire pudding is cooked by pouring a batter made from milk (or water), flour and eggs into preheated, oiled, baking pans, ramekins or muffin tins (in the case of miniature puddings). A basic formula uses 1/3 cup flour and 1/3 cup liquid per egg.

Next, put the flour and salt into a bowl, and make a space in the middle. Break in the egg, pour in half of the milk and a quarter of a teaspoonful of salt. Pour in half of the milk, and slowly mix thoroughly until it is full of bubbles. Stir in the rest of the milk. Finally, grease a dish. Pour in the mixture and place in a very hot oven for five minutes or until the mixture has risen and is a nice golden brown.

阅读辅助

约克郡布丁是英国的一种食品，为烤牛肉的配菜。首先，取四盎司的面粉，鸡蛋、半品脱牛奶和四分之一茶匙盐。其次将这几样东西搅拌，打成糊状物。最后，开始烹饪。将油抹在烤盘上，要抹匀。倒入布丁，放入预热好的烤箱（180~220°），烤5分钟左右，或者等到布丁隆起并转为漂亮的金黄色。

10 司康饼 *Scone*
——英式的快速面包

达人了解英美

◆ **History**

The original scone was round and flat, usually as large as a medium-sized plate. It was made with **unleavened**（未发酵的）oats and baked on a griddle (or girdle, inScots), then cut into **triangular**（三角形的）sections for serving. Today, many would call the large round cake a bannock, and call the triangles scones. In Scotland, the words are often used interchangeably. Scones sold commercially are usually round, although some brands are hexagonal as this shape may be **tessellated**（镶嵌成棋盘花纹的）for space efficiency. When prepared at home, they may take various shapes including triangles, rounds and squares. Baking scones at home is often closely tied to heritage baking. They tend to be made using family recipes rather than recipe books, since it is often a family member who holds the "best" and most-treasured recipe.

> **阅读辅助**
> 司康饼又称英国茶饼或英国松饼，传统的司康饼是由小麦、大麦或麦片制成，用烘焙粉作发酵剂烤制而成，之后切成三角形食用，今天也会做成圆形的薄饼。在苏格兰，通常圆形和三角形的茶饼都有。现在商家出售的大多是圆形的，而自家制作的是三角形的。

◆ Varieties

British scones are often lightly sweetened, but may also be **savoury** （开胃的菜肴）. They frequently include raisins, currants, cheese or dates. In Scotlandand Ulster, savory varieties of scone include soda scones, also known as soda farls, and potato scones, normally known as tat tie scones, which **resemble** （类似）small, thin savory pancakesmade with potato flour. Potato scones are most commonly served fried in afull Scottish breakfast or an Ulster fry. The griddle scone (or "girdle scone" in Scots) is a variety of scone which is fried rather than baked. Other common varieties include the dropped scone, or drop scone, like a pancake, after the method of dropping the batter onto the griddle or frying pan to cook it, and the lemonade scone, which is made with lemonade and cream instead of butter and milk. There is also the fruit scone or fruited scone, which contains currants, sultanas, peel and **glacé**（糖渍的）cherries, which is just like a plain round scone with the fruit mixed into the dough. In some countries one may also encounter savoury varieties of scone which may contain or be topped with combinations of cheese, onion, bacon, etc.

阅读辅助

司康饼与美式饼干极其类似，司康饼要比美国的饼干粘，通常包括甜葡萄干、无核小葡萄干、奶酪或枣。有食谱会加入牛奶，甚至直接用牛奶代替水。烘烤前，或在司康饼顶上涂上一层薄薄的蛋液。美国的食谱会使用蔓越橘或坚果等，而巧克力仁的司康饼在美国也很受欢迎。在一些国家中甚至有裹着或者顶上撒着些奶酪、洋葱或咸肉的司康饼类点心。

11 奶酪蛋糕 *Cheesecake*
——令人欲罢不能的美味

达人了解英美

◆ History

An ancient form of cheesecake may have been a popular dish in ancient Greece even prior to Romans' adoption of it with the conquest of Greece. The earliest attested mention of a cheesecake is by the Greek physician Aegimus, who wrote a book on the art of making cheesecakes. Cato the Elder's De Agri Cultura includes recipes for two cakes for religious uses: libumand placenta. Of the two, placenta is most like most modern cheesecakes, having a crust that is separately prepared and baked.

In 1872, William Lawrence from Chester, NY, along with other dairymen, came up with a way of making an "un-ripened" cheese that is heavier and creamier by accident, actually looking for a way to recreate the soft, French cheese, Neufchatel. Lawrence distributed the cheese in foil, becoming a brand that is familiarly recognized as "Philadelphia". Later on in 1912, James Kraft invented a form of this cream cheese, but **pasteurized**（巴氏消毒的）it — this is now the most commonly used cheese for cheesecake.

阅读辅助

芝士蛋糕据知是源于古希腊，在前776年时，为了供应雅典奥运所做出来的甜点。接着由罗马人将芝士蛋糕从希腊传播到整个欧洲。在19世纪跟着移民们，传到了美洲。而现在做奶酪蛋糕所用奶酪起源于1872年，由威廉·劳伦斯的制作。

✧ Cooking

Cheesecake is a dessert formed of a topping made with soft, fresh cheese upon a base made from biscuit, pastry or sponge. The topping is frequently sweetened with sugar and flavored or topped with fruit, nuts, and/or chocolate.

A common difficulty with baking cheesecakes is its tendency to "crack" when cooled. This is due to the **coagulation**（凝结）of the beaten eggs in its batter. There are various methods to prevent this. One method is to bake the cheesecake in a hot water bath to ensure even heating. Other methods include blending a little cornstarch into the batter or baking the cheesecake at a lower temperature and slow cooling it in the oven, turned off, with the door **ajar**（半开的）. If these methods fail, a common practice is to cover the top of the cheesecake with toppings such as fruit, whipped cream, or cookie crumbs.

> **阅读辅助**
>
> 芝士蛋糕是西方甜点的一种。有着柔软的上层，混合了特殊的奶酪再加上糖和其他的配料，如鸡蛋、奶油和水果等。奶酪蛋糕通常都以饼干做为底层，亦有不使用底层的，有固定的几种口味，表层常常以水果、干果或是巧克力做装饰，但也有不装饰或是只是在顶层简单抹上一层薄蜂蜜的样式。

12 苏格兰鲜鱼浓汤 Cullen Skink
——经典的苏格兰风味

达人了解英美

◆ **History**

Cullen skink is a thick Scottishsoup made of smoked **haddock**（黑线鳕）, potatoes and onions. An authentic Cullen skink will use finnan haddie, but it may be prepared with any other undyed smoked haddock. This soup is a local specialty, from the town of Cullen in Moray, on the north-east coast of Scotland. The soup is often served as a starter at formal Scottish dinners. Cullen skink is widely served as an everyday dish across the northeast of Scotland. Local recipes for Cullen skink have several slight variations, such as the use of milk instead of water or the addition of singlecream. Cullen skink was traditionally served with bread. It has been described as "smokier and more **assertive**（肯定的）than American chowder, heartier than classical French bisque".

阅读辅助

苏格兰鲜鱼浓汤是由烟熏线鳕，土豆和洋葱制成。正宗鲜鱼汤只使用烟熏黑线鳕鱼，这道汤是苏格兰东北海岸卡伦镇的特产。一般这个汤是在晚餐做头盘上菜的，之后这道汤开始作为家常菜在苏格兰东北部流行起来。只不过不同的地方对配料做了些轻微的变化，如用牛奶替代稀奶油等等。另外这道汤通常是配着面包使用的，它经常被誉为"比美国杂烩汤还好喝，比法国浓汤更丰富的美味"。

✧ Influence

Skink is a Scots word for a shin, knuckle, or hough of beef, which has developed the secondary meaning of a soup, especially one made from these. The word skink is ultimately derived from the Middle Dutch schenke "shin, hough".

Cullen skink appears in many traditional Scottish cookery books and appears in numerous restaurants and hotel menus throughout Scotland, the UK, and internationally. In 2012 a **Guardian columnist**（专栏作家）described the dish as "the milky fish soup which has surely replaced your haggises and **porridges**（麦片粥）as Scotland's signature dish".

> **阅读辅助**
>
> Skink 是个苏格兰词汇，表示牛的腕骨。升级其他的含义是指汤，里面包含了汤内的材料。鲜鱼汤是苏格兰的传统菜品，经常出现在苏格兰和英格兰风味的餐馆或者酒店的餐单上。2012年《卫报》的专栏作家称此汤已然取代了哈吉斯成为了苏格兰的招牌菜了。

读书笔记

Section 4-2 （美）垂涎欲滴的特色美食

美国，是世界上最著名的移民国家，也是拥有容纳百川心胸的国家。随着不同国家的移民的到来，各种馋涎欲滴的美食也接踵而至。经过时间的蹉跎将原先各国美食蜕变成为具有美国特色的食物，所以你来到美国可以品尝到似是而非的各国风情的珍馐佳肴，这种似是而非的感觉就是美国的美食文化。

1 鲁本三明治 *Reuben Sandwich*
——让人欲罢不能的三明治

达人了解英美

◇ Origins

Reuben Kulakofsky: One account holds that Reuben Kulakofsky, a Lithuanian-born grocer residing inOmaha, Nebraska, was the inventor perhaps as part of a group effort by members of Kulakofsky's weekly pokergame held in the Blackstone Hotelfrom around 1920 through 1935. The participants, who **nicknamed**（给……取绰号）themselves "the committee", included the hotel's owner, Charles Schimmel. The sandwich first gained local fame when Schimmel put it on the Blackstone's lunch menu, and its fame spread when a former employee of the hotel won a national contest with the **recipe**（食谱）. In Omaha, March 14 was **proclaimed**（宣布）as Reuben Sandwich Day.

Reuben's Delicatessen: Another account holds that the Reuben's creator was Arnold Reuben, the German owner of the famed yet **defunct**（死的）Reuben's Delicatessen in New York City who according to an interview with Craig Claiborne invented the "Reuben special" around 1914. The earliest references in print to the sandwich are New York–based but that is not **conclusive**（有说服力的）evidence, though the fact that the earliest, from a 1926 edition of Theatre Magazine, references a "Reuben special", does seem to take its cue from Arnold Reuben's menu.

Some sources name the actress in the above account as Annette Seelos, not Marjorie Rambeau, while noting that the original "Reuben special" sandwich did not contain corned beef or sauerkraut and was not grilled; still other **versions**（版本）give credit to Alfred Scheuing, Reuben's chef, and say he created the sandwich for Reuben's son, Arnold Jr., in the 1930s.

> **阅读辅助**
>
> 一种说法认为内布拉斯加州奥马哈的杂货铺老板鲁宾·库拉寇夫斯基于1920年至1935年间发明了鲁宾三明治。他制作的初衷是给自己周末打牌的牌友充饥。另一种说法认为纽约市的餐馆老板亚瑟·鲁宾在1914年发明了鲁宾三明治，是送给当时的电影明星的礼物。

✧ Recipes

Ingredients

☐ 2 tablespoons butter   ☐ 1/2 cup Thousand Island dressing
☐ 8 slices rye bread   ☐ 8 slices deli sliced corned beef
☐ 8 slices Swiss cheese   ☐ 1 cup sauerkraut, drained

Directions

1. Preheat a large **skillet**（平底锅）or griddle on medium heat.

2. Lightly butter one side of bread slices. Spread non-buttered sides with Thousand Island dressing. On 4 bread slices, layer 1 slice Swiss cheese, 2 slices corned beef, 1/4 cup sauerkraut and second slice of Swiss cheese. Top with remaining bread slices, buttered sides out.

3. Grill sandwiches until both sides are golden brown, about 15 minutes per side. Serve hot.

✧ Variations

Rachel sandwich：The Rachel sandwich is a variation on the standard Reuben sandwich, **substituting**（取代）pastrami for the corned beef, and coleslaw for the sauerkraut. Other recipes for the Rachel call for turkey instead of corned beef or pastrami. In some parts of the United States, especially Michigan, this turkey variant is known as a "Georgia Reuben" or "California Reuben", which sometimes uses **barbecue**（烤肉）sauce instead of Russian or Thousand Island.

West Coast Reuben：The West Coast Reuben is a variation on the standard Reuben sandwich, substituting Dijon **mustard**（芥末）as the dressing.

Montreal Reuben：The Montreal Reuben substitutes Montreal smoked meat for corned beef.

Reuben egg rolls：Reuben egg rolls, sometimes called "Irish egg rolls" or "Reuben balls", use the standard Reuben sandwich filling of corned beef, sauerkraut, and cheese inside a deep-fried egg roll wrapper. Typically served with thousand island dressing as an appetizer or snack, they originated at Mader's, a German restaurant in Milwaukee, Wisconsin, where chef Dennis Wegner created them for a summer festival in about 1990.

> 阅读辅助
>
> 鲁宾三明治有一个"姊妹"：Rachel，用火鸡肉代替粗盐腌牛肉，用凉拌卷心菜（Coleslaw）代替德国酸菜来制作。

2 烘肉卷 *Meatloaf*
—— 一道纯正的西餐狠菜

达人了解英美

✧ Origins

The meatloaf has European origins; meatloaf of **minced**（剁碎）meat was mentioned in the famous Roman cookery collection Apicius as early as the 5th century. Meatloaf is a traditional German and Belgian dish, and it is a cousin to the Dutchmeatball. American meatloaf has its origins in **scrapple**（玉米肉饼）, a mixture of ground pork andcornmeal served by German-Americans in Pennsylvania since Colonial times. However, meatloaf in the **contemporary**（当代的）American sense did not appear in cookbooks until the late 19th century.

In 2007, meatloaf was voted the seventh-favorite dish in the United States according to Good Housekeeping. During the Great Depression, cooking meatloaf was a way to stretch the food budget for families, using an inexpensive type of meat and other ingredients as **leftovers**（吃剩的食物）; along with spices, it was popular to add cereal grains to the meatloaf to stretch the meat. The tradition lives on with the merits of producing a lower-fat dish with superior binding and **consistency**（一致）.

The meatloaf is typically eaten with some kind of sauce or relish. Many of these recipescall for pasta sauce or tomato sauce to be poured over the loaf to form a crust during baking. The tomato-based sauce may be replaced with simple brown gravy or onion gravy, but the meatloaf is prepared in a similar manner. Barbecue sauce, tomato ketchup, or a mixture of both tomato ketchup and mustard may also be used. American meatloaf may be garnished with plain ketchup or a "meatloaf sauce" consisting of ketchup and brown sugar mixed.

Another variety of meatloaf is prepared by **frosting**（结霜）it with mashed potatoes, drizzling it with a small amount of butter, and browning in the oven.

The meatloaf is normally served warm as part of the main course, but can also be found sliced as a cold cut. Meatloaf can also be considered a typical comfort food and is served in many diners and restaurants today.

> 阅读辅助
>
> Meatloaf 是由意大利菜中的肉球（meatball）启发所制。基本上这又是一个加大加长版本的美国菜。但 Meatloaf 的成名却和美国的大萧条扯不开关系。

◇ Recipes

Ingredients

- 2 pounds lean ground beef
- 1 (10.75 ounce) cancondensed tomato soup
- 1/2 cup ketchup
- 3 tablespoons prepared mustard
- 2 eggs, beaten
- 1 onion, finely diced
- 1 tablespoon steak sauce
- 1 cup rolled oats

Directions

1. In a large bowl, combine ground meat, soup, chopped onion, rolled oats, eggs, steak sauce, ketchup and mustard. Mix well.

2. Shape into a loaf, and pat into a loaf pan.

3. Bake in a **preheated**（预先加热）350 degrees F (175 degrees C) oven for 1 hour or until done.

✧ Variations

Austria

The Austrian meatloaf version is called Faschierter Braten. Most of the time it is not filled (e.g., in Germany), but it is wrapped in ham before baking it. Often it is served with mashed potatoes (when warm) or with sauce cumberland (when cold).

Belgium

The Belgian version of meatloaf is called pain de viande (except in Flemish-speaking Flanders). It is usually served warm and can then be served with various sauces, but can also be eaten cold with a loaf of bread.

Cuba

The Cuban meatloaf is called pulpeta. It is made with ground beef and ground ham, and stuffed with hard boiled eggs, and it is cooked on the stove top. The dish was brought to public attention, **mistakenly**（曲解地）referred to as a sausage, in the second episode of the third season of *The Cosby Show* entitled "*Food for Thought*".

Germany

In Germany, meatloaf is referred to as Hackbraten, Faschierter Braten or Falscher Hase 'mock hare'. In some regions it often has boiled eggs inside.

Italy

In Italy, meatloaf is called polpettone and can be filled with eggs or ham and cheese.

Greece

In Greece, meatloaf is referred to as rolo (Ρολό) and it is usually filled with hard boiled eggs, although several other **variations**（变化）exist.

阅读辅助

　　Meatloaf 在不同国家，有着不同程度的改良。有的是材料变化，有的是蘸料的变化。

3 巴法罗鸡翅 *Buffalo wings*
—— 一道地道的纽约州美味

达人了解英美

◇ **History**

One of the more **prevalent**（流行的）claims is that Buffalo wings were first prepared at the Anchor Bar in Buffalo, New York, by Teressa Bellissimo, who owned the bar with husband Frank. Upon the unannounced, late-night arrival of their son, Dominic, with several of his friends from college, Teressa needed a fast and easy snack to present to her guests. It was then that she came up with the idea of deep frying chicken wings (normally thrown away or reserved for stock) and **tossing**（搅拌）them in **cayenne**（辣椒）hot sauce. Another claim is that a man named John Young served chicken wings in a special "mambo sauce" at his Buffalo restaurant in the mid-1960s. His wings were breaded. Young had registered the name of his restaurant, John Young's Wings 'n Things, at the county courthouse before leaving Buffalo in 1970.

> **阅读辅助**
>
> 布法罗辣鸡翅是在1964年10月3日在布法罗商业街近北大街的船锚吧首度面世的。身为其夫法兰克的合伙人，泰蕾莎·贝利西莫，为了招呼她的儿子多明尼克和他的朋友，把鸡翅炸了，配上酱汁而诞生。

◆ Recipes

Ingredients

☐ 1 quart vegetable oil for deep frying

☐ 1 tablespoon distilled white vinegar

☐ 24 chicken wings, tips removed and wings cut in half at joint

☐ 4 tablespoons butter

☐ salt and pepper to taste

☐ 5 tablespoons hot pepper sauce

Directions

1. Heat the oil in a large skillet or deep fryer to 375 degrees F (190 degrees C). Deep fry chicken wings in oil until done, about 10 minutes. Remove chicken from skillet or deep fryer and drain on paper towels.

2. Melt the butter in a large skillet. Stir in the, vinegar and hot pepper sauce. Season with salt and pepper to taste. Add cooked chicken to sauce and stir over low heat to coat. The longer the wings simmer in the sauce, the hotter they will be. Serve warm.

◆ Variations

The **appellation**（名称）"Buffalo" is also now commonly applied to foods other than wings, including chicken fingers,chicken fries, chicken nuggets, popcorn chicken,shrimp, and pizza that are seasoned with the Buffalo-style sauce or variations of it. The flavor of Buffalo wings is replicated by a number of dishes. A common variation on the "buffalo" sauce flavor is found in potato chips produced by a number of different companies. Many of these "Buffalo Chips" also incorporate a blue cheese flavoring to **simulate**（模仿）the complete Buffalo wing experience.

Today, there are many flavors of prepared wings (wingettes and drumettes) available, besides the original hot Buffalo style. Flavors include barbecue, lemon pepper, pepper Parmesan, garlic, sweet-and-sour, honey mustard, Thai chili, and Caribbean jerk. Since the first introduction, restaurants have introduced hundreds of different flavors of chicken wings.

> **阅读辅助**
>
> 鸡翅深入民心的程度，可以在其食法的发展体现出来。当中较多人采用的有把中翼较小的骨扭出或者以挤压法去骨以增加趣味及使食用更方便。

4 芝加哥式比萨 *Chicago-Style Pizza*
——极致奢华的芝加哥式馅饼

达人了解英美

✧ History

Deep-dish pizza: According to Tim Samuelson, Chicago's official cultural historian, there is not enough documentation to determine with certainty who invented Chicago-style deep-dish pizza. It is often reported that Chicago-style deep-dish pizza was invented at Pizzeria Uno in Chicago, in 1943, by Uno's founder Ike Sewell, a former University of Texas football star. However, a 1956 article from the Chicago Daily News **asserts**（断言）that Uno's original pizza chef Rudy Malnati developed the recipe.

Stuffed pizza: By the mid-1970s, two Chicago chains, Nancy's Pizza, founded by Rocco Palese, and Giordano's Pizzeria, operated by brothers Efren and Joseph Boglio, began experimenting with deep dish pizza and created the **stuffed**（塞满了）pizza. Palese based his creation on his mother's recipe for scarciedda, an Italian Easter pie from his hometown of Potenza. Chicago Magazine articles featuring Nancy's Pizza and Giordano's stuffed pizza popularized the dish.

阅读辅助

在1943年，Ike Sewell发明了一种深盘比萨（DeepDish），Ike相信如果你做的比萨带有大量的馅料（特别是香肠），它将会成为人们一顿丰盛美食的选择。之后在1970年中旬又出现了另一种芝加哥式的比萨。

◇ Styles of Pizza

Deep-dish pizza: The primary difference between deep-dish pizza and most other forms of pizza is that, as the name suggests, the **crust**（面包皮）is very deep, creating a very thick pizza that **resembles**（类似于）a pie more than aflatbread. Although the entire pizza is very thick, in traditional Chicago-style deep-dish pizzas, the crust itself is thin to medium in thickness. Deep-dish pizza is baked in a round, steel pan that is more similar to a cake or pie pan than a typical pizza pan. The pan is oiled in order to allow for easy removal as well as to create a fried effect on the outside of the crust. In addition to ordinary wheat flour, the pizza dough may contain semolina or food coloring, giving the crust a distinctly **yellowish**（淡黄色）tone. The dough is pressed up onto the sides of the pan, forming a bowl for a very thick layer of toppings.

Stuffed pizza: Stuffed pizzas are often even deeper than deep-dish pizzas, but otherwise, it can be hard to see the difference until it is cut into. A stuffed pizza generally has much deeper topping density than any other type of pizza. As with deep-dish pizza, a deep layer of **dough**（生面团）forms a bowl in a high-sided pan and the toppings and cheese are added. Then, an additional layer of dough goes on top and is pressed to the sides of the crust.

Thin-crust pizza: There is also a style of thin-crust pizza found in Chicago and throughout the rest of the Midwest. The crust is thin and firm enough to have a noticeable crunch, unlike a New York-style pizza. This pizza is cut into squares, also known as party cut or **tavern**（客栈）cut, as opposed to a pie cut into **wedges**（楔形）. Aurelios is a chain which specializes in this kind of pizza. Casa Bianca, located in the Eagle Rock section of Los Angeles, is also well known for this style of thin-crusted Chicago bar pizza.

（美）垂涎欲滴的特色美食 **Section 4-2**

> **阅读辅助**
>
> 　　制作这种比萨时，饼皮必须放在比较深的烤盘内，这样制作出的比萨侧沿很高，即所谓"深盘"。饼底像派皮那样包着模具的底部和四周，先烤完饼皮，然后在厚厚的饼皮内放上非常多的乳酪，加上有番茄颗粒的比萨酱，然后依照个人喜好增加肉、土豆、蔬菜等其他馅料，再放入炉内进行二次烘烤，烘焙时间比较长。

5 贝奈特饼 *Beignet*
—— 一道受人欢迎的开胃菜

达人了解英美

◇ Origin

Beignets are commonly known in New Orleans as a breakfast served with powdered sugar on top. They are traditionally prepared right before **consumption**（消耗）to be eaten fresh and hot. Variations of fried dough can be found across cuisines internationally; however, the origin of the term beignet is specifically French. In the United States, beignets have been popular within New Orleans Creole cuisine and are customarily served as a dessert or in some sweet variation. They were brought to New Orleans in the 18th century by French colonists, from "the old mother country", and became a large part of home-style Creole cooking, variations often including banana or plantain – popular fruits in the port city. Today, Café du Monde is a popular New Orleans food destination specializing in beignets with powdered sugar, coffee with **chicory**（菊苣）, and café au lait. Beignets were declared the official state **doughnut**（甜甜圈）of Louisianain 1986.

The tradition of deep-frying fruits for a side dish dates to the time of Ancient Rome, while the tradition of beignets in Europe is **speculated** （猜测）to have originated with a heavy influence of Islamic culinary tradition. The term beignet can be applied to two varieties, depending on the type of pastry. The French-style beignet in the United States, has the specific meaning of deep-fried **choux**（甘蓝）pastry. Beignets can also be made with yeast pastry, which might be called boules de Berlin in French, referring to Berliner doughnuts which have a spherical shape filled with fruit or jam.

> **阅读辅助**
>
> 贝奈特饼起源于法国，起初是为制作一种无孔的甜甜圈。法国移民定居路易斯安那后，将法式料理的传统与北美大陆的食材相结合，便催生出了今天的Cajun Cuisine和贝奈特饼。制作一个贝奈特饼，要先将泡芙糊油炸，然后撒上糖霜，而作为开胃菜时，新奥尔良人还会将虾或路易斯安那特产的小龙虾包裹其中做馅。它的口感绵密、松脆、香喷可口，在刚端到你面前时，热度恰到好处。贝奈特饼也被认为是世界上最美味的糕点之一。

◇ Recipes

Ingredients
- 2 1/4 teaspoons active dry yeast
- 1 cup evaporated milk
- 1 teaspoon salt
- 1 1/2 cups warm water (110 degrees F/45 degrees C)
- 7 cups all-purpose flour
- 1/2 cup white sugar
- 2 eggs
- 1/4 cup confectioners' sugar
- 1 quart vegetable oil for frying
- 1/4 cup shortening

Directions

1. In a large bowl, **dissolve**（溶解）yeast in warm water. Add sugar, salt, eggs, **evaporated**（蒸发）milk, and blend well. Mix in 4 cups of the flour and beat until smooth. Add the shortening, and then the remaining 3 cups of flour. Cover and chill for up to 24 hours.

2. Roll out dough 1/8 inch thick. Cut into 2 1/2 inch squares. Fry in 360 degree F (180 degrees C) hot oil. If beignets do not pop up, oil is not hot enough. Drain onto paper towels.

3. Shake confectioners' sugar on hot beignets. Serve warm.

6 龙萨饼 Runza
—— 一种俄罗斯、德国移民的民族美食

达人了解英美

✧ **History**

The runza sandwich originated in Russia during the 1800s and spread to Germany before appearing in the United States. Bierock comes from the Russian pirogi or pirozhki and is the term for any food consisting of a savory filling-stuffed dough. The recipe was passed down from generation to generation and is available throughout the Americas, particularly Argentina and the Canadian provinces of Alberta, Saskatchewan, Manitoba. The recipe was spread throughout the United States by the Volga Germans (Germans from Russia) and can be found in North and South Dakota, Michigan, Wisconsin, Minnesota, Illinois, Kansas, Oklahoma, and Nebraska. The term "runza" is registered as a **trademark**（商标）in the United States by Nebraska-based Runza Restaurants.

> **阅读辅助**
>
> Runza（龙萨饼）是一种俄罗斯、德国移民的民族饮食。它其实是一种类似于三明治的面团。传统的龙萨饼中包有碎牛肉、洋葱、卷心菜。现在也有许多新的口味，如奶酪、瑞士蘑菇、以及培根等。

✧ **Recipes**

Ingredients

☐ *1 (3 pound) package frozen white bread dough 1 pound shredded mozzarella che*

☐ 1 1/2 pounds ground beef salt and pepper to taste vegetable oil
☐ 1 medium head cabbage, shredded

Directions

1. Thaw out frozen bread dough; cut each roll into 3 pieces and set aside. Brown beef and cabbage in a large skillet, seasoning with salt and pepper to taste.

2. Preheat oven to 350 degrees F (175 degrees C).

3. Roll out bread dough and cut into squares. Place a spoonful of the beef/cabbage mixture onto the center of each dough square. Sprinkle cheese on top, fold over and pinch sides to seal. Rub a bit of oil on the outside of each pastry.

4. Place in a 9x13 inch baking dish and bake in the preheated oven for 45 to 60 minutes, or until golden brown.

7 斯派蒂斯 *Spiedies*
—— 一种传统的意大利烤肉串

达人了解英美

◇ Origins

The original idea for spiedie was brought by Italian immigrants to upstate New York in the early 1920s. The specific origin of the spiedie is disputed. Traditionally, the early Broome County spiedie was made only from spring lamb, but currently most commercial restaurants prepare spiedie using chicken or pork. The "chicken category" was added to the Spiedie Fest cook-off in 1987, and quickly became the most popular meat choice.

Camillo Iacovelli created the spiedie in Endwell, N.Y., but his brother Agostino "Augie" Iacovelli and Peter Sharak popularized spiedies, Iacovelli in his Endicott restaurant, and Sharak at Sharky's Bar and Grill in Binghamton. Iacovelli's **marinade**（卤汁）, which he called "zuzu", originally was made simply from wine vinegar, water, lemon juice, garlic and mint. Italian spices, olive oil, and minced onion were added later as regional tastes and the choice of meat began to vary.

阅读辅助

Spiedie 为宾汉姆顿当地发明的串烧肉，Spiedie 酱是由醋及多种香草料调制而成。将鸡肉或猪肉浸泡于酱汁中数时，将肉串起烧烤，即成为美味的串烧肉。酸酸顺口的味道，成为当地居民家常食肴，更吸引外地民众慕名前来品尝。

◆ Popularity

Through the 1960s and 1970s, spiedies also became popular with the families of deer hunters, since venison has a strong game quality and is similar to lamb. Many local families made their own marinade and enjoyed the wild game as a delicacy cooked on backyard grills. In 1975, Rob Salamida became the first person to bottle the sauce and sell it. He began by cooking spiedies outside a local tavern at 16. After a tornado nearly struck his stand in 1975, he decided it would be more **lucrative**（有利可图的）and safer to bottle a spiedie marinade.

Through the 1980s, Danny "Moonbeam" furthered the popularity of spiedies by selling them from porches of local bars at night in order to finance his motorcycle racing hobby. Lori Vesely featured spiedies straight off the grill at The Endwell Pub. Pork was especially good for long grilling times, making the bar spiedie a favorite of both staff and customers. In 1983, a few families got together and held a Spiedie Festthat was a tremendous hit. Coupled with a Balloon Rally, it quickly grew to an annual festival attracting more than 100,000 attendees.

> **阅读辅助**
>
> 宾汉姆顿地区有多家Spiedie烤肉餐厅，超市也有卖Spiedie酱供居民购买自行料理。活动另一焦点即为热气球，每年约有35个由企业提供的热气球参与施放活动，除了传统的形状，通常每年还会有几个不同以往的特殊设计气球。

◆ Recipes

Ingredients

☐ 5 pounds chicken, cubed ☐ 2 cups olive oil
☐ 1 cup white vinegar ☐ 2 teaspoons salt
☐ 2 tablespoons lemon juice ☐ 5 cloves garlic, minced
☐ 2 teaspoons dried oregano

- ☐ 3 tablespoons crushed dried mint
- ☐ 1 teaspoon fresh-ground black pepper
- ☐ 2 tablespoons dried basil
- ☐ 12 wooden skewers, soaked in water for 30 minutes
- ☐ 1 tablespoon garlic salt

Directions

1. Place the cubed chicken into a large resealable plastic bag or container, add the olive oil, vinegar, lemon juice, salt, garlic, garlic salt, oregano, garlic salt, mint, basil, and black pepper. Seal the container and shake until combined. Refrigerate for 1 to 3 days, shaking the container to turn the meat every 6 to 8 hours.

2. Preheat an outdoor grill for medium-high heat and lightly oil grate. When you are ready to cook, remove meat from the marinade and place on skewers.

3. Place the skewers on the preheated grill and cook, turning every three minutes until cooked through and the internal temperature of the meat reaches 170 degrees F (75 degrees C). Be careful not to overcook or the meat will be very dry. Serve the grilled meat on Italian bread or hot dog rolls.

8 牛油蛋糕 *Butter cake*
——不自觉流口水的美食

达人了解英美

◇ **History**

The invention of baking powder and other chemical leavening agents during the 19th century substantially increased the flexibility of this traditional pound cake by introducing the possibility of creating lighter, **fluffier**（毛绒绒的）cakes using these traditional combinations of ingredients, and it is this transformation that brought about the modern butter cake.

> **阅读辅助**
>
> 起源是英国的磅蛋糕，这种扁平、密实的奶油蛋糕最早起源于20世纪30年代，是非常常见的蛋糕，由于发酵粉的发现让这种蛋糕非常普及。

◇ **Craftsmanship**

Butter cakes are traditionally made using a creaming method, in which the butter and sugar are first beaten until fluffy to **incorporate**（合并）air into the butter. Eggs are then added gradually, creating an **emulsion**（乳剂），followed by alternating portions of wet and dry ingredients. Butter cakes are often considered to be unsurpassed in their richness and moistness when stored at room temperature, but they tend to stiffen, dry out, and lose flavor when refrigerated, making them unsuitable for filling or frosting in advance with ingredients that must be **refrigerated**（冷却的）, such as cream cheese frosting and pastry cream.

> 阅读辅助
>
> 　　这种蛋糕通常将蛋黄与蛋白分开，将蛋黄加入已打好的牛油中，用打蛋器打至奶油状。蛋白另外打至发泡，在加面粉之后轻轻拌入打匀了的蛋黄，再倒入模子中。焗三十分钟即成。

◆ Recipes

Ingredients

- 1 1/2 cups all-purpose flour
- 2 teaspoons baking powder
- 1 cup white sugar
- 1 teaspoon vanilla extract
- 1/2 teaspoon salt
- 1/2 cup butter, room temperature
- 2 eggs, room temperature
- 3/4 cup milk, room temperature

Directions

1. Preheat oven to 350 degrees F (175 degrees C). Lightly grease an 8-inch square baking pan. Line bottom with **parchment**（羊皮纸）or wax paper, or dust lightly with flour.

2. Sift together the flour, salt, and baking powder.

3. Beat butter and white sugar until fluffy and light in color. Gradually add eggs, beating well after each addition; stir in vanilla. Add the sifted dry ingredients to the creamed mixture alternately with the milk. Stir until just blended (see Cook's Note for Blueberry Cake variation). Pour batter into prepared pan.

4. Bake at 350 degrees F (175 degrees C) for until cake springs back when lightly touched, about 30 minutes. Let cool in pan for 10 minutes before inverting onto wire rack to cool completely.

9 新泽西猪肉卷 *Pork roll*
——特色的新泽西早餐

达人了解英美

◇ Origin

It was developed in 1856 by John Taylor of Trenton, New Jersey, and sold as "Taylor Ham". While a similar item, packed minced ham, may have been produced at the time of the Battle of Trenton, John Taylor is credited with creating his secret recipe for the product in 1856. George Washington Case, a farmer and butcher from nearby Belle Mead, New Jersey, created his own recipe for pork roll in 1870. Case's was reportedly packaged in corn **husks**（外皮）. Taylor originally called his product "Taylor's Prepared Ham", but was forced to change the name after it failed to meet the new legal definition of "ham" established by the Pure Food and Drug Act of 1906. Marketed as both "Taylor's Pork Roll" and "Trenton Pork Roll", it saw competition from products with similar names like "Rolled Pork" and "Trenton style Pork Roll". When their makers were **sued**（请求）by Taylor a 1910 legal case ruled that the words "Pork Roll" could not be trademarked. In North Jersey, residents continue to use the term Taylor Ham.

阅读辅助

新泽西猪肉卷是你在新泽西最容易吃到的美食之一，其实也就是我们经常看到的泰勒火腿，这道美食是1856年由新泽西泰勒开发，泰勒自创秘方产出了有特色的火腿，之后自成品牌而风行于世。

✧ Preparation

In this suit it was described as "a food article made of pork, packed in a cylindrical cotton sack or bag in such form that it could be quickly prepared for cooking by slicing without removal from the bag." Some people compare the modern article's taste and/or texture to Treet, bologna, mild salami, or US-style Canadian bacon. Pork roll is generally sliced and pan-fried or grilled, but can also be microwaved. It is commonly given one to four cuts along its outer edge to prevent the slices from curling in the middle and cooking unevenly. It is typically eaten as part of a sandwich, with popular **condiments**（香料）including salt, pepper, ketchup, mustard, hot sauce, lettuce, and tomato. It is also incorporated in many other recipes, notably a popular breakfast sandwich known in the region as a "Jersey Breakfast", "Taylor Ham, Egg, and Cheese", or "Pork Roll, Egg, and Cheese". In these fried pork roll is joined with a fried egg and American cheese and served on a hard roll or bagel. When a slice or two is put on top of a grilled hamburger it is referred to as a "Trenton Burger."

阅读辅助

这是一种略带烟熏口味的早餐肉，新泽西人非常喜欢将它切片后，搭配煎鸡蛋或者奶酪卷，制成特色的新泽西早餐三明治。

10 巧克力豆曲奇 Chocolate Chip Cookie
——龙卷风般的味觉感受

达人了解英美

◆ **History**

The chocolate chip cookie was invented by Ruth Graves Wakefield. She owned the Toll House Inn, in Whitman, Massachusetts, a very popular restaurant that featured home cooking in the 1930s. Her cookbook, Toll House Tried and True Recipes, was first published in 1936 by M. Barrows & Company, New York. The 1938 edition of the cookbook was the first to include the recipe "Toll House Chocolate Crunch Cookie" which rapidly became a favorite cookie in American homes. Ruth Wakefield stated that she **deliberately**（谨慎地）invented the cookie. She said, "We had been serving a thin butterscotch nut cookie with ice cream. Everybody seemed to love it, but I was trying to give them something different. So I came up with Toll House cookie." A different version of events says that Wakefield is said to have been making chocolate cookies and on running out of regular baker's chocolate, substituted broken pieces of semi-sweet chocolate from Nestlé thinking that they would melt and mix into the batter. They did not and the chocolate chip cookie was born.

A still different history of the cookie derives from George Boucher, who was at one time head chef at the Toll House Inn, and his daughter, Carol Cavanagh, who also worked there. Contradicting Nestlé's claim that Wakefield put chunks of chocolate into cookie dough hoping they would melt, the daughter stated that the owner, already an accomplished chef and author of a cookbook, knew enough about the **properties**（性能）of chocolate to realize it would not melt and mix into the batter while baking.

> **阅读辅助**
>
> 巧克力片饼干是由露丝·格雷夫斯·韦克菲尔德所发明。露丝·韦克菲尔德说巧克力片饼干是她的发明。她说:"我们一直提供有冰淇淋的坚果饼干,大家都很喜欢,不过我想提供一些不一样的东西,所以就发明了巧克力片饼干。"

◆ Composition

Chocolate chip cookies are commonly made with white sugar; brown sugar; flour; a small portion of salt; eggs; a leavening agent such as baking powder; a fat, typically butter or shortening; vanilla extract; and semi-sweet chocolate pieces. Some recipes also include milk or nuts in the dough. Depending on the ratio of ingredients and mixing and cooking times, some recipes are **optimized**(最佳化的)to produce a softer, chewy style cookie while others will produce a crunchy/crispy style. Regardless of ingredients, the procedure for making the cookie is fairly consistent in all recipes: First, the sugars and fat are creamed, usually with a wooden spoon or electric mixer. Next, the eggs and vanilla extract are added followed by the flour and leavening agent. Depending on the additional flavoring, its addition to the mix will be determined by the type used: peanut butter will be added with the wet ingredients while cocoa powder would be added with the dry ingredients. The titular ingredient, chocolate chips, as well as nuts are typically mixed in towards the end of the process to **minimize**(最小化)breakage, just before the cookies are scooped and positioned on a cookie sheet. Most cookie dough is baked, although some eat the dough as is, or use it as an addition to vanilla ice cream to make chocolate chip cookie dough ice cream.

(美）垂涎欲滴的特色美食 **Section 4-2**

> **阅读辅助**
>
> 　　这款曲奇没有那么甜，没有那么软，但是香味不减，巧克力豆的配搭，更加丰富了它的味道。巧克力片饼干的材料包括白糖、砂糖、面粉、少量的盐、鸡蛋、膨松剂（例如泡打粉）、脂肪（通常是黄油）、香草精及和半甜巧克力片。一些食谱会在面团中加入牛奶或坚果（如切碎的核桃）。

235

读书笔记

Section 5-1　（英）受人追捧的知名品牌

漫步在英国的城市街道到处都是有历史的品牌，只要现在还存在的英国品牌，那都是著名品牌。从日用品，饮料汽车、服饰、体育用品，英国的品牌都是那么严谨，一丝不苟。还有就是英国这个金字招牌了，英国这个弥足珍贵的历史品牌，让英国的东西凡是有大英二字的就是品牌了，所以只要英国现在还在的老品牌那都是著名品牌。

1 皇家壳牌石油 *Royal Dutch Shell*
——油气行业领导者

达人了解英美

◇ **History**

The Royal Dutch Shell Group was created in February 1907 through the **amalgamation**（混合）of two rival companies: Royal Dutch Petroleum Company and the "Shell" Transport and Trading Company Ltd of the United Kingdom. It was a move largely driven by the need to compete globally with Standard Oil. Royal Dutch Petroleum Company was a Dutch company founded in 1890 to develop an oilfield in Sumatra. For various reasons, the new firm operated as a dual-listed company, whereby the merging companies maintained their legal existence, but operated as a single-unit partnership for business purposes. The terms of the merger gave 60 percent ownership of the new group to the Dutch arm and 40 percent to the British.

The "Shell" Transport and Trading Company was a British company, founded in 1897. The founder had owned an **antique**（古董）company in Houndsditch, London, which expanded in 1833 to import and sell sea-shells, after which the company "Shell" took its name.

阅读辅助

荷兰皇家壳牌集团是目前世界第一大石油公司，始创于1907年，是由荷兰皇家石油与英国的壳牌两家公司合并组成。它是国际上主要的石油、天然气和石油化工产品的生产商。荷兰皇家石油于1890年创立，并获得荷兰女王特别授权，因此被命名为荷兰皇家石油公司。为了与当时最大的石油公司美国的标准石油竞争，1907年荷兰皇家石油公司与英国壳牌运输和贸易公司合并成立荷兰皇家壳牌集团。公司实行两总部控股制，其中荷兰资本占60%，英国占40%。

◆ Company

Shell is also one of the world's most valuable companies. As of January 2013 the largest **shareholder**（股东）is Capital Research Global Investors ahead of BlackRock in second. Shell topped the 2013 Fortune Global 500 list of the world's largest companies. Royal Dutch Shell revenue was equal to 84% of the Netherlands' GDP at the time.

Shell is vertically integrated and is active in every area of the oil and gas industry, including exploration and production, **refining**（精炼）, distribution and marketing, petrochemicals, power generation and trading. It has minor **renewable**（可再生的）activities in the form of biofuelsand wind.It has operations in over 90 countries, produces around 3.1 million barrels of oil equivalent per day and has 44,000 service stations worldwide. Shell Oil Company, its **subsidiary**（子公司）in the United States, is one of its largest businesses.

> **阅读辅助**
>
> 壳牌也是世界上最具价值的公司之一。是世界500强公司中最大的一家公司。也为荷兰的GDP做出了巨大的贡献。壳牌是石油、能源、化工和太阳能领域的重要竞争者。壳牌拥有五大核心业务，包括勘探和生产、天然气及电力、煤气化、化工和可再生能源。壳牌在全球140多个国家和地区拥有分公司或有业务往来。

◆ Affair

In the 1990s, protesters criticized the company's environmental record, particularly the possible pollution caused by the proposed disposal of the Brent Spar platform into the North Sea. Despite support from the UK government, Shell reversed the decision under public **pressure**（压力）but maintained that sinking the platform would have been environmentally better. Shell subsequently published an **unequivocal**（明确的）commitment to sustainable development, supported by executive speeches reinforcing this commitment.

In 2004 Shell overstated its oil reserves, resulting in loss of confidence in the group, a £17 million fine by the Financial Services Authority and the departure of the chairman Philip Watts. A lawsuit resulted in the payment of $450 million to non-American shareholders in 2007.

> **阅读辅助**
>
> 1990年,环保人士对公司Brent Spar平台可能造成的污染提出抗议,壳牌首先阐明平台的安全性,并出具相关数据承诺一定保证做到。后来在2004年由于壳牌夸大其储量,而让公众对其丧失信心,英国当局对其开出了1700万英镑的高额罚单。

2 阿斯顿马丁 *Aston Martin*
——英国豪华跑车制造商

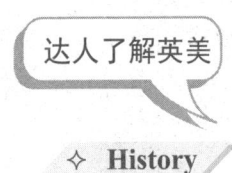

达人了解英美

◆ **History**

Aston Martin was founded in 1913 by Lionel Martin and Robert Bamford. The two had joined forces as Bamford & Martin the **previous**（以前的）year to sell cars made by Singer from premises in Callow Street, London where they also serviced GWK and Calthorpe vehicles. Martin raced specials at Aston Hill near Aston Clinton, and the pair decided to make their own vehicles. The first car to be named Aston Martin was created by Martin by fitting a four-cylinder Coventry-Simplex engine to the chassis of a 1908 Isotta-Fraschini.

They acquired premises at Henniker Mews in Kensington and produced their first car in March 1915. Production could not start because of the outbreak of World War I, and Martin joined the Admiralty and Bamford the Royal Army Service Corps. All machinery was sold to the Sopwith Aviation Company. After the war, the company was refunded at Abingdon Road, Kensington and a new car designed to carry the Aston-Martin name. Bamford left in 1920 and the company was **revitalized**（恢复）with funding from Count Louis Zborowski. In 1922, Bamford & Martin produced cars to compete in the French Grand Prix, which went on to set world speed and endurance records at Brooklands.

> **阅读辅助**
>
> 阿斯顿·马丁公司由莱昂内尔·马丁和罗伯特·班姆福德创建于1913年，起先的品牌叫做"班姆福德和马丁"，开始时两人只是为GWK和Calthorpe汽车提供服务。之后两人决定自己生产自己的汽车，第一辆"阿斯顿·马丁"品牌的汽车诞生于1915年，但是由于一战的爆发，马丁不得不进入英国海军服役，而班姆福德则进入英国皇家陆军服役，公司就此停产。一战后，公司重组并重新使用"阿斯顿·马丁"的品牌设计了一款新车。1920年，班姆福德离开公司。1922年开始生产跑车，并创造了多项速度纪录。

✧ Nowadays

The firm became associated with luxury grand touring cars in the 1950s and 1960s, and with the fictional character James Bond following his use of a DB5 model in the 1964 film Goldfinger. The company has had a **chequered**（多变的）financial history, including bankruptcy in the 1970s, but has also enjoyed long periods of success and stability, including under the ownership of David Brown, from 1947 to 1972 and of the Ford Motor Company from 1994 to 2007.

In March 2007, a **consortium**（财团）of investors, led by David Richards, purchased 92% of Aston Martin, with Ford retaining a £40 million stake. David Richards became chairman of Aston Martin. In December 2012, the Italian private equity fund Invest industrial signed a deal to buy 37.5% of Aston Martin.

> **阅读辅助**
>
> 该公司的跑车开始为人们熟知是在五六十年代，起源于一部电影《金手指》里的男主角邦德驾驶的跑车。该公司随后也经历多次破产，1947年，大卫·布朗公司收购了阿斯顿·马丁公司，阿斯顿·马丁开始生产其里程碑式的经典车型。1987年，福特汽车购得阿斯

顿·马丁75%的股份,并逐渐掌控了该公司。福特一直控股阿斯顿·马丁直到2007年,Prodrive的老板大卫·理查兹以9.25亿美元的价格从福特手中购得阿斯顿·马丁。

3 宾利 *Bentley*
——熠熠生辉顶级英国豪华汽车

达人了解英美

✧ History

Bentley Motors Limited was founded by W. O. Bentley on 18 January 1919 in Cricklewood near London and was acquired by Rolls-Royce in 1931. Before World War I in Cricklewood near London, Walter Owen Bentley had been in partnership with his brother Horace Millner Bentley selling French DFP cars, but he had always wanted to design and build his own range of cars bearing his name. It was on a visit to the DFP factory in 1913 that W.O. noticed an aluminium **paperweight**（镇纸）, and had the inspired idea of using the lightweight metal instead of cast iron to make engine pistons. The first Bentley aluminium pistons went into service in aero engines for the Sopwith Camel during World War I. In August 1919, Bentley Motors Ltd. was **registered**（注册的）, and a chassis with dummy engine was exhibited at the London Motor Show in October of that year.

Bentley Motors Limited is the direct successor of Rolls-Royce Motors, which Volkswagen AG purchased in 1998. The purchase included the vehicle designs, model **nameplates**（铭牌）, production and administrative facilities, the Spirit of Ecstasy and Rolls-Royce grille shape trademarks, but not the rights to the use of the Rolls-Royce name or logo, which are owned by Rolls-Royce Holdings plc and were later licensed to BMW AG.

(英) 受人追捧的知名品牌　Section 5-1

> **阅读辅助**
>
> 宾利汽车是由沃尔特·欧文·宾利在1919年于英格兰创立的。宾利的创办人早年是以在一战中制造供应皇家空军飞机引擎而闻名。宾利先生在1925正式成为公司的主席，可是好景不常，在1931年只得将车厂卖给劳斯莱斯。在1998年劳斯莱斯以及宾利都被大众买下，自20世纪90年代末BMW就一直为宾利提供引擎所以交易后制造分配并不单纯，而且大众并没有劳斯莱斯品牌使用权，因为它仅将品牌使用权卖给了BMW。

◇ Bentley Boys

A group of wealthy British motorists known as the "Bentley Boys" kept the marque's reputation for high performance alive. Bentley, located at Cricklewood, north London, was noted for its four **consecutive**（连贯的）victories at the 24 Hours of Le Mans from 1927 to 1930.

In 1929, Birkin had developed the lightweight Blower Bentley, including five racing specials that started with the Brooklands racing designed Bentley Blower No.1. In March 1930, Woolf Barnato drove against the train from Cannes to Calais, then by ferry to Dover, and finally London, travelling on public highways, and won. Barnato drove his H.J. Mulliner–bodied formal saloon in the race against the Blue Train. Both cars became known as the "Blue Train Bentleys"; the latter is regularly mistaken for, or **erroneously**（错误地）referred to as being, the car that raced the Blue Train, while in fact Barnato named it in memory of his race.

> **阅读辅助**
>
> 当时在英国有一群富裕的汽车爱好者，他们有个别名叫做"宾利男孩"，就是因为他们对宾利的热衷和狂热，塑造宾利高速与高贵的品牌形象。当时Barnato驾驶着宾利6.5 L和Le Train Bleu火车比赛看谁先由戛纳到伦敦，结果他获胜了。此后宾利6.5 L又被称Blue Train Bentley。

4 巴宝莉 *Burberry*
——极具英国传统风格的奢侈品牌

达人了解英美

◇ History

Burberry was founded in 1856 when 21-year-old Thomas Burberry, a former draper's apprentice, opened his own store in Basingstoke, Hampshire, England. By 1870, the business had established itself by focusing on the development of outdoors attire. In 1880, Burberry introduced in his brand the gabardine, a hardwearing, water-resistant yet breathable fabric, in which the yarn is **waterproofed**（防水的）before weaving. "Burberry" was the original name, but then the company soon switched to using the name "Burberrys", after many customers from around the world began calling it "Burberrys of London". This name is still visible on many older Burberry products. In 1891 Burberry opened a shop in the Haymarket, London.

In 1901, the Burberry Equestrian Knight Logo was developed containing the Latin word "Prorsum", meaning forwards, and registered as a trademark. In 1914, Burberry was **commissioned**（委任）by the War Office to adapt its officer's coat to suit the conditions of contemporary warfare, resulting in the "trench coat". After the war, the trench coat became popular with civilians. The iconic Burberry check was created in the 1920s and used as a lining in its **trench**（战壕）coats.

阅读辅助

Burberry 品牌创建于1856年，由当时只有21岁的在布衣店做学徒的托马斯·勃贝雷创立，他在英国英格兰汉普郡东北部的小镇开了自己的店铺。到1870年的时候，依靠注重开发户外服饰，勃贝雷的生意成为知名店铺。在1880年，勃贝雷开始以"Burberry"品牌推出华达呢，华达呢的出现受到欢迎，并在1888年获得专利。"Burberry"是公司原来的名字，但很快因为来自世界各地的顾客开始称它为"伦敦勃贝雷记"，后来公司就改用"Burberrys"至今在很多较老的勃贝雷产品上依然能够看到这个名字。

◇ **Brands**

Burberry Group plc is a British luxury fashion house, distributing outerwear, fashion accessories, fragrances, sunglasses, and cosmetics. Its distinctive tartan pattern has become one of its most widely copied trademarks. Burberry is most famous for its trench coat, which was designed by founder Thomas Burberry. The company has branded stores and **franchises**（特许权）around the world and also sells through **concessions**（让步）in third-party stores. Queen Elizabeth II and the Prince of Wales have granted the company Royal Warrants, which have been maintained despite Burberry's closure of its factory in Wales. Christopher Bailey has been the CEO and Chief Creative Officer since 2014. The company is listed on the London Stock Exchange and is a constituent of the FTSE 100 Index. In 2014, Burberry ranked 73rd in Interbrand's 'Best Global Brands' report, listing the world's most valuable brands.

阅读辅助

巴宝莉是英国奢侈时尚用品公司，销售服装和配饰，并拥有冠名香水。它独具特色的花呢格纹图案是其最受仿冒所累的商标之一。Burberry 以其风衣而著称，最早由创始人 Thomas Burberry 为军方设计的款式。Burberry 公司在世界各地经营自身品牌门店、授权特许经营商店，并在第三方店铺里通过特许专柜形式销售。Burberry 获得英国女王伊丽莎白二世与威尔士亲王查尔斯王子颁授的皇家御用徽章。

5 特易购 *Tesco*
——英国最大的零售公司

达人了解英美

◇ **History**

Jack Cohen, the son of Jewish migrants from Poland, founded Tesco in 1919 when he began to sell war-surplus groceries from a stall at Well Street Market, Hackney, in the East End of London. The Tesco brand first appeared in 1924. The name came about after Jack Cohen bought a **shipment**(装货) of tea fromThomas Edward Stockwell. He made new labels using the first three letters of the supplier's name (TES), and the first two letters of his surname (CO), forming the word TESCO. The first Tesco store was opened in 1929 in Burnt Oak, Edgware, Middlesex. His business expanded rapidly, and by 1939 he had over 100 Tesco stores across the country. Tesco were **floated**(漂浮) on the London Stock Exchange in 1947 as Tesco Stores Limited. The first self-service store opened in St Albans in 1956, and the first supermarket in Maldon in 1956. In 1961 Tesco Leicester made an appearance in the Guinness Book of Records as the largest store in Europe.

阅读辅助

　　1919年杰克·科恩，一个波兰移民的儿子，他将战后物资摆摊到街上进行销售。1924年，他引进了他的第一个自有品牌产品——特易购茶，而特易购的名字则来自于他的原料供应商T.E.Stockwell和他的名字Cohen的前两个字母。1929年第一家特易购店在伦敦开业，到20世纪30年代末已经拥有超过100家店铺，但都主要位于伦敦。而在20世纪30年代中期他却对美国的自助超市模式产生了兴趣，就决定采用相同的模式。

◆ Nowadays

Originally a UK-focused grocery retailer, since the early 1990s Tesco has increasingly **diversified**（多样化的）geographically and into areas such as the retailing of books, clothing, electronics, furniture, toys, petrol and software; financial services; telecoms and internet services. The 1990s saw Tesco reposition itself, from its perception as a down-market "pile 'em high, sell 'em cheap" retailer, to one which appeals across a wide social group, from its Tesco Value to its Tesco Finest ranges. This was successful, and saw the chain grow from 500 stores in the mid-1990s to 2,500 stores fifteen years later.

> **阅读辅助**
>
> 特易购最早以销售食品起家，逐渐延伸至服装、电器、客户财经服务、互联网服务、汽车保险及电信业务。之后他对美国的自助超市模式产生了兴趣，决定采用"堆得高卖得便宜"原则开始特易购的美国之旅。1947年第一家美国风格的特易购开业，这一繁荣的财富链以此模式迅速扩张。

◆ Advertising

Tesco have used many television adverts over the years. In July 2007 a DVD containing adverts from 1977–2007 was given to all members of staff. Early advertising stressed cheap prices and how to keep "The cost of living in check." Tesco's main advertising slogan is "Every little helps". Its advertisements in print and on television mainly consist of product shots against a white background, with a price or appropriate text **superimposed**（重迭的）on a red circle. On television, voiceovers are provided by recognizable actors and presenters. Tesco's in-store magazine is one of the largest-circulation magazines in the United Kingdom, with a circulation of 1.9 million as of 2013.

阅读辅助

　　特易购经常在电视上播放广告，而其早期的广告主要强调如何降低生活成本。之后特易购的主要广告口号就是"每一个小帮助"。其具有特色的印刷广告让人记忆犹新，另外在电视的画外音也通常由知名的演员和主持人配音，此外还在发行量很高的杂志上做广告。

6 吉百利 *Cadbury*
——老牌糖果制造商

达人了解英美

◆ History

In 1824, John Cadbury began selling tea, coffee, and drinking chocolate in Bull Street in Birmingham, England. From 1831 he moved into the production of a variety of cocoa and drinking chocolates, made in a factory in Bridge Street and sold mainly to the wealthy because of the high cost of production. In 1847 John Cadbury became a partner with his brother Benjamin and the company became known as "Cadbury Brothers". The brothers opened an office in London, and in 1854 they received the Royal Warrant as manufacturers of chocolate and cocoa to Queen Victoria. The company went into decline in the late 1850s.

John Cadbury's sons Richard and George took over the business in 1861. At the time of the **takeover**（接管）, the business was in rapid decline. By 1864 Cadbury was profitable again. The firm's first major **breakthrough**（突破性进展）occurred in 1866 when Richard and George introduced an improved cocoa into Britain. In the 1880s the firm began to produce chocolate **confectioneries**（蜜饯）. In 1878 the brothers decided to build new premises in countryside four miles from Birmingham. In 1897, following the lead of Swiss companies, Cadbury introduced its own line of milk chocolate bars. In 1899 Cadbury became a private limited company.

> **阅读辅助**
>
> 吉百利创立于1824年，是英国伯明翰老牌糖果制造商，是英国历史最悠久的巧克力品牌之一。吉百利开始时以卖茶、咖啡、巧克力饮品为主业，之后在1831年，开始生产各种各样的巧克力产品，因为这种食品生产成本高，所以主要购买人主要是富人。在1847年，约翰·吉百利和他的兄弟开始合伙创办吉百利兄弟公司，并在伦敦开设了办公室。在1854年收到皇家授权后为维多利亚女王生产巧克力。但是该公司却在1850年进入衰退期，之后随着他的儿子接管公司，公司虽然还在盈利但是还是挡不住衰退。在1866年一个重大的突破彻底改变了现状，一种改良过的可可进入了英国，随后公司在伯明翰的农村设厂批量生产自己的牛奶巧克力。

◇ Nowadays

Cadbury merged with drinks company Schweppes to form Cadbury Schweppes in 1969. The benefits of the merger were to prove **elusive**（易忘的）. The merger put an end to Cadbury's close links to its Quaker founding family and its perceived social ethos by instilling a capitalist venturer philosophy in management. In 1978 the company acquired Peter Paul, the third largest chocolate manufacturer in the United States for $58 million, which gave it a 10 percent share of the world's largest **confectionery**（糖果店）market.

In 1986, Cadbury Schweppes sold its Beverages and Foods division to a management known as Premier Brands. This saw the company divest itself of such brands as Typhoo Tea, Kenco, Smash and Hartley Chivers jam. Meanwhile, Schweppes switched its **alliance**（联盟）in the UK from Pepsi to Coca-Cola, taking a 51 percent stake in the joint venture Coca-Cola Schweppes. As a result of these **acquisitions**（兼并）, Cadbury Schweppes became the third largest soft drinks manufacturer in the world.

(英）受人追捧的知名品牌 Section 5-1

阅读辅助

1969年，吉百利和史威士合并成为一家国际性公司，之后又在1978年收购了美国第三大巧克力制造商，这让它在糖果市场的份额占到了10%。随后在1986年公司又进军饮料市场收购了Premier Brands，并占有百事可乐和可口可乐51%的股份，这些收购让吉百利史威士成为世界第三大饮料制造商。

7 联合利华 *Unilever*
——为世人带来美好生活

达人了解英美

✧ History

Unilever was formed in September 1929 by a merger of the operations of British soapmaker Lever Brothers and Dutch margarine producer Margarine Unie. The merger made sound commercial sense, aspalm oil was a major raw material for both **margarines**（人造奶油）and soaps, and could be imported more efficiently in larger quantities. In the 1930s business grew and new ventures were launched in Africa and Latin America. The Nazi occupation of Europe during the Second World War meant that Unilever was unable to **reinvest**（再投资于）its capital into Europe, so it instead acquired new businesses in the UK and the US. In 1943 it acquired T. J. Lipton, a majority stake in Frosted Foods and Batchelors Peas, one of the largest vegetables canners in the UK.

During the second half of the 20th century the company increasingly diversified from being a maker of products made of oils and fats, and expanded its operations worldwide. It has made numerous corporate **acquisitions**（并购）. Unilever divested its specialty chemicals businesses to ICI in 1997. In the 2010s, under leadership of Paul Polman, the company gradually shifted its focus toward health and beauty brands and away from food brands showing slow growth.

(英) 受人追捧的知名品牌　**Section 5-1**

> **阅读辅助**
>
> 　　1929年英国Lever肥皂制造商与荷兰Margarine Unie人造黄油生产商签订协议，组建Unilever公司。由于棕榈油是肥皂和人造黄油的主要原料，所以需要大量的进口。于是公司在1930进军非洲和拉美。随着纳粹在二战期间对欧洲的蹂躏，造成了联合利华在欧洲销售不理想，因而转战到英国和美国。随后在1943年收购英国一家最大的蔬菜罐头公司，此后一直到20世纪的下半叶公司的产品日益多样化，并将其业务扩展到全球，而且并购了多家企业。随着公司在1997年放弃化学成分的日用品配方之后，公司逐渐转向了健康食品和美容用品。

✧ Unilever

　　Unilever is a British–Dutch multinational consumer goods company, Its products include food, beverages, cleaning agents and personal care products. It is the world's third-largest consumer goods company measured by 2012 revenue, after Procter & Gambleand Nestlé. Unilever is the world's largest producer of food spreads, such as margarine. One of the oldest **multinational**（跨国公司）companies, its products are available in around 190 countries.

　　Unilever owns over 400 brands, but focuses on 14 brands with sales of over 1 billion euros. It is a dual-listed company consisting of Unilever N.V., based in Rotterdam, and Unilever plc, based in London. The two companies operate as a single business, with a common board of directors. Unilever is organized into four main divisions - Foods, Refreshment, Home Care, and Personal Care. It has research and development **facilities**（设施）in the United Kingdom, the Netherlands, China, India and the United States.

> **阅读辅助**
>
> 联合利华这家拥有多个世界知名食品、饮料、清洁剂和个人护理产品的品牌的上市公司，是世界上第三大消费品公司，还是最大粮食生产公司，还是最古老的合资公司之一，其产品在世界上190多个国家销售。联合利华拥有超过400个品牌，其中有14个品牌有着黄金般的销售业绩。联合利华被分成四个主要部门，食品、点心、家庭护理、个人护理。它的研发基地在英国、荷兰、中国、印度和美国都有。

◆ Logo

The current Unilever corporate logo was introduced in 2004 and was designed by the brand consultancy Wolff Olins. It is composed of 25 icons woven together to create a U shape, with each icon representing one of the company's sub-brands or its corporate values. The brand identity was developed around the idea of "adding vitality to life."

> **阅读辅助**
>
> 当前的商标是在2004年开始使用的，该Logo是由Wolff Olins设计，它是由25个图标编制在一起写成一个字母U，里面的每一个图标都是公司旗下的一个品牌，这体现了公司的价值观"增加生活的活力"。

8 君皇仕 Gieves & Hawkes
——为欧洲的贵族量身打造

达人了解英美

◆ **History**

Gieves & Hawkes' business was originally based on catering for the needs of the British Army and the Royal Navy, and hence by association theBritish Royal family. After coming to London in 1760, Thomas Hawkes set up his first shop in 1771 in Brewer Street. Catering for gentlemen, his main clients were **commanders**（指挥官）of the British Army, through which King George III became a customer. Having expanded his retail operation by moving to No.17 Piccadilly in 1793, Hawkes gained the first of many Royal Warrants in 1809.

In 1835, James Watson Gieve was employed by 'Old Mel' Meredith, a Portsmouth-based tailor by appointment to the Royal Navy. In 1852, Gieve partnered with Joseph Galt, and in 1887, Gieve purchased the remaining shares to form Gieves & Co. He died in 1888. In 1912, Hawkes & Co. bought No. 1 Savile Row from the Royal Geographical Society ,in part because the firm had dressed so many explorers. In 1974, Gieves Ltd acquired Hawkes & Co., and the **freehold**（不动产所有权）of 1 Savile Row. The company was renamed Gieves & Hawkes. In 2009, Kathryn Sargent of Gieves and Hawkes became the first female head **cutter**（刀具）in Savile Row.

> **阅读辅助**
>
> 　　君皇仕最开始的业务是为英国陆军和皇家海军服务，Hawkes 成立于1771年，并在 Brewer Street 开设第一家店，专制军帽。而他的主要客户都是英国军队的指挥官，通过他们的介绍 Hawkes 有幸让国王乔治三世成为他的客户。之后他的西服深得英国皇室推崇，更被授予皇室勋章。Gieve 则是在1835年受雇于 'Old Mel' Meredith，给皇家海军制作军服。随后在1852年 Gieve 购买了 Gieves & Co. 部分股份。随后 Gieves 和 Hawkes 在1974年正式合并，成为唯一与皇家关系密切的服饰品牌。

✧ Royal Warrants

　　Gieves & Hawkes have a strong history of both service to the military, and hence to the British Royalty. Hawkes & Co. were granted their first Royal Warrant in 1809, during the reign of King George III. Gieves & Hawkes presently have all three main Royal Warrants, appointed to HM The Queen, HRH The Duke of Edinburgh and HRH The Prince of Wales.

　　Customers past and present include: Winston Churchill, Admiral Lord Nelson, The Duke of Wellington, Charlie Chaplin, Michael Jackson, David Beckham, Mikhail Gorbachev, Bill Clinton, George W. Bush and Diana, Princess of Wales.

> **阅读辅助**
>
> 　　Gieves 成立于1785年，以裁制军装闻名；Hawkes 成立于1771年，专制军帽。合并后的 G & H 在二百多年来，深得英国皇室推崇，更被授予皇室勋章。在 Gieves & Hawkes 的专卖店里，必定会看到三个大大的徽章，分别是由英国英国女皇伊利沙白二世、其夫婿爱丁堡公爵以及威尔斯亲王授予的皇家徽章，代表着 G & H 作为这三者御用服装供应商的地位。

9 芝华士 Chivas Regal
——威士忌三重调和的创造者

达人了解英美

◆ **History**

    Chivas Brothers traces its roots to the opening of a grocery store at 13 King St, Aberdeen in 1801. The store sold luxury foodstuffs such as coffee, exotic spices, French brandies, and Caribbean rums to a wealthy **clientele**（客户）. In 1842, Chivas Brothers was retained to supply provisions to the royal family at Balmoral Castle upon Queen Victoria's first visit to Scotland. In 1843, Chivas Brothers was granted a Royal Warrant to supply goods to Queen Victoria. The May 8, 1890 edition of Scotland Magazine described Chivas Brothers as "undoubtedly the finest purveying business in the north of Scotland".

    During the 1850s, James Chivas decided to respond to his **affluent**（富裕的）customers' demands for a smoother whisky, by beginning to blend whiskies to create a blend proprietary to Chivas Brothers. The firm's first blended Scotch whisky, Royal Glen Dee, was launched, followed in the 1860s by a second proprietary blended Scotch whisky, Royal Strathy than. In the early 1900s, Chivas Brothers decided to create its most aged blended Scotch whisky to export to the U.S, where the booming economy after the turn of the century was **fueling**（加燃料）demand for luxury goods. The whisky was named Chivas Regal.

> **阅读辅助**
>
> 芝华士兄弟公司的历史可追溯至1801年位于苏格兰的一家杂货店。这家商店出售奢侈食品,如咖啡,充满异国情调的香料,法国白兰地酒,和加勒比朗姆酒。1842年,当维多利亚女王首次访问苏格兰的巴尔莫勒尔城堡时,芝华士兄弟被要求给王室供应商品。1843年,芝华士兄弟便收到了为维多利亚女王提供货物的皇家御用保证。在19世纪50年代,芝华士决定满足那些富裕客户们的要求,通过调和几种最好的陈年威士忌,制造出了一种口感爽滑、味道浓醇的酒。他们第一个混合苏格兰威士忌名为"皇家格伦 Dee"随后在19世纪60年代的第二个混合苏格兰威士忌——皇家 Strathythan。直到20世纪初,芝华士兄弟决定创建自己的混合型苏格兰威士忌并出口到美国,随后被命名为芝华士威士忌。

◆ **Strathisla distillery**

The home of Chivas Regal and location of its visitor centre is located at the Strathisla distillery. The distillery was founded in 1786, and is the oldest working distillery in the Highlands of Scotland - Strathisla Distillery, located in Speyside. The Strathisla **distillery**(酿酒厂)is owned by Chivas Brothers, and Strathisla Single Malt is one of the malt whiskies used within the Chivas Regal blend. Strathisla Single Malts have a natural sweetness and help to define the taste of Chivas Regal.

> **阅读辅助**
>
> 芝华士的酿酒基地是在 Strathisla 酒厂,酒厂成立于1786年,是最古老的在苏格兰高地酒厂,酒厂位于 Speyside,该酒厂属于芝华士兄弟,这里的酒大多是由麦芽制成的麦芽威士忌,这是用来酿芝华士的原料。这里的麦芽威士忌有种天然的甜味,对芝华士的味道起到了关键的作用。

家用电脑操作系统市场上获取长足进步,后来出现的Windows使得微软逐渐统治了家用桌面电脑操作系统市场。同时微软也开始扩张业务,进军其他行业和市场。

◆ Culture

Technical reference for developers and articles for various Microsoft magazines such as Microsoft Systems Journalare available through the Microsoft Developer Network. Helpful people can be elected by peers or Microsoft employees for Microsoft Most Valuable Professional (MVP) status, which entitles them to a sort of special social status and possibilities for awards and other benefits. Noted for its internal **lexicon**(词典), the expression "eating our own dog food" is used to describe the policy of using pre-release and beta versions of products inside Microsoft in an effort to test them in "real-world" situations. Another bit of jargon, FYIFV or FYIV, is used by an employee to indicate they are financially independent and can avoid work anytime they wish. The company is also known for its hiring process, **mimicked**(模仿)in other organizations and dubbed the "Microsoft interview", which is **notorious**(臭名昭著的)for off-the-wall questions such as "Why is a **manhole**(人孔)cover round?" Microsoft is an outspoken **opponent**(对手)of the cap on H1B visas, which allow companies in the U.S. to employ certain foreign workers.

阅读辅助

微软创立了多所培训中心,旨在训练出精通各样微软及配合公司环境的专家。MVP(Most Valued Professional)是微软为在电脑社区中有杰出成就人士而设之奖励,为微软有关产品提出建议。公司有很多特殊的文化被世人谈论,如招聘问的奇怪问题,和内部测试的过程,还有常用语等等。

◆ **Logo**

Microsoft adopted the so-called "Pac-Man Logo", designed by Scott Baker, in 1987. Baker stated "The new logo, in Helvetica italic typeface, has a **slash**（削减）between the o and s to emphasize the "soft" part of the name and convey motion and speed." Microsoft's logo with the "Your potential. Our passion." tagline below the main corporate name, is based on a slogan Microsoft used in 2008. In 2002, the company started using the logo in the United States and eventually started a TV campaign with the slogan, changed from the previous **tagline**（标语）of "Where do you want to go today?" During the private MGX conference in 2010, Microsoft unveiled the company's next tagline, "Be What's Next." 2012, Microsoft **unveiled**（原形毕露）a new corporate logo, the new logo also includes four squares with the colors of the then-current Windows logo which have been used to represent Microsoft's four major products.

> **阅读辅助**
>
> 微软自从1987年以来重新设计的第一个标识中应用了较少的颜色，在简单的微软名字旁边使用一个新的多颜色的方块，取代了陈旧的斜体字风格的标识。之后几十年，微软更换了多个不同的公司标识，最近微软又推出了新的公司标识。微软在新 Logo 中首次加入了符号标志：即四个小方块，分别采用蓝色、橙色、绿色和黄色设计，这四种颜色同时也代表着微软的产品和服务群体的多样性。

2 可口可乐 The Coca-Cola Company
——让碳酸饮料深入人心

达人了解英美

◇ **History**

The Coca-Cola Company is best known for its flagship product Coca-Cola, invented in 1886 by pharmacist John Stith Pemberton in Columbus, Georgia. The Coca-Cola formula and brand was bought in 1889 by Asa Griggs Candler, who incorporated The Coca-Cola Company in 1892. The company operates a **franchised**（授权）distribution system dating from 1889 where The Coca-Cola Company only produces syrup concentrate which is then sold to various bottlers throughout the world who hold an exclusive territory. The Coca-Cola Company owns its anchor bottlerin North America, Coca-Cola Refreshments.

The company has a long history of acquisitions. Coca-Cola acquired Minute Maid in 1960, the Indian cola brand Thums Up in 1993 and Barq's in 1995. In 2001, it acquired the Odwalla brand of fruit juices, smoothies and bars for $181 million. In 2001, it acquired the Odwalla brand of fruit juices, smoothies and bars for $181 million. The company's 2009 bid to buy a Chinese juice maker ended when China rejected its $2.4 billion bid for the Huiyuan Juice Group on the grounds that it would be a virtual **monopoly**（垄断）.

阅读辅助

可口可乐公司是一家跨国无酒精饮料生产，销售商，也是世界第一个可乐品牌，其最出名的产品：Coca-Cola 的配方和名字由合伙人与 Asa Candler 1892年发明。但当初命名时是直接将该饮料称为"Coca-Cola",日后也就直接成为该公司品牌名称。之后公司就开始了收购兼并世界上不同类型的饮料企业。

◆ Products

The Coca-Cola Company offers more than 500 brands in over 200 countries, aside from its namesake Coca-Cola beverage. Tab was Coca-Cola's first attempt to develop a diet soft drink, using saccharin as a sugar substitute. Introduced in 1963, the product is still sold today, although its sales have dwindled since the introduction of Diet Coke. The Tab soft drink is difficult to locate in recent times, due to its de **facto**(事实上的)replacement by Diet Coke. The Coca-Cola Company also produces a number of other soft drinks including Fanta and Sprite.

Fanta's origins date back to World War II during a trade embargo against Germany on cola **syrup**(糖浆), making it impossible to sell Coca-Cola in Germany. Max Keith, the head of Coca-Cola's German office during the war, decided to create a new product for the German market, made from products only available in Germany at the time, which they named Fanta. The drink proved to be a hit, and when Coke took over again after the war, it adopted the Fanta brand as well. In 1961 Coca-Cola introduced Sprite, another of the company's bestsellers and its response to 7 Up.

阅读辅助

可口可乐公司在超过200个国家销售其500中品牌的饮料产品,有可口可乐、雪碧、芬达、醒目、爽健美茶等等。

3 迪斯尼 The Walt Disney Company
——因一只老鼠而成为传奇

达人了解英美

◆ History

Disney was founded on October 16, 1923, by Walt Disney and Roy O. Disney as the Disney Brothers Cartoon Studio, and established itself as a leader in the American **animation**（活泼）industry before diversifying into live-action film production, television, and theme parks. The company also operated under the names The Walt Disney Studio, then Walt Disney Productions. Taking on its current name in 1986, it expanded its existing operations and also started divisions focused upon theater, radio, music, publishing, and online media. In addition, Disney has since created corporate divisions in order to market more **mature**（成熟的）content than is typically associated with its flagship family-oriented brands. The company is best known for the products of its film studio, the Walt Disney Studios, which is today one of the largest and best-known studios in American cinema. Disney also owns and operates the ABC broadcast television network; cable television networks such as Disney Channel, ESPN, A+E Networks, and ABC Family; publishing, **merchandising**（销售规划）, music, and theatre divisions; and owns and licenses 14 theme parks around the world. The company has been a component of the Dow Jones Industrial Average since May 6, 1991. An early and well-known cartoon creation of the company, Mickey Mouse, is a primary symbol of The Walt Disney Company.

> **阅读辅助**
>
> 迪士尼公司成立于1923年10月16日，由华特·迪士尼和洛伊·迪士尼所建立。公司最初名为"迪士尼兄弟动画工作室"，在进行真人电影、主题公园及广播电视等多元化发展之前，便已经确立了其在美国动画电影行业里的领导者地位。此外，迪士尼公司创建了新的品牌来面对那些成熟的盈利市场，而其旗舰品牌则依旧着力于家庭消费者。

✧ Parks and Resort

When Walt Disney opened Disneyland on July 17, 1955, he created a unique **destination**（目的地）built around storytelling and immersive experiences, **ushering**（传达）in a new era of family entertainment. More than 55 years later, Walt Disney Parks and Resorts (WDP&R) has grown into one of the world's leading providers of family travel and leisure experiences, providing millions of guests each year with the chance to spend time with their families and friends making memories that will last forever.

At the heart of WDP&R are five world-class vacation destinations with 11 theme parks and 44 resorts in North America, Europe and Asia, with a sixth destination currently under construction in Shanghai. WDP&R also includes the Disney Cruise Line with its four ships - the Disney Magic, Disney Wonder, Disney Dream and Disney Fantasy; Disney Vacation Club, with 12 properties and approaching a total of 200,000 member families; and Adventures by Disney, which provides guided family vacation experiences to destinations around the globe.

> **阅读辅助**
> 迪士尼乐园是由华特迪士尼公司所创立与营运的一系列主题乐园与度假区，内有许多迪士尼人物，如米奇老鼠，及迪士尼电影场景。此后，在美国和海外又陆续开了5家，分布在4个国家和地区的迪士尼主题公园。

◆ The Walt Disney Studios

For over 90 years, The Walt Disney Studios has been the foundation on which The Walt Disney Company was built. Today, the Studio brings quality movies, music and stage plays to consumers throughout the world. Feature films are released under the following banners: Disney, including Walt Disney Animation Studios and Pixar Animation Studios; Disneynature; Marvel Studios; Lucasfilm; and Touchstone Pictures, the banner under which live-action films from DreamWorks Studios are distributed. The Disney Music Group **encompasses**（包含）the Walt Disney Records and Hollywood Records labels, as well as Disney Music Publishing. The Disney Theatrical Group produces and licenses live events, including Disney on Broadway, Disney On Ice and Disney Live!

> **阅读辅助**
> 华特迪士尼工作室电影部门负责发行、行销和宣传华特迪士尼影业集团旗下各公司制作的电影。在此品牌下，迪士尼发行了许多优秀的动画片与真人片。动画片当中，截至目前，由迪士尼动画片场制作了53部经典动画长片。

◆ Disney Consumer Products

Disney Consumer Products (DCP) is the business **segment**（分割）of The Walt Disney Company (NYSE:DIS) and its **affiliates**（联播电台）

that delivers innovative and engaging product experiences across thousands of categories from toys and apparel to books and fine art. As the world's largest licensor, DCP inspires the imaginations of people around the world by bringing the magic of Disney into consumers' homes with products they can enjoy year-round. DCP is comprised of three business units: Licensing, Publishing and Disney Store. The Licensing business is aligned around five strategic brand priorities: Disney Media, Classics & Entertainment, Disney & Pixar Animation Studios, Disney Princess & Disney Fairies, Lucasfilm and Marvel. Disney Publishing Worldwide (DPW) is the world's largest publisher of children's books, magazines, and digital products and also includes an English language learning business, consisting of over 40 Disney English learning centers across China and a **supplemental**（补充的）learning book program. DPW's growing library of digital products includes best-selling eBook titles and original apps that leverage Disney content in innovative ways. The Disney Store retail chain operates across North America, Europe and Japan with more than 350 stores worldwide and is known for providing consumers with high-quality, unique products.

阅读辅助

迪士尼消费品生产部门，包含利用公司品牌及版权人物进行开发生产的玩具、服饰及其他产品；给世界的孩子们带去了童话般的快乐。

4 耐克 *Nike Inc.*
——给体育界带来了一场革命

达人了解英美

◆ **History**

The company was founded on January 25, 1964, as Blue Ribbon Sports, by Bill Bowerman and Phil Knight, and officially became Nike, Inc. on May 30, 1971. The company takes its name from Nike, the Greek goddess of victory. Nike markets its products under its own brand. In 1964, in its first year in business, BRS sold 1,300 pairs of Japanese running shoes grossing $8,000. By 1965 the **fledgling**（初出茅庐）company had acquired a full-time employee, and sales had reached $20,000. In 1966, BRS opened its first retail store, in 1967, due to rapidly increasing sales, BRS expanded retail and **distribution**（分配）operations on the East Coast, in Wellesley, Massachusetts.

By 1971, the relationship between BRS and Onitsuka Tiger was nearing an end. BRS prepared to launch its own line of footwear, which would bear the Swoosh newly designed by Carolyn Davidson. The Swoosh was first used by Nike on June 18, 1971, and was registered with the U.S. Patent and Trademark Office on January 22, 1974. Nike has acquired several apparel and **footwear**（鞋类）companies over the course of its history, some of which have since been sold.

> **阅读辅助**
>
> 1962年，Phil Knight 在取得 MBA 学位后，前往日本，与生产商 Onitsuka Tiger 的管理人员会面，试图说服他们让 Knight 拥有的蓝带体育公司成为 Tiger 在美国西岸的代理商。1964年，Knight 把 Tiger 鞋子的样板送到一位田径教练那里，之后这位教练成为了日后的合伙人。两人握手并各出资500美元开设新公司。耐克的名称源自希腊神话中的胜利女神尼刻。

✧ Products

Nike produces a wide range of sports equipment. Their first products were track running shoes. They currently also make shoes, jerseys, shorts, cleats, baselayers, etc. for a wide range of sports, including track and field, baseball, ice hockey, tennis, association football (soccer), **lacrosse**（曲棍球）, basketball, and cricket.

Nike sells an assortment of products, including shoes and apparel for sports activities like association football, basketball, running, combat sports, tennis, American football, athletics, golf, and cross training for men, women, and children. Nike also sells shoes for outdoor activities such as tennis, golf, skateboarding, association football, baseball, American football, cycling, volleyball, wrestling, cheerleading, aquatic activities, auto racing, and other **athletic**（运动的）and recreational uses.

Nike is well known and popular in youth culture, chav culture and hip hop culture for their supplying of urban fashion clothing. Nike recently teamed up with Apple Inc. to produce the Nike+ product that monitors a runner's performance via a radio device in the shoe that links to the iPod nano.

> **阅读辅助**
>
> 耐克以自己的品牌销售,包括耐克、Air Jordan、耐克Golf、Team Starter等,亦包括属下全资拥有的品牌匡威等。耐克一贯的目标都是根据运动员的实际需求而推出更能提升运动表现的产品,让运动员得以最大限度地发挥自己的独特技能。

◆ Marketing Strategy

Advertising: In 1982, Nike aired its first national television ads, created by newly formed ad agency Wieden+Kennedy, during the broadcast of the New York Marathon. Nike also has earned the Emmy Award for best commercial twice since the award was first created in the 1990s. The first was for "The Morning After," a **satirical**(讽刺性的)look at what a runner might face on the morning of January 1, 2000 if every dire prediction about the Y2K problem came to fruition. The second was for a 2002 spot called "Move," which featured a series of famous and everyday athletes in a variety of athletic pursuits. Beatles song: Nike was criticized for its use of the Beatles song "Revolution" in a 1987 commercial against the wishes of Apple Records, the Beatles' recording company.

> **阅读辅助**
>
> 耐克的市场销售战略独具特色,它是最有特色的广告推广之一,另外还用具有争议的披头士音乐作为主题音乐等等。

5 星巴克 *Starbucks*
——将丑小鸭变成白天鹅的奇迹

达人了解英美

◆ **History**

From Starbucks' founding in 1971 as a Seattle [coffee bean] roaster and **retailer**（零售商）, the company has expanded rapidly. Between 1987 and 2007, Starbucks opened on average two new stores every day. Starbucks had been profitable as a local company in Seattle in the early 1980s but lost money on its late 1980s expansion into the Midwest and British Columbia. Its fortunes did not reverse until the fiscal year of 1989-1990, when it registered a small profit of $812,000. By the time it expanded into California in 1991 it had become trendy. The first store outside the United States or Canada opened in Tokyo in 1996, and overseas stores now constitute almost one third of Starbucks' stores. The company planned to open a net of 900 new stores outside of the United States in 2009, but has announced 300 store **closures**（停业）in the United States since 2008.

> 阅读辅助
>
> 　　星巴克其成立于1971年，最初仅专卖咖啡豆，在转型为现行的经营型态后开始快速展店，并成为美式生活的象征之一，部分店铺甚至与超级市场、书店等异业结盟，以复合式商店经营。星巴克目前在全球有约2万1千家分店，其中有1万2千家位于美国境内。

◆ **Products**

Starbucks locations serve hot and cold **beverages**（饮料）, whole-bean coffee, micro ground instant coffee, full-leaf teas, pastries, and snacks. Most stores also sell pre-packaged food items, hot and cold sandwiches, and items such as mugs and tumblers. Starbucks Evenings locations also offer a variety of beers, wines, and **appetizers**（开胃菜）after 4pm. Through the Starbucks Entertainment division and Hear Music brand, the company also markets books, music, and film. Many of the company's products are seasonal or specific to the locality of the store. Starbucks-brand ice cream and coffee are also offered at **grocery**（食品杂货店）stores.

阅读辅助

星巴克提供多样的咖啡种类，他们以一周为期，每周更换不同种类的咖啡豆，让消费者以简单的方式喝到不同种咖啡豆调和的咖啡。星巴克还有一系列的热饮；包含咖啡类和非咖啡类。除咖啡之外，亦有茶饮等饮料，以及三明治、糕点等点心类食品。

◆ **Logo**

The logo is an image of a "twin-tailed mermaid, or siren as she's known in Greek **mythology**（神话）". The logo has been significantly **streamlined**（使合理化）over the years. In the first version, In the first version, the Starbucks siren was topless and had a fully visible double fish tail. The image also had a rough visual texture and has been likened to a melusine. In the second version, which was used from 1987–92, her breasts were covered by her flowing hair, but her navel was still visible. The fish tail was cropped slightly, and the primary color was changed from brown to green, a nod to the Alma Mater of the three founders, the University of San Francisco. In the third version, used between 1992 and 2011, her navel and **breasts**（胸脯）are not visible at all, and only **vestiges**（痕迹）remain of the fish tails. The original "woodcut" logo has been moved to the Starbucks' Headquarters in Seattle.

> **阅读辅助**
>
> 　　星巴克的商标有2种版本，第一种版本的棕色的商标由来是一幅16世纪斯堪地那维亚的双尾美人鱼木雕图案，她有赤裸乳房和一条可清楚看见的双重鱼尾巴。第二版之商标，沿用了原本的美人鱼图案，但做了少许的修改，她没有赤裸乳房，并把商标颜色改成代表每日咖啡的绿色，就这样融合了原始星巴克与每日咖啡的特色的商标就诞生了。

6 雅诗兰黛 Estée Lauder Companies
——奉行为每个女性带来美丽的原则

达人了解英美

◆ History

The company began in 1946 when Estée Lauder and her husband Joseph Lauder began producing cosmetics in New York City. They first carried only four products: Super-Rich All Purpose Creme, Creme Pack, Cleansing Oil, and Skin Lotion. Two years later, they established their first department store account with Saks Fifth Avenue in New York. Over the next 15 years, they expanded the range and continued to sell their products in the United States. In 1960, the company started its first international account in the London department store Harrods. The following year it opened an office in Hong Kong.

In 1964, they started Aramis Inc., designed by Arame Yeranyan, with the **fragrance**(芬芳) named after Yeremes - a city inArmenia, producing fragrances and grooming products for men. In 1967, Estée Lauder herself was named one of ten Outstanding Women in Business in the United States by business and financial editors. in 1968, the company expanded again, opening Clinique Laboratories, Inc. Clinique was the first **dermatologist**(皮肤科医生) guided, the company expanded again, opening Clinique Laboratories, Inc. Clinique was the first dermatologist guided.

> **阅读辅助**
>
> 雅诗·兰黛主要出售四种护肤品。它就是由雅诗·兰黛和约瑟夫·兰黛建立的雅诗·兰黛公司的前身，现在已经发展成为全球最大的护肤、化妆品和香水公司，并且仍在不断拓展业务。1946年，雅诗兰黛夫人创立了雅诗兰黛，她以自己的名字命名公司。

◆ Brand

For over 60 years, the Estée Lauder Companies has built an unrivaled **portfolio**（文件夹）of brands. Its products are sold in more than 150 countries and range from entry-level prestige to ultra-premium **luxury**（奢侈品）.

Clinique: Clinique, founded in 1968, is the first dermatologist-created, prestige cosmetics brand. Its customized approach and **innovative**（创新的）products have made it one of the world's leading skin care authorities. Sold in 130 countries and territories, its mission is to provide the highest quality, most effective products to **enhance**（增加）every skin type and concern.

Aramis：Introduced in 1964, Aramis was the first prestige men's fragrance to be sold in department stores. Today, it remains successful through its strong brand identity and continues as a symbol of classic **masculinity**（阳刚之气）and **sophistication**（老练）. It is now sold in more than 130 countries and territories worldwide.

> **阅读辅助**
>
> Estée Lauder 雅诗兰黛创立于1946年。产品涵盖广泛的女士化妆、香水和护肤品以及男士香水和护肤品。雅诗兰黛品牌的产品享有技术先进、富有创新精神及品质卓著的声誉。

克莱斯勒 *Chrysler*
——汽车工业的领导性品牌

达人了解英美

◆ History

The Chrysler Corporation was founded by Walter Chrysler in 1925 out of what remained of the Maxwell Motor Company. Chrysler greatly expanded in 1928, when it **acquired**（后天习得的）the Fargo truck company and the Dodge Brothers Company and began selling vehicles under those brands; that same year it also established the Plymouth and DeSoto automobile brands.

In the 1960s the company expanded into Europe, creating the Chrysler Europe division, formed from the **acquisition**（获得）of French, British and Spanish companies. In the 1970s, a number of factors including the 1973 oil crisis impacted Chrysler's sales, and by the late 1970s, Chrysler was on the verge of **bankruptcy**（破产）, forcing its retreat from Europe in 1979. Lee Iacocca was brought in as CEO and is credited with returning the company to profitability in the 1980s. In 1987, Chrysler acquired American Motors Corporation (AMC), which brought the profitable Jeep brand under the Chrysler umbrella. In 1998, Chrysler merged with German automaker Daimler-Benz AG to form DaimlerChrysler; the merger proved **contentious**（有争议的）with investors and Chrysler was sold to Cerberus Capital Management and renamed Chrysler LLC in 2007. Like the other Big Three automobile manufacturers, Chrysler was hit hard by the automotive industry crisis of 2008–2010.

> **阅读辅助**
>
> 该公司为沃尔特·克莱斯勒于1925年6月6日利用马克斯韦尔汽车公司剩下的资产所创建的。1927年推出普利茅斯品牌并合并道奇兄弟汽车公司。1929年克莱斯勒成为全美前三大车厂。1998年，克莱斯勒与戴姆勒-奔驰合并为戴姆勒-克莱斯勒，2007年克莱斯勒集团的股份被出售，再度成为独立集团。2013年，意大利菲亚特入股投资。

◇ **Brand**

Chrysler is an American automobile manufacturer headquartered in Auburn Hills, Michigan and owned by Italian automaker Fiat. Chrysler is one of the "Big Three" American automobile manufacturers. It sells vehicles worldwide under its flagship Chrysler brand, as well as the Dodge, Jeep and Ram. Other major divisions include Mopar, its automotive parts and **accessories**（附件）division, and SRT, its performance automobile division. In 2014, FCA US LLC is the seventh biggest automaker in the world by production. Chrysler is the smallest of the "Big Three" U.S. automakers. In 2013 Chrysler sold9% up from 2012, and fourth largest in sales behind GM, Ford and Toyota. Chrysler is the world's 11th largest vehicle manufacturer as ranked by OICA in 2012.

> **阅读辅助**
>
> 克莱斯勒集团与福特汽车、通用汽车，合称美国汽车制造三大龙头。其旗下有多个汽车品牌，包括克莱斯勒（Chrysler）、道奇（Dodge）、吉普（Jeep）等。克莱斯勒旗下销售量最大的厂牌是道奇汽车，近年来则是Jeep销量最多，克莱斯勒本身厂牌则针对价位较高的市场与国际市场。普利茅斯与老鹰等品牌后来在产品整合中取消。

苹果 *Apple Inc.*
——砸醒世人的第三颗苹果

达人了解英美

◆ **History**

Apple was founded by Steve Jobs, Steve Wozniak, and Ronald Wayne on April 1, 1976, to develop and sellpersonal computers. It was incorporated（合并）as Apple Computer, Inc. on January 3, 1977, and was renamed as Apple Inc. on January 9, 2007, to reflect its shifted focus towards consumer electronics. Apple (NASDAQ:APPL) joined the Dow Jones Industrial Average on March 19, 2015.

Apple is the world's second-largest information technology company by revenue after Samsung Electronics, and the world's third-largest mobile phone maker. On November 25, 2014, in addition to being the largest publicly traded corporation in the world by market capitalization, Apple became the first U.S. company to be valued at over $700 billion. As of 2014, Apple employs 72,800 **permanent**（永恒的）full-time employees, maintains 437 retail stores in fifteen countries, and operates the online Apple Store and iTunes Store, the latter of which is the world's largest music retailer.

阅读辅助

苹果公司由史蒂夫·乔布斯、史蒂夫·沃兹尼克、罗纳德·韦恩创立于1976年4月1日，开发和销售个人计算机。该公司于1977年1月3日正式称为苹果电脑公司，并于2007年1月9日改名为苹果公司，以反应该公司将业务重点转向消费电子领域。

◆ **Logo**

According to Steve Jobs, the company's name was inspired by his visit to an apple farm while on a **fruitarian**（果食主义者）diet. Jobs thought the name "Apple" was "fun, spirited and not **intimidating**（吓人的）". Apple's first logo, designed by Ron Wayne, depicts Sir Isaac Newton sitting under an apple tree. It was almost immediately replaced by Rob Janoff's "rainbow Apple", the now-familiar rainbow-colored **silhouette**（剪影）of an apple with a bite taken out of it. However, Jobs insisted that the logo be colorized to humanize the company. The logo was designed with a bite so that it would not be confused with a cherry. In 1999, Apple officially dropped the rainbow scheme and began to use **monochromatic**（单色的）logos nearly identical in shape to the previous rainbow incarnation.

> **阅读辅助**
>
> 在史蒂夫·乔布斯决定成立公司时，他向沃兹建议把公司命名为"苹果电脑"。最初的标志在1976年由创始人三人之一韦恩设计，为牛顿坐在苹果树下看书的钢笔绘画。本次标志确定使用了彩虹色、具有一个缺口的苹果图像。这个标志一直使用至1998年，2007年再次变更为金属带有阴影的银灰色，使用至今。

◆ **Slogan**

Apple's first slogan, "Byte into an Apple", was coined in the late 1970s. From 1997 to 2002, the **slogan**（标语）"Think Different" was used in advertising campaigns, and is still closely associated with Apple. Apple also has slogans for specific product lines — for example, "iThink, therefore iMac" was used in 1998 to promote the iMac, and "Say hello to iPhone" has been used in iPhone advertisements. "Hello" was also used to introduce the original Macintosh, Newton, iMac ("hello (again)"), and iPod. From the introduction of the Macintosh in 1984 with the 1984 Super Bowl commercial to the more modern 'Get a Mac' adverts, Apple has been recognized in for its efforts towards effective advertising and marketing for its products.

> **阅读辅助**
>
> 苹果的每一次口号的发出，都意味苹果向前更进一步了。让人们更加了解苹果，让苹果更加走向世界。

肯德基 *KFC*
——一只鸡，改变了人们的饮食世界

达人了解英美

✧ History

KFC was founded by Harland Sanders, an entrepreneur who began selling fried chicken from his roadside restaurant in Corbin, Kentucky, during the Great Depression. Sanders identified the potential of the restaurant **franchising**（特许专营）concept, and the first "Kentucky Fried Chicken" franchise opened in Utah in 1952. KFC popularized chicken in the fast food industry, diversifying the market by challenging the established **dominance**（统治）of the hamburger. By branding himself as "Colonel Sanders," Harland became a prominent figure of American cultural history, and his image remains widely used in KFC advertising. However, the company's rapid expansion saw it **overwhelm**（压垮）the ageing Sanders, and in 1964 he sold the company to a group of investors led by John Y. Brown, Jr. and Jack C. Massey.

KFC was one of the first fast food chains to expand internationally, opening **outlets**（销售点）in Canada, the United Kingdom, Mexico, and Jamaica by the mid-1960s. Throughout the 1970s and 1980s, KFC experienced mixed **fortunes**（机遇）domestically, as it went through a series of changes in corporate ownership with little or no experience in the restaurant business. The chain continued to expand overseas however, and in 1987 KFC became the first Western restaurant chain to open in China.

Section 5-2

> 阅读辅助
>
> 肯德基是由哈兰德·桑德斯创办的,桑德斯在大萧条时期开始在位于肯塔基州科尔宾市的路边餐厅卖炸鸡。桑德斯认识到餐厅特许经营的概念的潜力,1952年,第一家"肯德基炸鸡"的特许经营餐厅在犹他州开门营业。桑德斯以"桑德斯上校"的名字闻名,成为美国文化历史的著名人物,肯德基广泛以桑德斯作为广告形象。

✧ **Specialists**

KFC's original product is pressure fried chicken pieces, seasoned with Sanders' recipe of 11 herbs and spices. The constituents of the recipe represent a notable trade secret. Larger portions of fried chicken are served in a cardboard "bucket," which has become a well known feature of the chain since it was first introduced by franchisee Pete Harman in 1957. Since the early 1990s, KFC has expanded its menu to offer other chicken products such as chicken fillet burgersand wraps, as well as salads and side dishes, such as French fries and coleslaw, desserts, and soft drinks, the latter often supplied by Pepsi Co. KFC is known for the slogan"finger lickin' good," which has since been replaced by "Nobody does chicken like KFC" and "So good."

> 阅读辅助
>
> 肯德基的原产是加压炸鸡块,以桑德斯的11种草药和香料的配方调味。配方的成分是著名的商业机密。自1990年代初以来,肯德基扩展了菜单,提供其他鸡肉产品如鸡柳包,还有沙拉和小菜。

✧ **Logo**

The first KFC logo was introduced in 1952 and featured a "Kentucky Fried Chicken" **typeface**(字型)and a logo of the Colonel. It was designed by the Lippincott & Margulies corporate identity agency. Lippincott & Margulies were hired to redesign it in 1978, and used a similar typeface and a slightly different Sanders logo. The "KFC" initialism logo was designed by Schechter & Luth of New York and was introduced in 1991, and the Colonel's face logo was switched from brown to blue ink. Landor redesigned the logo in 1997, with a new image of the Colonel. The new Colonel image was more thinly lined, less cartoonish and a more realistic **representation**（表现）of Sanders. In 2006, the Colonel logo was updated by Tesser of San Francisco, replacing his white suit with an apron, bolder colors and a better defined **visage**（面貌）.

> **阅读辅助**
>
> 　　肯德基广泛以桑德斯作为广告形象，白色西装，打着黑色蝴蝶结，一身南方绅士打扮的白发上校，他的打扮已经成为肯德基独一无二的注册商标。

10 沃尔玛 *Walmart*
——世界上最大的连锁零售企业

达人了解英美

✧ History

The company was founded by Sam Walton in 1962 and incorporated on October 31, 1969. It began trading stock as a publicly held company on October 1, 1970, and was soon listed on the New York Stock Exchange. In the 1980s, Walmart continued to grow rapidly, and by its 25th anniversary in 1987. By the mid-1990s, it was far and away the most powerful **retailer**（零售商）in the U.S. and expanded into Mexico in 1991 and Canada in 1994. It spread to New England, Maryland, Delaware, Hawaii, Alaska and the Pacific Northwest last, Vermont being the last state to get a store in 1995. It has over 11,000 stores in 27 countries, under a total 71 banners. The company operates under the Walmart name in the United States and Puerto Rico.

阅读辅助

1962年，山姆·沃尔顿于美国阿肯色州罗杰斯开设第一家商店至今，沃尔玛已发展成为全世界最大的零售业巨头。1972年在纽约证券交易所公开交易。

✧ Brand

Walmart is the world's largest company by revenue, according to the Fortune Global 500 list in 2014, as well as the biggest private employer in the world with 2.2 million employees. Walmart is a family-owned business, as the company is controlled by the Walton family, who own over 50 percent of Walmart through their holding company, Walton Enterprises. It is also one of the world's most valuable companies by market value, and is also the largestgrocery retailer in the U.S. In 2009, it **generated**（产生）51 percent of its US$258 billion (equivalent to $284 billion in 2015) sales in the U.S. from its grocery business.

Sam's Club is a chain of warehouse clubs that sell groceries and general merchandise, often in bulk. Sam's Club stores are "membership" stores and most customers buy annual memberships. There are three kinds of memberships of Sam's Club, Sam's Plus, Sam's Business and Sam's Savings. Each of those memberships provides customers various benefits and **convenience**（便利）.

> **阅读辅助**
>
> 沃尔玛公司有8500家门店，分布于全球15个国家。沃尔玛在美国50个州和波多黎各运营。沃尔玛主要有沃尔玛购物广场、山姆会员店、沃尔玛商店、沃尔玛社区店等四种营业方式。

◆ Charity

Founder Sam Walton held the belief that the company's contribution to society was the fact that it operated efficiently, thereby lowering the cost of living for customers, and therefore in that sense was a "powerful force for good", despite his **refusal**（驳回）to contribute cash to philanthropic causes. Since Sam Walton's death in 1992, however, Walmart and the Walmart Foundation dramatically increased charitable giving. For example, in 2005, Walmart donated $20 million in cash and **merchandise**（商品）for Hurricane Katrina relief. Today, Walmart's charitable donations approach $1 billion each year.

(美)受人追捧的知名品牌 **Section 5-2**

阅读辅助

2011年,沃尔玛公司和沃尔玛基金会慈善捐赠资金累计3.19亿美元、物资累计超过4.8亿美元。2014年,沃尔玛公司以4762.94亿美元的销售额力压众多石油公司而再次荣登《财富》世界500强榜首。

读书笔记

Section 6-1　（英）影响世界的励志名人

人生往往充满了矛盾和痛苦，而智者熠熠生辉的智慧可以帮助人们生活得更有意义，更加自然和谐，亦可以让世界更加美丽。都说一千个人眼中有一千个哈姆雷特，这对文学和影视来说又何尝不是呢？让我们打开眼前这扇窗，全方位多维度地看到这些在英国一展宏图的名人们，他们留下的是他们思想的种子，演绎的是多彩的人生，书写的是理想的国度。

1 查尔斯·狄更斯 Charles Dickens
——展现英国底层生活的文学巨匠

达人了解英美

✧ Early Life

Born in Portsmouth, When Charles was four, they relocated to Sheerness, and thence to Chatham, Kent, where he spent his **formative**（形成的）years until the age of 11. His early life seems to have been idyllic, Charles spent time outdoors but also read voraciously, including the **picaresque**（流浪汉）of Tobias Smollett and Henry Fielding, as well as Robinson Crusoe and Gil Blas. He retained **poignant**（辛酸的）memories of childhood, helped by an excellent memory of people and events, which he used in his writing. Dickens left school to work in a factory when his father was incarcerated in adebtors' prison. Despite his lack of formal education, he edited a weekly journal for 20 years, wrote 15 novels, five novellas, hundreds of short stories and non-fiction articles, lectured and performed extensively, was an **indefatigable**（不知疲倦的）letter writer, and **campaigned**（活动）vigorously for children's rights, education, and other social reforms.

阅读辅助

查尔斯·狄更斯1812年2月7日出生于朴次茅斯市郊。他很小的时候家境还比较富裕，但是9岁那年，他的家庭陷入债务危机，从此他便开始了艰辛的生活。这段生活经历在他的心里留下了无法磨灭的伤痕，15岁的时候他开始做法务助理，之后又担任采访记者。

◆ Career

Dickens' writing career started in the 1830s when she used the pen name Boz and his first publication was a short story collection named Sketches By Boz in 1836. However, it was The Pickwick Papers (1837) that gained him widely **popularity**（普及）.

Generally speaking, Dickens' writing career can be divided into three periods. All the work finished before 1841 were included into the first period including *The Pickwick Papers* (1837), *Oliver Twist* (1838), *The Old Curiosity Shop* (1839) and *Nicholas Nickleby* (1841). In this period, Dickens' works were featured by gentle social criticism and fantastic optimism The second period of Dickens' writing career was from 1842 to 1847 during which *American Notes* (1842), *A Christmas Carol* (1843) and *Martin Chuzzlewit* (1843) were published. In this period, there was a more fiercecriticism towards the society and the plots and structures of the novels were more unified and **sophisticated**（复杂的）. Dickens' writing career arrived at its prosperity at the time between 1850 and 1870. Most of Dickens' greatest works were created in this period such as *David Copperfield* (1852), *Bleak House* (1853), *Hard Times* (1854), *Little Dorrit* (1857), *A Tale of Two Cities*, *Great Expectations* (1861), and *Our Mutual Friend* (1865). In the late period, Dickens' criticism of the society was extremely poignant and his mastery of works also reached the highest level.

阅读辅助

19世纪30年代狄更斯用笔名鲍兹开始创作，这也是他写作生涯的开始。在1836年他发表了短篇小说集《鲍兹随笔》，同时这本小说集也是他的第一份出版物。通常来说，狄更斯的写作生涯可以划分为三个时期。

✧ Evaluation

He created some of the world's best-known fictional characters and is regarded as the greatest novelist of the Victorian era. His works enjoyed unprecedented popularity during his lifetime, and by the twentieth century critics and scholars had recognized him as a literary **genius**（天才）. His novels and short stories enjoy lasting popularity.

Charles Dickens was at his best in writing using critical realism and his protagonists were mostly from the lower class. It was his critically realistic **description**（描述）of the lower class people that made him one of the greatest writers in the British literary history.

> **阅读辅助**
>
> 狄更斯是杰出的批判现实主义小说家，他的作品的主人公绝大部分来自社会底层。也正是他对社会底层人民生活的采用批判现实主义手法的描述使得他成为英国历史上最杰出的一位作家。

2 简·奥斯汀 *Jane Austin*
——独立自主的"道德教育家"

达人了解英美

◆ Personal Life

Jane Austin was born on 16 December 1775 at the rectory in the village of Steventon in Hampshire. As the seventh child of a **clergyman**（教士）, Jane was educated at home because her father taught several live-in children. Spending most of her time with her brothers and sisters as well as her father's students, Jane had a very happy childhood. Jane loved reading very much and thanks to her father's library, she read **extensively**（广阔地）which provided materials for her own writing. Jane spent most of her life at home and her life was quiet and **uneventful**（平凡的）. She never married and died when she was only 41 years old.

阅读辅助

简·奥斯汀1775年12月16日生于罕布什尔乡村小镇斯蒂文顿的一个牧师家庭。她是七个孩子中最小的一个。她的父亲是当地的教区牧师，他与父亲的学生一起接受了家庭式教育。她与其他兄弟姐妹和父亲的学生一起度过了非常愉快的童年。简非常喜欢阅读，这得益于她父亲的大量藏书，从中她涉猎了大量书籍，这也为她日后自己的创作积累了大量素材。简的一生几乎是在家中度过的，而且生活一直都很平静，没有波澜壮阔的经历。直到41岁去世她一生都未婚。

✧ Career

Jane Austin started her writing career at the age of 14 and produced six well-received novels throughout her life: Sense and Sensibility, Pride and Prejudice, Northanger Abbey, Mansfield Park, Emma and Persuasion. All of Jane Austen's novels were published **anonymously** (不具名地). In her works, Jane drew many realistic and vivid pictures of everyday life of the ordinary people in the country society and her focus was on the relationship between family members and neighbors. Though Jane never married her life, her perception of marriage was widely accepted. For Jane, there were three kinds of marriage; marriage for money, marriage out of passion as well as marriage based on love with the consideration of economic and social status.

Jane Austin's novels have always been the favorites of the film makers. All of her six famous novels have been adapted in films before. In recent years, some of them were re-adapted into films, such as *Sense and Sensibility* (1995) starred by Emma Thompson and Kate Winslet and *Emma* (1996) with the leading actor of Gwyneth Paltrow as well as *Pride and Prejudice* (2005) starred by Keira Knightley. There were also films on the author Jane Austin, *The Jane Austen Book Club* (2007) co-stared acted by Emily Blunt and Hugh Dancy as well as *Becoming Jane* (2007) co-starred by Anne Hathaway and James Andrew McAvoy.

阅读辅助

简·奥斯汀14岁时开始了她的写作生涯，一生中创作了6部受到广泛认可和欢迎的作品：《理智和情感》《傲慢与偏见》《诺桑觉寺》《曼斯菲尔德花园》《爱玛》。简·奥斯汀的所有作品都是匿名发表的。在她的作品中，简刻画了很多真实的普通人日常生活的场景，她描绘的重点是亲人以及邻里直接的关系。尽管简自己一生未婚，但是她在作品中对婚姻的深刻认识却被大家广泛认同。简·奥斯汀的作品一直以来都是电影制作者的最爱。她的6部作品很早就已经全部被改编成电影。

3 威廉·莎士比亚 William Shakespeare
——被喻为"人类文学奥林匹斯山上的宙斯"

达人了解英美

✧ Personal Life

William Shakespeare was born on 23 April 1564 in Stratford-upon-Avon in a wealthy family. However, his family met with financial crisis when he was 13, so he went for London and did odd jobs to earn money, such as stable boy, servant at the theater, actor, and playwright and finally became **stockholder**（股东）of the theatre. However, all of these were inferred from the existed documents and without accurate evidence. The next sure thing was Shakespeare's marriage with Anne Hathaway in 1582 followed by the birth of his twin daughters three years later. From the year 1585 to 1592 was a period of "lost years" for Shakespeare because there's no sign of any kind as to where Shakespeare was and what did he do. Shakespeare reappeared in 1592 in a London theatre. Shakespeare's acting career was in the Lord Chamberlain's Company where he became a partner later. The theatre was quite popular at the time and renamed the King's Company in 1603 when James came to power. It was the original form of the renowned the Royal Shakespeare Theatre. According to various documents and records, Shakespeare gradually grew richer in London and bought a house in London's wealthiest parts as well as the biggest house in his hometown.

> **阅读辅助**
>
> 威廉·莎士比亚于1564年4月23日生于英国中部埃文河畔斯特拉特福的一位富裕的市民家庭。但是他13岁的时候家里遭受了经济危机,他曾做过马倌,在剧院做过服务生、演员和剧作家,最终成为了剧院的股东。但是这些都是从现有的资料推断出来的,并没有精确的证据证明这些。但是可以确定的是莎士比亚在1582年与安妮·海瑟薇结婚,他们的双胞胎女儿在1585年出生。据史料记载,莎士比亚在伦敦逐渐富裕起来,并在伦敦最繁华的地方买了房子。

◇ Works

His extant works, including some **collaborations**(协作), consist of about 38 plays,154 sonnets, two long **narrative**(叙事的)poems, and a few other verses, of which the authorship of some is uncertain. His plays have been translated into every major living language and are performed more often than those of any other playwright.

Shakespeare's writing career could be divided into three phases: the early phase was from 1590 to 1600 in which historical plays and comedies were produced, such as *Richard III*, *Henry III* and *A Midsummer Night's Dream*, *The Merchant of Venice* and *Twelve Night*. The famous tragedy *Romeo and Juliet* was also produced in this period; in the middle phase of 1601-1607, Shakespeare's works were mainly tragedies. Shakespeare's four tragedies *Hamlet*, *Othello*, *King Lear*, and *Macbeth* were all written in this period. Some of his comedies in this period were also showed flashes of tragedy like *All's Well that Ends Well* and *Measure for Measure*; the late phase lasted from 1608 to 1612 when **tragicomedies**(悲喜剧), also known as romances were created such as *Cymbeline*, *The Winter's Tale* and *The Tempest* and etc.

> **阅读辅助**
>
> 他流传下来的作品包括38部戏剧、155首十四行诗、两首长叙事诗和其他诗歌。他的戏剧有各种主要语言的译本，而且表演次数远远超过其他任何戏剧家的作品。莎士比亚的写作生涯可以分成三个阶段：早期——从1590到1600年，主要作品是历史剧和喜剧，中期——1601到1607年，他的作品主要是悲剧，末期——是从1608到1612年，在这期间他开始创作悲喜剧，又称为传奇剧，并与其他剧作家合作。

◆ Influence

Shakespeare's influence on the English-speaking world is reflected in the ready recognition afforded many **quotations**（语录）from Shakespearean plays, the titles of works based on Shakespearean phrases, and the frequent performance of his plays. Shakespeare's work has made a lasting impression on later theatre and literature. In particular, he expanded the dramatic potential of characterisation, plot, language, and genre. Until Romeo and Juliet, for example, romance had not been viewed as a worthy topic for tragedy. Soliloquies had been used mainly to convey information about characters or events; but Shakespeare used them to explore characters' minds. His work heavily influenced later poetry.

Scholars have identified 20,000 pieces of music linked to Shakespeare's works. Shakespeare has also **inspired**（激发）many painters, including the Romantics and the Pre-Raphaelites. In Shakespeare's day, English grammar, spelling and pronunciation were less standardized than they are now, and his use of language helped shape modern English.

阅读辅助

莎士比亚的著作对后来的戏剧和文学有着持久的影响。实际上，他对戏剧人物刻画、情节叙述、语言表达和文学体裁多个方面都有不同程度的扩展，直到《罗密欧与朱丽叶》。这部传奇剧并没有被视作悲剧。另外独白以前主要用于人物或场景切换信息，但是莎士比亚则用来探究人物的思想，他的作品对后来的诗歌影响重大。学者们鉴定出2万首音乐和莎士比亚的作品相关，莎士比亚对很多画家也有影响。在莎士比亚时期，英语语法和拼写没有标准化，所以他对语言的运用影响了现代英语。

4 J.K. 罗琳 J.K. Rowling
——挥动魔法棒的"灰姑娘"

达人了解英美

✧ **Name**

Although she writes under the pen name "J. K. Rowling", her name, before her remarriage, was simply "Joanne Rowling". Anticipating that the target audience of young boys might not want to read a book written by a woman, her publishers asked that she use two **initials**（缩写）, rather than her full name. As she had no middle name, she chose K (for "Kathleen") as the second initial of her pen name, from her paternal grandmother. She calls herself "Jo". Following her marriage, she has sometimes used the name Joanne Murray when conducting personal business. During the Leveson Inquiry she gave **evidence**（证据）under the name of Joanne Kathleen Rowlingand her entry in Who's Who (UK) lists her name as Joanne Kathleen Rowling.

阅读辅助

虽然罗琳大多数时候都用她的笔名"J.K. 罗琳",但实际上在《哈利·波特与魔法石》出版时却直接使用本名"乔安娜·罗琳"。而出版社考虑此书的目标读者群为小男孩,恐怕他们不会买女作家写的书,遂建议她改用两个字母缩写作为笔名;但罗琳没有中间名,于是选择奶奶凯瑟琳的"K"作为她笔名的第二个缩写字母。

◆ Personal Life

J.K. Rowling is a British novelist best known as the author of the Harry Potter fantasy series. The books have gained worldwide attention, won **multiple**（多样的）awards, and sold more than 400 million copies. They have become the best-selling book series in historyand been the basis for a series of films which became the highest-grossing film series in history. Rowling had overall approval on the scripts and **maintained**（保持）creative control by serving as a producer on the final instalment.

Born in Yate, Gloucestershire, Rowling was working as a researcher and bilingual secretary for Amnesty International when she conceived the idea for the Harry Potter series on a delayed train from Manchester to London in 1990. The seven-year period that followed saw the death of her mother, divorce from her first husband and relative poverty until Rowling finished the first novel in the series, Harry Potter and the Philosopher's Stone in 1997. There were six **sequels**（续篇）, the last, Harry Potter and the Deathly Hallows in 2007. Rowling has led a "rags to riches" life story, in which she progressed from living on state benefits to multi-millionaire status within five years. She is the United Kingdom's best-selling living author, with sales in excess of £238m. She has supported charities including Comic Relief, One Parent Families, Multiple Sclerosis Society of Great Britain and Lumos, and in politics supports the Labour Party and Better Together.

阅读辅助

J.K. 罗琳是一位英国知名奇幻小说家，代表作为《哈利·波特》系列作品。她的《哈利·波特》畅销全球，热卖超过4亿本，成为史上最畅销的书籍之一，其作品被改编为同名电影也成为电影史上票房收入最高的电影之一，该系列电影获得罗琳的完整授权。J.K. 罗琳生于英国格洛斯特郡叶特，她曾是国际特赦组织的研究员兼双语秘书。在撰写《哈利·波特与魔法石》期间，罗琳经历贫穷、母亲过世与首次离婚，终于在1997年出版第一本《哈利·波特》系列小说。其后续集逐年出版，直到最后一部《哈利·波特与死亡圣器》在2007年出版后宣告全书完结。J. K. 罗琳的人生宛如《灰姑娘》故事般，在短短5年内从接受政府济助的贫穷单亲妈妈成为富有的畅销作家。

5 查尔斯·卓别林 Charles Chaplin
——奠定了现代喜剧电影的基础

达人了解英美

✧ Personal Life

Chaplin's childhood in London was defined by poverty and **hardship** (苦难). As his father was absent and his mother struggled financially, he was sent to a workhouse twice before the age of nine. When he was 14, his mother was committed to a mental asylum. Chaplin began performing at an early age, touring music halls and later working as a stage actor and comedian. At 19 he was signed to the prestigious Fred Karno company, which took him to America. Chaplin was scouted for the film industry, and began appearing in 1914 for Keystone Studios. He soon developed the Tramp **persona**（人物角色）and formed a large fan base. Chaplin directed his films from an early stage, and continued to hone his craft as he moved to the Essanay, Mutual, and First National corporations. By 1918, he was one of the best known figures in the world.

阅读辅助

卓别林出生于英国伦敦，在他很小的时候父母就分居了，他的母亲因嗓子突然失声而失业，致使他的家境每况愈下，随后他被送入伦敦兰贝斯区的一个贫童习艺所。在卓别林14岁时，母亲被诊断出患有精神病，此后他就开始做不同的工作了。卓别林从小就喜欢表演，这让他最终成为了一名舞台演员，19岁的他与著名的Karno公司签约。而卓别林的电影事业真正的开始形成规模是在1914年，他建立了自己的电影公司。之后创造出了一个经典的流浪汉形象，从狄更斯式的伦敦童年一直达到了电影工业的世界顶端，卓别林已成为了一个文化偶像。

✦ Achievement

Chaplin was an English comic actor and filmmaker who rose to fame in the silent film era. Chaplin became a worldwide icon through his screen persona "the Tramp" and is considered one of the most important figures of the film industry.

Chaplin wrote, directed, produced, edited, starred in, and composed the music for most of his films. He was a **perfectionist**（完美主义者）, and his financial independence enabled him to spend years on the development and production of a picture. His films are characterized by slapstick combined with pathos, typified in the Tramp's struggles against adversity. Many contain social and political themes, as well as autobiographical elements. In 1972, as part of a renewed appreciation for his work, Chaplin received an Honorary Academy Award for "the **incalculable**（无数的）effect he has had in making motion pictures the art form of this century". He continues to be held in high regard, with *The Gold Rush*, *City Lights*, *Modern Times*, and *The Great Dictator* often ranked among industry lists of the greatest films of all time.

> **阅读辅助**
>
> 在无声电影时期，卓别林是最有才能和最具影响力的人物之一。而卓别林演得最好的角色是一个外貌为流浪汉，内心则一副绅士气度的形象。他自己编写、导演、表演和发行他自己的电影。从在英国的大剧院作为孩童演员登台演出，到他88岁高龄逝世为止，他的电影职业生涯超过70年。卓别林两次获得奥斯卡荣誉奖，在有声电影被发明后他还拍了两部最著名的无声电影《城市之光》和《摩登时代》，此后他开始转向有声电影。

✧ Influence

Chaplin believed his first influence to be his mother, who entertained him as a child by sitting at the window and **mimicking**(模仿)passers-by: "it was through watching her that I learned not only how to express emotions with my hands and face, but also how to observe and study people." Chaplin's early years in music hall allowed him to see stage comedians at work; he also attended the Christmas **pantomimes**(哑剧)at Drury Lane, where he studied the art of clowning through performers like Dan Leno. Chaplin's years with the Fred Karno Company had a formative effect on him as an actor and filmmaker. Simon Louvish writes that the company was his "training ground", and it was here that Chaplin learnt to vary the pace of his comedy. The concept of mixing pathos with **slapstick**(趣剧)was learnt from Karno, who also used elements of **absurdity**(荒谬)that became familiar in Chaplin's gags. From the film industry, Chaplin drew upon the work of the French **comedian**(喜剧演员)Max Linder, whose films he greatly admired. In developing the Tramp costume and persona, he was likely inspired by the American vaudeville scene, where tramp characters were common.

阅读辅助

卓别林个人认为能够成为演员是受到他母亲的影响，从小他就喜欢坐在窗户前去模仿路人，从母亲那里不仅学会了如何表达感情也学会了如何观察和学习别人。此外他早期在音乐厅的工作也让他有机会向别人学习，之后他还常参加了哑剧的聚会，从中学习如何表演。之后在Karno公司的发展，最终让他站上了成功的舞台。

6 费雯丽 Vivien Leigh
——妩媚动人的"好莱坞的珍珠"

达人了解英美

✧ Personal Life

Leigh was born Vivian Mary Hartley in British India on the campus of St. Paul's School. Her mother, a devout Roman Catholic, may have been of Irish and Parsi Indian ancestry. Her parents were married in 1912 in Kensington, London.

After her drama school education, Leigh appeared in small roles in four films in 1935 and progressed to the role of **heroine**（女主角）in Fire Over England. Lauded for her beauty, Leigh felt that it sometimes prevented her from being taken seriously as an actress. Despite her fame as a screen actress, Leigh was primarily a stage performer. During her 30-year stage career, she played roles ranging from the heroines of Noël Coward and George Bernard Shaw comedies to classic Shakespearean characters such as Ophelia, Cleopatra, Juliet and Lady Macbeth. Later in life, she played character roles in a few films.

To the public at the time, Leigh was strongly identified with her second husband Laurence Olivier, to whom she was married from 1940 to 1960. Leigh and Olivier starred together in many stage productions, with Olivier often directing, and in three films. She earned a reputation for being difficult to work with, as for much of her adult life, she suffered from **bipolar**（有两极的）disorder, as well as **recurrent**（周期性的）bouts of chronic tuberculosis, first diagnosed in the mid-1940s, which ultimately claimed her life at the age of 53.

> **阅读辅助**
>
> 她出生于英属印度西孟加拉邦大吉岭。1912年，她的父母在伦敦肯辛顿结婚。她在毕业之后就出演话剧《道德的面具》从而声名鹊起，之后费雯丽来到美国发展并获得很大的成功。晚年的费雯·丽身心上受肺结核和抑郁症困扰，在1967年7月8日病逝于英国家中，享年53岁。巨星殒落，让全世界喜爱她的影迷们不胜唏嘘。

◇ Awards

She won two Academy Awards for Best Actress for her performances as "Southern belle" Scarlett O'Hara in *Gone with the Wind* (1939) and Blanche DuBois in the film version of *A Streetcar Named Desire* (1951), a role she had also played on stage in London's West End in 1949. She also won a Tony Award for her work in the Broadway version of Tovarich. Although her career had periods of **inactivity**（静止）, in 1999, the American Film Institute ranked Leigh as the 16th greatest female movie star of all time.

> **阅读辅助**
>
> 费雯丽是两届的奥斯卡影后，分别是第12届的《乱世佳人》和第23届的《欲望街车》。1999年，费雯·丽被美国电影学会选为百年来最伟大的女演员之一。同时她也是奥斯卡史上第一位英国籍影后。

7 休·格兰特 *Hugh Grant*
——风度翩翩的英伦绅士

达人了解英美

✧ **Personal life**

Grant was born on 9 September, 1960, in Hammersmith, London. Young Grant was fond of literature and acting. He won a scholarship to Oxford, going up to New College in 1979 where he starred in his first film, Privileged, produced by the Oxford University Film Foundation in 1982. After Oxford, he turned down a scholarship to do postgraduate studies in Art History at the Courtauld **Institute**（协会）in London, and focused on his acting career. Grant's breakthrough came with the leading role in Richard Curtis's sleeper hit Four Weddings and a Funeral (1994), a role which won him a Golden Globe Award, as well as a BAFTA Film Award for Best Actor. During the 1990s Grant established himself as a very original and **resourceful**（资源丰富的）actor. He played a string of characters projecting a positive mindset, showing how to stay optimistic when you are actually worried about a **cascade**（小瀑布）of troubles.

Outside of his acting profession, Grant has been a good athlete, he played cricket and football in his younger years. He currently enjoys playing golf, frequently taking part in Pro-Am tournaments. He has been an avid art lover since his younger years, and has been collecting fine art, a passion he inherited from his father.

阅读辅助

格兰特于1960年9月9日出生于伦敦的哈默史密斯市。年轻的时候，格兰特喜欢文学与演戏。他曾获得了牛津大学的奖学金，并于1979年开始就读于牛津大学新学院。他在牛津大学出演了自己的第一部电影——是由牛津大学电影基金会于1982年制作的《牛津之爱》。格兰格的演艺突破来自于理查德·科蒂斯的一部票房黑马电影《四个婚礼一个葬礼》，他凭借在该片中的表演获得了金球奖以及英国电影学院奖最佳男主角。在演艺事业之外，格兰特还是一个不错的运动员，他在年轻的时候曾玩过板球和足球。

◇ Achievement

Hugh Grant has received a Golden Globe Award, a BAFTA, and an Honorary César. His movies have earned more than $2.4 billion from 25 theatrical releases worldwide. He is best known for his roles in *Notting Hill* (1999), opposite Julia Roberts, and in *Music and Lyrics* (2007), opposite Drew Barrymore, among his other works.

In 1995, Grant played a leading role as Emma Thompson's suitor in Ang Lee's Academy Award-winning **adaptation**（适应）of Jane Austen's *Sense and Sensibility*. In 1999, he paired with Julia Roberts in *Notting Hill*, which was a commercial as well as relative critical success. Indeed, the romantic comedy seemed to be simply the most natural fit for the actor, and he found more success in new millennium with returns to this genre in *Bridget Jone's Diary* (2001), *Two Weeks Notice* (2002), *About a boy* (2002), *Love Actually* (2003), *Bridget Jones: The Edge of Reason* (2004) and *Music and Lyrics* (2007).

阅读辅助

休·格兰特到目前为止获得一次金球奖，一次英国电影学院奖，一次凯撒荣誉奖。而他共有25部在世界各地的影院上映，共获得24亿美元的票房收入。他最著名的电影有《诺丁山》与《K歌情人》等等。事实上，浪漫爱情喜剧似乎是最适合休·格兰特的电影类型。

8 温斯顿·丘吉尔 Winston Churchill
——大英帝国的"帝国之心"

达人了解英美

◇ Evaluation

Churchill was a British politician who was the Prime Minister of the United Kingdom from 1940 to 1945 and again from 1951 to 1955. Widely regarded as one of the greatest wartime leaders of the 20th century, Churchill was also an officer in the British Army, a historian, a, and an artist. He won the Nobel Prize in Literature, and was the first person to be made **an honorary**(荣誉的)citizen of the United States. He is generally regarded as greatest British leader of the 20th century and one of the greatest politicians in the world history because he led Britain through one of the darkest times in the British history, the World War II. Besides, he is also a good writer and a painter as well as an excellent orator.

阅读辅助

丘吉尔是英国政治家、演说家、军事家和作家,曾两次出任英国首相。丘吉尔被认为是20世纪最重要的政治领袖之一,对英国乃至于世界均影响深远。此外,他在文学上也有很高的成就,曾于1953年获诺贝尔文学奖。他带领着英国人走过了英国历史上最黑暗的二战时期。

✧ Personal Life

Churchill was born into the **aristocratic**（贵族的）family of the Dukes of Marlborough, a branch of the Spencer family. His father, Lord Randolph Churchill, was a charismatic politician who served as Chancellor of the Exchequer, one of the greatest British military commanders of the 17th century; his mother, Jennie Jerome, was an American socialite.

As a young army officer, he saw action in British India, the Sudan, and the Second Boer War. He gained fame as a war correspondent and wrote books about his campaigns. Churchill entered Royal Military College at Sandhurst at the age of 18 and was appointed a second **lieutenant**（副官）in a proud cavalry **regiment**（大量）. From 1896, Churchill travelled to many countries as a journalist and wrote books and reports, such as Cuba, India, and Sudan. During the Boer War, Churchill was hired by a newspaper to report the war but was captured. He escaped from prison and walked 480 kilometers of enemy territory before reached safe place. He became famous for this experience. After the Boer War, Churchill entered politics. His early political career was full of ups and downs. Before the World War II began, Churchill was appointed first lord of the **admiralty**（海军部）. In the following year, Chamberlain was forced to resign; Churchill took his place as the prime minister of the Great Britain at the age of 66. Churchill made many wise critical decisions in the WWII to resist Hitler's invasion, which enabled Britain to become the last fort to defend Germany. Churchill made many **stirring**（激起）war speech that inspired the British people greatly. Everywhere he went; he held up two fingers and made the victory gesture which became the symbol for final victory for British people as well as people of the Allied nations.

阅读辅助

温斯顿·丘吉尔是17世纪英国伟大军事领袖约翰·丘吉尔的后裔，他母亲名叫珍妮·杰罗姆，是美国富豪之女。18岁的他进入桑德赫斯特的皇家军事学院学习，1895年在一个荣誉骑兵团任少尉。从1896年开始，丘吉尔以记者身份去过很多国家并写出相关的书籍或报道，在布尔战争期间，丘吉尔受派于一家报社到南非进行报道。布尔战争之后，丘吉尔决定从政。他的早期政治生涯较为坎坷。在二战即将爆发之际，丘吉尔被任命为海军大臣。丘吉尔以其杰出的领导才能在战时做了很多抵抗希特勒的正确决策，使英国成为欧洲战场上抗德的最后一个堡垒。丘吉尔在战时发表了很多精彩的讲话，极大鼓舞了英国人民的斗志。无论丘吉尔到哪里，他都会高举两个手指做出胜利的"V"字，象征着英国人民，乃至同盟军最终的胜利。

❖ Honors

In 1953 Queen Elizabeth II made Churchill Sir Winston Churchill by made him a knight of the Order of the Garter, the highest honor of knighthood. Churchill also won the Nobel Prize for literature for his works and his **oratory**（雄辩）. In 1963 Churchill was made an honorary citizen of the United States. Two months after the celebration of his 90th birthday, Winston Churchill died peacefully at his home. Upon his death aged ninety in 1965, Elizabeth II granted him the honor of a state funeral, which saw one of the largest **assemblies**（装配）of world statesmen in history. Churchill is widely regarded as being among the most influential people in British history, **consistently**（一贯地）ranking well in opinion polls of Prime Ministers of the United Kingdom.

阅读辅助

为了表彰丘吉尔的卓越功勋，伊丽莎白二世女王授予他最高荣誉---嘉德勋章。丘吉尔还因他的著作和演讲获得诺贝尔文学奖。1963年，美国国会授予丘吉尔美国荣誉公民的称号。他90岁生日的两个月后，丘吉尔在家中安详辞世。丘吉尔死后，女王特赐予举行国葬仪式，这显示出丘吉尔被视为有史以来最伟大的英国人。

9 撒切尔夫人 Margaret Hilda Thatcher
——英国永远的"铁娘子"

达人了解英美

◇ **Evaluation**

Margaret Hilda Thatcher, was the longest-serving British Prime Minister of the 20th century and is the only woman to have held the office. A Soviet journalist called her the "Iron Lady", a nickname that became associated with her **uncompromising**（不妥协的）politics and leadership style. As Prime Minister, she implemented policies that have come to be known as Thatcherism. She changed the general opinion about woman and proved to the world that women could achieve as much as men do and women could even **undertake**（承担）what might be impossible for most men. Till now, Thatcher is still regarded as one of greatest statesmen in the history of Britain and many of her policies still have great influences on their country.

阅读辅助

格丽特·希尔达·撒切尔，人称"铁娘子"，是英国20世纪连续执政时间最长的首相。也是迄今为止英国唯一的一位女首相。其政治哲学与政策主张被通称为"撒切尔主义"。她改变了人们对女性的普遍看法，向世人证明，女性不仅能够完成和男性一样的工作，而且能做到很多男性无法做到的事情。时至今日，撒切尔夫人仍被人们认为是英国历史上最伟大的政治领袖之一。她实施的很多政策对今天的英国依然有着重大的影响。

✧ Personal Life

Thatcher was born on 13 October 1925 in England. Graduated from Oxford University with a Science bachelor degree and then a Master of Arts degree, Thatcher worked as a barrister before being selected into the House of Commons and elected the leader of her party. When the Conservative Party **defeated**（被击败）the Labour Party in 1979 election, Thatcher became the first woman prime minister of the Britain. Her service as the prime minister lasted from 1979 to 1990 made her the longest prime minister in the 20th century.

Thatcher's service as a prime minister ended in 1990, succeeded by John Mayor due to her disagreement with several Cabinet ministers. Thatcher submitted her **resignation**（辞职）on 28 October 1990. In 1992, she was made a baroness for her contribution to the country and also became a member of the House of Lords.

阅读辅助

撒切尔出生于1925年10月13日。先后获得牛津大学理学学士和文学硕士学位，毕业后成为一名律师直到被选入下议院。之后成为保守党领袖。1979年，撒切尔夫人也成为了英国历史上第一位女首相。她的执政时间从1979年持续到1990年，这也使她成为20世纪执政时间最长的英国首相。由于与几位内阁大臣在经济外交政策出现分歧，撒切尔夫人于1990年10月28日辞去首相职位，由约翰·梅杰继任。1992年，撒切尔夫人因其对国家做出的突出贡献被册封为女男爵并成为上院议员。

✧ Achievement

The Thatcher government was dedicated to reduce the government control over the economy. The private ownership was encouraged for many government interests were sold to the private citizens or businesses, namely,

privatization（私有化）. The government also adopted monetarist policies to control inflation which involved controlling the money supply to reduce inflation. With the implementation of these policies, inflation was reduced; however, the unemployment rate increased greatly and many British enterprises were on the edge of **bankruptcy**（破产）. Many people began to doubt or even criticize the government. But Thatcher stuck to her policies all along and won herself the nickname of "Iron Lady".

With the revival of the world economy, British economy was also improved. Many of Thatcher's policies gained her popularity such as her sensible and **decisive**（决定性的）handling of Britain's conflict with Argentina; the government under Thatcher attached great importance to its relationship with US as well as its defense system with Western Europe. All of Thatcher's polices were named Thatcherism.

阅读辅助

撒切尔夫人领导下的政府致力于减少政府对经济的控制力度。政府支持个体和私营经济的发展，同时政府把很多国有的所有权出售给私人或企业。为了控制通货膨胀，撒切尔政府推行以控制通货膨胀为主的货币主义政策，包括减少货币供应。随着这些政策的实施，通货膨胀受到抑制；然而，失业率猛增，很多企业面临破产。人们开始对撒切尔夫人的领导产生质疑甚至批判，但撒切尔毫不动摇。她的坚定为她赢得了"铁娘子"的称号。随着世界经济的复苏，英国经济也得到了改善。撒切尔夫人的很多决策开始赢得人们的肯定，尤其是她果断处理了英国与阿根廷的冲突为她获得了无数的好评。

10 艾萨克·牛顿 Isaac Newton
——百科全书式的"全才"

达人了解英美

✧ Personal Life

Born at Woolsthorpe, near Grantham in Lincolnshire, where he attended school, Newton entered Cambridge University in 1661. Since 1669, Newton had held the prestigious post of Lucasian Professor of Mathematics until 1696 when he was appointed warden of the Royal Mint, settling in London. He took his duties at the Mint very seriously and campaigned against **corruption**（腐败）and inefficiency within the organization. In 1703, he was elected president of the Royal Society, an office he held until his death. He was knighted in 1705. Newton has been regarded for almost 300 years as the founding exemplar of modern physical science, his achievements in experimental investigation being as **innovative**（创新的）as those in mathematical research. With equal, if not greater, energy and originality he also plunged into chemistry, the early history of Western civilization, and theology.

Newton was a difficult man, prone to depression and often involved in bitter arguments with other scientists, but by the early 1700s he was the dominant figure in British and European science. He never married and lived **modestly**（谨慎地）, but was buried with great pomp in Westminster Abbey.

> **阅读辅助**
>
> 牛顿出生于林肯郡格兰瑟姆附近的伍兹索普,并在那里开始了求学生涯。牛顿于1661年进入剑桥大学。从1669年开始,牛顿担任了颇具名望的卢卡斯数学教授一职,一直持续到1696年他被任命为皇家造币厂督察员。1703年他被选举为皇家学会主席,并担任此职直至去世。1705年,他被授予爵士爵位。近300年来,牛顿一直被认为是现在物理学的奠基人。牛顿终生未婚,为人谦逊,但死后却以盛况空前的葬礼葬于威斯敏斯特大教堂。

✧ Achievement

His **monograph**(专题著作)"Mathematical Principles of Natural Philosophy", published in 1687, lays the foundations for most of classical mechanics. In this work, Newton showed how a universal force, gravity, applied to all objects in all parts of the universe. This book is generally considered to be one of the most important scientific books ever written. Widely regarded as one of the most influential people in human history, Newton built the first practical reflecting **telescope**(望远镜)and developed a theory of color based on the observation that a prism decomposes white light into the many colors that form the visible spectrum. He also formulated an empirical law of cooling and studied the speed of sound. In mathematics, Newton shares the credit with Gottfried Leibniz for the development of differential and integral calculus. He also demonstrated the generalized **binomial**(二项式)theorem, developed Newton's method for approximating the roots of a function, and contributed to the study of power series.

> **阅读辅助**
>
> 他的著作《自然哲学的数学原理》出版于1687年，为经典力学奠定了的绝大部分基础。在这部作品中，他展示了宇宙中的力——重力——是如何作用于宇宙中各部分的所有实体的。这本书普遍被认为是史上最重要的科学著作之一。他制造了第一台实用型反射式望远镜。他用棱镜把白色的光分解成多种不同的颜色，形成可见光谱，从而提出了颜色理论。他还建立了冷却定律，并研究了声音的速度。数学方面，牛顿与莱布尼兹共同发明了微积分。他还论证了二项式定理，建立了用于求方程近似的根的牛顿方法。他还致力于幂级数的研究。

❖ Apple Incident

Newton himself often told the story that he was inspired to **formulate** （规划）his theory of gravitation by watching the fall of an apple from a tree. Although it has been said that the apple story is a myth and that he did not arrive at his theory of gravity in any single moment, acquaintances of Newton (such as William Stukeley, whose manuscript account of 1752 has been made available by the Royal Society) do in fact confirm the **incident** （事件）, though not the cartoon version that the apple actually hit Newton's head.

It is known from his notebooks that Newton was grappling in the late 1660s with the idea that **terrestrial** （陆地的）gravity extends, in an inverse-square proportion, to the Moon; however, it took him two decades to develop the full-fledged theory. The question was not whether gravity existed, but whether it extended so far from Earth that it could also be the force holding the Moon to its orbit. Newton showed that if the force **decreased** （减小）as the inverse square of the distance, one could indeed calculate the Moon's orbital period, and get good agreement. He guessed the same force was responsible for other orbital motions, and hence named it "universal gravitation".

阅读辅助

一则著名的故事称，牛顿在受到一颗从树上掉落的苹果启发后，阐示出了他的万有引力定律。漫画作品更认为，掉落的苹果正好砸中了牛顿的脑门，它的碰撞让他不知何故地明白了引力。问题不在于引力是否存在，而在于它是否能从地球延伸到如此远，还能够成为保持月球在轨道运行的力。牛顿发现，如果让该力随距离的平方反比而减少，所计算出的月球轨道周期能与真实情况非常好地吻合。他猜想同样的力也导致了其他的轨道运动，并因此将之命名为"万有引力"。

斯蒂芬·威廉·霍金 Stephen William Hawking
——最杰出的"宇宙之王"

达人了解英美

✧ Personal Life

Stephen Hawking was born on 8 January 1942 in Oxford, England. When he was eight, his family moved to St. Albans. At the age of eleven, Stephen went to St. Albans School and then on to his father's old college, University College, Oxford. Stephen wanted to study Mathematics, which was not **available**（有效的）at University College, so he pursued Physics instead. After getting his degree in 1962, Hawking moved to Cambridge University. In 1973 he joinedthe Applied Mathematics and Theoretical Physics department at Cambridge, where in 1977 he became Professor of Gravitational Physics. Since 1979, Hawking has held the post of Lucasian professor of **mathematics**（数学）at Cambridge University.

At the age of 21, Hawking was **diagnosed**（诊断）with ALS (amyotrophic lateral sclerosis) or Lou Gehrig's disease, a neuromuscular disease that progressively weakens muscle control. Doctors gave him about two years to live. He not only exceeded their **estimate**（估计）, but also earned his doctorate, married, had three children, was appointed an Honorary Fellow of the Royal Society of Arts, a lifetime member of the Pontifical Academy of Sciences, and in 2009 was awarded the Presidential Medal of Freedom, the highest civilian award in the United States.

> **阅读辅助**
>
> 史蒂芬·霍金于1942年1月8日出生于英格兰的牛津。8岁时，举家迁往圣奥尔本斯。11岁时进入圣奥尔本斯学校学习，之后霍金本打算进入他父亲的母校——牛津大学学习数学专业未果，于是转而学习物理学，在1962年取得学位后到剑桥大学继续学习。1973年，他加入了牛津大学应用数学与理论物理系，并在那里于1977年成为了引力物理学教授。霍金21岁的时候，他被诊断出患上了肌萎缩性脊髓侧索硬化症，当时医生预言他最多还有2年寿命。但他不仅延长了这一预言，还取得了博士学位，结了婚并诞有3个孩子，并被推选为皇家学会荣誉会员，梵蒂冈教皇科学学会终身成员。

◇ Achievement

Stephen William Hawking is an English theoretical physicist and **cosmologist**（宇宙论者）who is world famous for his theory of exploding black holes. Stephen Hawking is generally considered as one of the most celebrated scientists and greatest minds of the present time. His work helped tore configure models of the universe and to redefine what's in it. In additionto being a brilliant scientist, Hawking is a great popularize of science.

Hawking's key scientific works to date have included providing, with Roger Penrose, theorems regarding gravitational **singularities**（奇异性）in the framework of general relativity, and the theoretical prediction that black holes should emit radiation, which is today known as Hawking radiation. He has also achieved success with works of popular science in which he discusses his own theories and **cosmology**（宇宙论）in general; these include the best seller *A Brief History of Time*, which stayed on the British Sunday Times best-sellers list for a record-breaking 237 weeks.

（英）影响世界的励志名人 **Section 6-1**

> **阅读辅助**
>
> 　　史蒂芬·威廉姆·霍金是英国理论物理学家和宇宙学家，以其黑洞爆炸理论而闻名于世。史蒂芬·霍金被普遍认为是当今最著名的科学家以及最伟大的智者之一。他的研究帮助我们重新认识了宇宙的模型，重新定义了宇宙的内容。他不但是一位杰出的科学家，还是一位伟大的科学普及者。

12 弗朗西斯·培根 Francis Bacon
——英国唯物主义和整个现代实验科学的真正始祖

达人了解英美

◆ Personal Life

Bacon was born in January 1561 in London. His family held high position in court. His father Sir Nicholas Bacon was the Lord Keeper of the Privy Seal for Elizabeth I and his mother was the daughter of Edward VI's tutor. Born in such a well-connected family, Bacon was naturally expected to pursuit a political career.

Bacon received early education at home and entered Trinity College; Cambridge in 1573 when he was only twelve and was admitted to Gray's Inn to study law and later became a big lawyer. At the age of 23, Bacon was elected as a MP in House of Commons. However, his opposition of certain new taxes offended Elizabeth I and didn't come to a high position at her reign. When James I came to power, Bacon was greatly favored and ascended from one post to another until he became Lord Chancellor. In the course of rising, he made many enemies who later charged him of **bribery** （贿赂）, an accepted custom of the time and there's not necessarily evidence of his deeply corrupt behavior and was admitted by himself. Consequently, he was deprived of office, fined and banished from London in 1621 and died five years later.

> **阅读辅助**
>
> 培根在1561年出生于伦敦,他家的门第很高,他的父亲是尼古拉斯爵士而母亲是爱德华六世女儿的家庭老师。出生于名门的培根对政治自然是有追求的。培根的早期教育是在家里完成的,之后进入了三一学院。在1573年考入了剑桥大学学习法律,毕业之后成为一个大律师。23岁的培根成为下议院议员,然而他对伊丽莎白一世的一些税收制度表达了反对意见。直到詹姆士一世继位,他的政治生涯才开始有起色,他成为大法官。随后由于有人指控他有受贿行为而被制裁,判了罚款并流放。

◆ Achievement

Bacon has been called the father of **empiricism**(经验主义). His works established and popularized inductive methodologies for scientific inquiry, often called the Baconian method, or simply the scientific method. His demand for a planned procedure of investigating all things natural marked a new turn in the rhetorical and theoretical framework for science, much of which still surrounds conceptions of proper **methodology**(方法学) today.

Bacon's major works on philosophy included *The Proficiency and Advancement of Learning* (1605), *Magna Instauratio* (1620) and *The New Atlantis* (1626) and etc. His works **advocated**(提倡)the scientific revolution and established an inductive methodology for scientific inquiry. Bacon was also the inventor of a method involving collecting data and interpreting them judiciously as well as carrying out experiments to learn the secrets of nature by organized observation of its regularities. This idea had a great influence on the scientific research in the 17th Europe.

> **阅读辅助**
>
> 培根在著作中提出科学革命，并建立了科学研究的推衍方法。培根还发明了一种收集数据、进行缜密的分析，并通过有组织的实验观察其规律来了解事物本质的方法。这种方法对17世纪欧洲的科学研究产生了巨大影响。

✧ Influence

Bacon's ideas were influential in the 1630s and 1650s among scholars, in particular Sir Thomas Browne, who in his encyclopedia Pseudodoxia Epidemica (1646–72) frequently adheres to a Baconian approach to his scientific enquiries. During the 18th-century French Enlightenment, Bacon's non-metaphysical approach to science became more influential than the dualism of his French **contemporary**（当代的）Descartes, and was associated with criticism of the ancien regime. In 1733 Voltaire introduced him as the "father" of the scientific method" to a French audience, an understanding which had become widespread by 1750. In the 19th century his emphasis on induction was revived and developed by William Whewell, among others. He has been **reputed**（被普遍认为……的）as the "Father of Experimental Science".

> **阅读辅助**
>
> 培根的思想在1630那个年代的学者之中极具影响力，特别是对汤玛斯爵士的百科全书的编写，据他所说他编写此书是按照科学调查归纳法罗列的。另外对18世纪的法国启蒙运动，培根的科学法更具有影响力，如笛卡尔的二元论。在1733年伏尔泰将培根视为科学方法之父，并将此普及给法国的民众。

Section 6-2　（美）影响世界的励志名人

美国，一个开明创新的民主强国。任何国家的进步和发展都是由于人的努力而实现的，人们从中可以获得难以想象的存在感。美国有知名的名人堂，其主旨在于纪念美国那些为艺术、体育、商业、教育、慈善、科学做出巨大贡献的人们，这无疑更加体现美国精神。

1 亚伯拉罕·林肯 *Abraham. Lincoln*
——洋溢神性光辉的政客

达人了解英美

◇ Life Story

Lincoln grew up on the western frontier in Kentucky and Indiana. As a youth, Lincoln disliked the hard labor associated with frontier life. Some of his neighbors and family members thought for a time that he was lazy for all his "reading, scribbling, writing, ciphering, writing Poetry, etc. "He was an avid reader and **retained**（保存）a lifelong interest in learning. Lincoln's first romantic interest was Ann Rutledge, they were in a relationship but not formally engaged. But she died at the age of 22. In 1840, Lincoln became engaged to Mary Todd, who was from a wealthy slave-holding family in Lexington, Kentucky.

阅读辅助

林肯来自一个美国西部一个贫困的家庭，他的青年时代热爱读书，他夜读的灯火总要闪烁到很晚很晚。他通过自学使自己成为一个博学而充满智慧的人。他的初恋并没有最终成为他的妻子，因为她在22岁时去世了。之后林肯与玛丽·托德结婚并育有子女。

◇ Career

Largely self-educated, he became a lawyer in Illinois, a Whig Party leader, and a member of the Illinois House of Representatives, where he served from 1834 to 1846. Because he had originally agreed not to run for a second term in Congress, and his opposition to the Mexican–American War was unpopular among Illinois voters, Lincoln returned to Springfield and resumed his successful law practice. Reentering politics in 1854, he became a leader in building the newRepublican Party, which had a statewide **majority**（成年）in Illinois. In 1860 Lincoln secured the Republican Party presidential nomination as a moderate from a swing state. With very little support in the **slaveholding**（拥有奴隶）states of the South, he swept the North and was elected president in 1860. His election prompted seven southern slave states to form the Confederate States of America before he was sworn into office.

> **阅读辅助**
>
> 在伊利诺伊州自学成才成为律师，在1830年代为辉格党领袖和州众议员，并在1840年代在国会担任过一任议员。1850年，美国的奴隶主势力大增，林肯退出国会，继续当律师。1856年，林肯因强烈反对扩大奴隶制而退出辉格党，参加新成立的反对奴隶制的共和党，并很快成为该党主要领导人。1860年，作为一个来自摇摆州的温和派，林肯获得了共和党的总统提名。就任总统初期，林肯为避免国家分裂与战乱，他曾试图需求以和平的方式废除奴隶制。但随着战争的深入，林肯真正地认识到，要想真正废除奴隶制，就必须要流血牺牲，和平的方式根本解决不了任何问题。

◇ Spark Words

Four score and seven years ago our fathers brought forth on this continent, a new nation, conceived in Liberty, and dedicated to the proposition that all men are created equal. Now we are engaged in a great civil war, testing whether that nation, or any nation so **conceived**（构思）and so dedicated, can long endure. We are met on a great battle-field of that war.

We have come to dedicate a portion of that field, as a final resting place for those who here gave their lives that that nation might live. It is altogether fitting and proper that we should do this. But, in a larger sense, we can not dedicate - we can not **consecrate**（奉献）- we can not hallow - this ground.

> 阅读辅助
>
> 林肯诉诸独立宣言所支持的"凡人生而平等"之原则，并重新定义这场内战：不只是为联邦存续而奋斗，亦是"自由之新生"，将真平等带给全体公民。林肯在宾夕法尼亚州葛底斯堡的葛底斯堡国家公墓，哀悼在长达五个半月的葛底斯堡之役中阵亡的将士。

2　埃尔维斯·普雷斯利 Elvis Presley
——世界人民眼中永远的猫王

达人了解英美

✧ Early years

　　Presley was born in Tupelo, Mississippi, and when he was 13 years old, he and his family **relocated**（迁移）to Memphis, Tennessee. His music career began there in 1954, when he recorded a song with producer Sam Phillips at Sun Records. Accompanied by guitarist Scotty Moore and bassist Bill Black, Presley was an early popularizer of rockabilly, an uptempo, backbeat-driven fusion of country music and rhythm and blues.

　　RCA Victor acquired his contract in a deal arranged by Colonel Tom Parker, who managed the singer for more than two decades. Presley's first RCA single, "Heartbreak Hotel", was released in January 1956 and became a number-one hit in the United States. He was regarded as the leading figure of rock and roll after a series of successful network television appearances and **chart-topping**（在排行榜榜首的）records. His energized interpretations of songs and sexually **provocative**（刺激的）performance style, combined with a singularly potent mix of influences across color lines that coincided with the dawn of the Civil Rights Movement, made him enormously popular—and **controversial**（有争议的）.

阅读辅助

　　普雷斯利出生于密西西比州图珀洛，13岁时随家人搬至田纳西州的孟菲斯居住。10岁的埃尔维斯首次登台表演，他在密西西比州的唱歌比赛中演唱了乡村歌曲，获得二等奖。他从未接受过正规的音乐训练，也不会识谱，完全是通过收音机听音乐自学成才的。1953年埃尔维斯来到太阳唱片公司录下两首歌，当时的公司老板很欣赏埃尔维斯。1954年埃尔维斯发行生平第一张单曲唱片他舞台上独特的扭臀动作，加上将黑人的节奏布鲁斯和白人的乡村歌曲融为一体，让听众如痴如醉。

◆ Become well known

In November 1956, he made his film debut in Love Me Tender. In 1958, he was drafted into military service: He resumed his recording career two years later, producing some of his most commercially successful work before devoting much of the 1960s to making Hollywood movies and their accompanying **soundtrack**（声道）albums, most of which were critically **derided**（嘲弄）. In 1968, following a seven-year break from live performances, he returned to the stage in the **acclaimed**（欢呼）televised comeback special Elvis, which led to an extended Las Vegas concert **residency**（住处）and a string of highly profitable tours. In 1973, Presley was featured in the first globally broadcast concert via satellite, Aloha from Hawaii. Several years of prescription drug abuse severely damaged his health, and he died in 1977 at the age of 42.

阅读辅助

1956年9月，RCA公司将猫王的7首单曲同时发行。1957年出版了专辑《埃尔维斯的圣诞集锦》。1957年派拉蒙公司为拍摄了新片。1960年以后猫王突出的作品非常少，很明显在走下坡。这时英国的披头士征服了欧美流行音乐市场，使猫王的地位备受威胁。1970年代以后健康、经济、艺术方面都遇到了严重的问题，在1977年被发现晕倒在浴室，之后因心律严重失常导致心脏病突发过世，享年42岁。

◇ Award

Presley is one of the most celebrated and influential musicians of the 20th century. Commercially successful in many genres, including pop, blues and gospel, he is the best-selling solo artist in the history of recorded music, with estimated record sales of around 600 million units worldwide. He won three Grammys, also receiving the Grammy Lifetime Achievement Award at age 36, and has been inducted into multiple music halls of fame. Forbes named Elvis Presley as the 2nd top earning dead **celebrity**（名声）with $55 million as of 2011.

> **阅读辅助**
>
> 猫王经常被认为是摇滚乐历史上影响力最大的歌手，有摇滚乐之王的誉称。从1969年至1977年猫王共举行1,100场演唱会。共演出31部电影。因为他的魅力，摇滚乐成为美国的全民运动。猫王开辟了摇滚乐艰难的前进道路，之后摇滚开始成为对美国社会影响最深远的文化之一。

◇ Influence

Presley's earliest musical influence came from **gospel**（信条）. His mother recalled that from the age of two, at the Assembly of God church in Tupelo attended by the family, "he would slide down off my lap, run into the aisle and scramble up to the platform. There he would stand looking at the choir and trying to sing with them." As a teenager, Presley's musical interests were wide-ranging, and he was deeply informed about African American musical **idioms**（惯用语）as well as white ones. Though he never had any formal training, he was blessed with a remarkable memory, and his musical knowledge was already considerable by the time he made his first professional recordings in 1954 at the age of 19.

阅读辅助

猫王最早的音乐方面的影响是在教堂的唱诗班演唱形成的,教堂里布道者和做礼拜的人们情绪激昂的摇摆晃动、载歌载舞为普雷斯利那著名的胯部扭动动作提供了基础。

迈克尔·杰克逊 *Michael Jackson*
——心怀大爱的流行天王

达人了解英美

◇ **Success**

He began his solo career in 1971. In the early 1980s, Jackson became a dominant figure in popular music. The music videos for his songs were credited with breaking down racial barriers and with transforming the medium into an art form and promotional tool. The popularity of these videos helped to bring the then-relatively-new television channel MTV to fame. He continued to innovate the medium throughout the 1990s, as well as forging a reputation as a touring solo artist. His **distinctive**（有特色的）sound and style has influenced numerous hip hop, post-disco, **contemporary**（当代的）R&B, pop, and rock artists. Jackson is one of the few artists to have been inducted into the Rock and Roll Hall of Fame twice. He was also inducted into the Songwriters Hall of Fame and the Dance Hall of Fame as the first and only dancer from pop and rock music.

阅读辅助

在他8岁时，他与杰梅因成了主唱，乐队就此更名为杰克逊五人组。并于1964年初次登上职业音乐舞台，后于1971年开始单飞。20世纪80年代初期，杰克逊成为流行音乐的主导人物。他歌曲的音乐影片，将媒体转化为一种艺术形式和宣传工具，也对打破种族障碍有着巨大的贡献。些音乐影片的流行促使当时创立不久的电视频道"音乐电视网"名扬天下。他独特的声音和风格影响了很多嘻哈音乐、后期迪斯科、现代节奏布鲁斯、流行音乐及摇滚音乐的艺术家。杰克逊是为数不多的已两次入选摇滚名人堂的艺术家之一，是唯一一位进入舞蹈名人堂的流行艺人。

✧ Childhood

Michael Joseph Jackson was born in 1958, he was the eighth of ten children in an African-American working-class family. Jackson had a troubled relationship with his father; he acknowledged that he regularly whipped Jackson as a boy. His father was also said to have verbally abused his son, often saying that he had a "fat nose". Jackson stated that he was physically and **emotionally**（感情上）abused during incessant **rehearsals**（排练）, though he also credited his father's strict discipline with playing a large role in his success. Jackson has won hundreds of awards, making him the most awarded recording artist in the history of popular music.

> **阅读辅助**
>
> 迈克尔·杰克逊于1958年，杰克逊一家属于非裔美国工薪阶层。杰克逊与他父亲约瑟夫的关系紧张，约瑟夫在2003年承认他在杰克逊小的时候经常对他进行鞭打。杰克逊声称他在不断的排练中身体上和精神上深受虐待，尽管他也相信他父亲严格的纪律与他的成功有着很大的关系。杰克逊的父亲也表示曾经口头虐待杰克逊，称他在许多场合都有大鼻子。杰克逊赢得了数百个奖项，使他成为流行音乐历史上获奖最多的艺人。

✧ Spark Spirit

My childhood was completely taken away from me. There was no Christmas, there were no birthdays, it was not a normal childhood, nor the normal pleasures of childhood - those were exchanged for hard work, struggle, and pain, and eventually material and professional success. But as an awful price, I cannot re-create that part of my life. However, today, when I create my music, I feel like an instrument of nature. I wonder what delight nature must feel when we open our hearts and express our God-given talents. The sound ... of approval rolls across the **universe**（宇宙），

and the whole world abounds in magic. Wonder fills our hearts, for what we have glimpsed, for an instant, the **playfulness**（嬉闹）of life.

And that's why I love children and learn so much from being around them. I realize that many of our world's problems today - from the inner city crime, to large scale wars and terrorism, and our **overcrowded**（过度拥挤的）prisons - are a result of the fact that children have had their childhood stolen from them. The magic, the wonder, the mystery, and the innocence of a child's heart, are the seeds of creativity that will heal the world. I really believe that.

> **阅读辅助**
>
> 杰克逊讲述了他的童年，人生经历，并且表明是音乐让他感到幸福和快乐，另外他对孩子们的爱是纯洁无私的，希望能够真正地帮助到他们。

4 伊丽莎白·泰勒 Elizabeth Taylor
——好莱坞性感端庄的代名词

达人了解英美

✧ Early Life

Elizabeth Rosemond Taylor was born at Heathwood in 1932. Her Daddy was an art dealer, and her mom was a former actress whose stage name was "Sara Sothern". Colonel Victor Cazalet, one of their closest friends, had an important influence on the family. He was a rich, well-connected bachelor, a Member of Parliament and close friend of Winston Churchill. Additionally, as a Christian Scientist and lay **preacher**（传教士）, his links with the family were spiritual. He also became Elizabeth's godfather. A dual citizen of the United Kingdom and the United States, she was born British through her birth on British soil and an American citizen through her parents. At the age of three, Taylor began taking ballet lessons. Shortly before the beginning of World War II, her parents decided to return to the United States to avoid hostilities.

阅读辅助

伊丽莎白·泰勒1932年出生于英国伦敦，父亲是艺术品商人，而母亲则是一名舞台剧演员。她自幼学习跳舞，但1939年第二次世界大战的爆发逼使她全家移居到美国洛杉矶好莱坞。1942年，年仅十岁的伊丽莎白·泰勒便登上银幕，演出处女作翌年，她转投米高梅公司，在该公司拍摄电影近20年。

✧ Acting career

Soon after settling in Los Angeles, Taylor's mother discovered that Hollywood people "**habitually**（习惯地）saw a movie future for every pretty face". Finally, MGM gave her a seven-year contract. Taylor appeared in her first motion picture at the age of nine in There's One Born Every Minute, her only film for Universal. MGM cast Taylor in Lassie Come Home with child-star Roddy McDowall, with whom she would share a lifelong friendship. The film received **favorable**（良好的）attention for both actors, and MGM signed Taylor to a **conventional**（传统的）seven-year contract, starting at $100 a week with regular raises.

The teenage Taylor was **reluctant**（勉强的）to continue making films. Her stage mother forced Taylor to relentlessly practice until she could cry on cue and watched her during filming, signaling to change her delivery or a mistake. Taylor met few others her age on movie sets, and was so poorly educated that she needed to use her fingers to do basic **arithmetic**（算法）. When, at age 16, Taylor told her parents that she wanted to quit acting for a normal childhood. 1948, Taylor sailed aboard the RMS Queen Mary to England to begin filming **Conspirator**（阴谋者）. Unlike some other child actors, Taylor made an easy transition to adult roles.

> 阅读辅助
>
> 　　在60年的银幕生涯中，她与众多的好莱坞明星合拍了不少名经典电影，并且凭借1960年的《青楼艳妓》和1966年的《谁怕弗吉尼亚·沃尔夫》两度获得奥斯卡最佳女主角奖，还获得过三次提名。伊丽莎白·泰勒自1980年代开始投身于慈善事业。

✧ Personal Life

Taylor was married eight times to seven husbands. When asked why she married so often, she replied, "I don't know, honey. It sure beats the hell out of me," but also said that, "I was taught by my parents that if you fall in love, if you want to have a love affair, you get married. I guess I'm very old-fashioned."

She had two sons, a daughter and adopted a two-year-old girl from Germany. In 1971, Taylor became a grandmother at the age of 39. At the time of her death, she was survived by her four children, ten grandchildren, and four great-grandchildren.

阅读辅助

泰勒一生共结过八次婚,有过七个丈夫,其中与理查德·伯顿的婚姻持续的时间最长,也最被外界所关注。她精采多姿的婚姻生活是她传奇人生的一大特色。

5 拉尔夫·爱默生 Ralph Emerson
——美国的孔子般的灵魂人物

达人了解英美

◇ Career

Emerson gradually moved away from the religious and social beliefs of his **contemporaries**（同辈人）, formulating and expressing the philosophy of Transcendentalism in his 1836 essay, Nature. Following this groundbreaking work, he gave a speech entitled "The American Scholar", which Oliver Wendell Holmes, Sr. considered to be America's "Intellectual Declaration of Independence". Emerson wrote on a number of subjects, never **espousing**（嫁娶）fixed philosophical tenets, but developing certain ideas such as individuality, freedom, the ability for humankind to realize almost anything, and the relationship between the soul and the surrounding world. He remains among the **linchpins**（关键）of the American Romantic Movement, and his work has greatly influenced the thinkers, writers and poets that have followed him.

阅读辅助

他在1836年9月创作了第一本小品文《论自然》。当作品成为超越论的基本原则时，爱默生又以《美国学者》为题发表了一篇著名的演讲辞，宣告美国文学已脱离英国文学而独立。另外这篇讲辞还抨击了美国社会的拜金主义，强调人的价值。被誉为美国思想文化领域的"独立宣言"。三年后，《论文集》第二集也出版了。这部著作为爱默生赢得了巨大的声誉，他的思想被称为超验主义的核心，他本人则被冠以"美国的文艺复兴领袖"之美誉。

✧ Life Story

Emerson was born in Boston, Emerson was raised by his mother, his aunt in particular had a profound effect on Emerson. Emerson's formal schooling began at the Boston Latin School when he was nine. At 14, Emerson went to Harvard College and was appointed freshman messenger for the president, requiring Emerson to fetch **delinquent**（怠忽的）students and send messages to faculty. Emerson served as Class Poet; as was custom, he presented an original poem on Harvard's Class Day. Emerson's religious views were often considered radical at the time. He believed that all things are connected to God and, therefore, all things are divine.

阅读辅助

生于波士顿的思想家、文学家，诗人爱默生，是美国文化精神的代表人物。他是由母亲和姑母抚养他成人。隔年他被送到了波士顿拉丁学校就读。在1817年10月爱默生14岁时，他入读哈佛大学并且被任命为新生代表，这个身份让他获得免费住宿的机会。他是一名无神论者，他认为耶稣是一个人并不是神。

✧ Spark words

We live in succession, in division, in parts, in particles. Meantime within man is the soul of the whole; the wise silence; the universal beauty, to which every part and particle is equally related, the eternal ONE. And this deep power in which we exist and whose **beatitude**（祝福）is all accessible to us, is not only self-sufficing and perfect in every hour, but the act of seeing and the thing seen, the seer and the spectacle, the subject and the object, are one. We see the world piece by piece, as the sun, the moon, the animal, the tree; but the whole, of which these are shining parts, is the soul.

（美）影响世界的励志名人 Section 6-2

> **阅读辅助**
> 艾默生的超验主义是最著名的，强调人与上帝间的直接交流和人性中的神性，具有强烈的批判精神，是重要的一次思想解放运动。

6 迈克尔·乔丹 Michael Jordan
——飞起来的 23 号球衣

达人了解英美

◇ Own Story

Jordan was born in Brooklyn, New York, his family moved to North Carolina, when he was a **toddler**（学步的小孩）. Jordan attended Emsley A. Laney High School in Wilmington, where he **anchored**（抛锚）his athletic career by playing baseball, football, and basketball. He tried out for the **varsity**（大学，大学运动代表队）basketball team during his sophomore year, but at 180 m, he was deemed too short to play at that level. Motivated to prove his worth, Jordan became the star of Laney's junior varsity **squad**（小队）. As a senior, he was selected to the McDonald's All-American Team after averaging a triple-double. In 1981, Jordan accepted a basketball scholarship to North Carolina, where he majored in cultural geography. He was selected by **consensus**（舆论）to the NCAA All-American First Team in both his sophomore and junior seasons.

阅读辅助

乔丹出生在纽约布鲁克林区，五岁的时候，乔丹一家人便搬到了北卡罗来纳州。威尔明顿兰尼高中是乔丹篮球生涯的起点，不过年幼的乔丹并不引人注目，第二年时，他的身高只有5尺11寸。不过乔丹没有放弃，到了高三的时候，他入选了全美高中生阵容。乔丹作为北卡罗莱那大学的一名新生，在NCAA联赛的决赛里投进制胜球，帮助北卡大学战胜了乔治城大学。1982-1983赛季，乔丹被《体育新闻》评为年度大学生球员及全美第一阵容队员。

◆ **Success**

Jordan's individual **accolades**（赞美）and accomplishments include five Most Valuable Player (MVP) Awards, ten All-NBA First Team designations, nine All-Defensive First Team honors, fourteen NBA All-Star Game appearances, three All-Star Game MVP Awards, ten scoring titles, three steals titles, six NBA Finals MVP Awards, and the 1988 NBA Defensive Player of the Year Award. Among his numerous accomplishments, Jordan holds the NBA records for highest career regular season scoring average and highest career playoff scoring average. In 1999, he was named the greatest North American athlete of the 20th century. He is a two-time inductee into the Basketball Hall of Fame – in 2009 for his individual career, and in 2010 as a member of the 1992 United States men's Olympic basketball team. Jordan is also known for his product **endorsements**（推荐）. He fueled the success of Nike's Air Jordan sneakers. Jordan also starred in the 1996 feature film Space Jam as himself.

> 阅读辅助
>
> 在15年中，乔丹总共获得6次总冠军，5次最有价值球员，6次总决赛最有价值球员，10次入选年度NBA年度第一队，更史无前例地获得十届NBA得分王，其中有七届是蝉联。他目前仍保持NBA常规赛球员职业生涯的场均得分最高纪录是蝉联。他目前仍保持NBA常规赛球员职业生涯的场均得分最高纪录和季后赛场均得分最高纪录。他在2009年入选篮球名人堂。

◆ **Spark Words**

I retired the first time when Phil Jackson was the coach. And I think that even with Phil being the coach I would have had a tough time, mentally finding the challenge for myself, although he can somehow present challenges for me. I don't know if he could have presented the challenge for me to continue on to this season. Even though middle way of this season I wanted to continue to play a couple more years, but at the end of this season I was mentally **drained**（流干）and tired. So I can't say that he would have restored that. I think the game itself is a lot bigger than Michael Jordan. I've been given an opportunity by people before me, to name a few, Kareem Abdul Jabbar, Doctor J, Eljohn Baylor, Jerry West. These guys played the game way before Michael Jordan was born and Michael Jordan came on the heels of all that activity. I played it to the best I could play it, I tried to enhance the game itself. I've tried to be the best basketball player that I could be.

> **阅读辅助**
>
> 我觉得这项运动本身比乔丹重要得多。我的前辈给了我很多机会，这些人早在乔丹出生前就活跃在赛场上了，乔丹是踩着他们的脚步来的。我尽了自己的所能，努力地推动篮球事业的发展，也尽了最大的努力成为最好的球员。

7 伊利莎白·雅顿 Elizabeth Arden
——让世界充满了芬芳

达人了解英美

◇ Biography

Arden was born in 1878 in Ontario, Canada. Her parents had **emigrated**（移居）to Canada from United Kingdom in the 1870s. Her father was Scottish and her mother was Cornish and had arranged for a wealthy aunt in Cornwall to pay for her children's education. Arden dropped out of nursing school in Toronto. She then joined her elder brother in Manhattan, working briefly as a bookkeeper for the E.R. Squibb Pharmaceuticals Company. While there, Arden spent hours in their lab, learning about **skincare**（护肤用的）. She then worked—again briefly—for Eleanor Adair, an early beauty culturist, as a "treatment girl".

In her salons and through her marketing campaigns, Elizabeth Arden stressed teaching women how to apply makeup, and pioneered such concepts as scientific **formulation**（规划）of cosmetics, beauty makeovers, and **coordinating**（协调的）colors of eye, lip, and facial makeup. Elizabeth Arden was largely responsible for establishing makeup as proper and appropriate—even necessary—for a ladylike image, when before makeup had often been associated with lower classes and such professions as prostitution. She **targeted**（把……作为目标）middle age and plain women for whom beauty products promised a youthful, beautiful image. In politics, Elizabeth Arden was a strong conservative who supported Republicans.

> **阅读辅助**
>
> 伊丽莎白·雅顿1878年出生在加拿大多伦多。她年轻时来到美国，先在纽约一家化妆品公司工作，1910年，她从亲戚手中借了6000美元，在美国时尚中心纽约第五大道开设了自己的美容沙龙。不久后，弗洛伦丝·南丁格尔·格雷厄姆改名为伊丽莎白·雅顿，并以此作为美容沙龙的名称。

◇ Career

In 1909 Arden formed a partnership with Elizabeth Hubbard, another **culturist**（培养者）. When the partnership dissolved, she coined the business name "Elizabeth Arden" from her former partner and from Tennyson's poem "Enoch Arden". With a $6,000 loan from her brother, she then used the shop space to open her first salon on 5th Avenue. In 1912 Arden travelled to France to learn beauty and facial massage techniques used in the Paris beauty salons. She returned with a collection of rouges and tinted powders she had created. She began expanding her international operations in 1915, and started opening salons across the world. In 1934, she opened the Maine Chance residential spa in Rome, Maine, the first destination beauty spa in the United States. It operated until 1970.

In recognition of her contribution to the **cosmetics**（化妆品）industry, she was awarded the Légion d'Honneur by the French government in 1962. Arden died at Lenox Hill Hospital in Manhattan in 1966; she was interred in the Sleepy Hollow Cemetery in Sleepy Hollow, New York, under the name Elizabeth N. Graham.

> **阅读辅助**
>
> 起先，伊丽莎白·雅顿只卖别人生产的香水。直到1922年，第一款由伊丽莎白·雅顿自己配制的香水正式推出。此后，雅顿夫人与化学家们合作开发了许多化妆品配方，并推出了一系列安全有效的护肤用品。1932年伊丽莎白·雅顿已在全球一些大都市设立了29家高档专卖店。伊丽莎白·雅顿女士凭借完美主义的性格和执着精神，成功创造了国际最知名的化妆品品牌之一。

8 阿尔伯特·爱因斯坦 Albert Einstein
——震撼世界的超级大脑

达人了解英美

✦ Career

Near the beginning of his career, Einstein thought that Newtonian mechanics was no longer enough to **reconcile**（调停）the laws of classical mechanics with the laws of the electromagnetic field. This led to the development of his special theory of relativity. He realized, however, that the principle of relativity could also be extended to **gravitational**（重力的）fields, and with his **subsequent**（随后的）theory of gravitation in 1916, he published a paper on the general theory of relativity. He continued to deal with problems of statistical mechanics and **quantum**（量子论）theory, which led to his explanations of particle theory and the motion. He also investigated the thermal properties of light which laid the foundation of the photon theory of light. In 1917, Einstein applied the general theory of relativity to model the large-scale structure of the **universe**（宇宙）.

Einstein published more than 300 scientific papers along with over 150 non-scientific works. Einstein's intellectual achievements and originality have made the word "Einstein" **synonymous**（同义的）with genius so that in a sense he may be regarded as the greatest genius who ever lived.

阅读辅助

年近26岁的爱因斯坦连续发表了三篇论文（《光量子》《布朗运动》和《狭义相对论》），在物理学三个不同领域中取得了历史性成就，特别是狭义相对论的建立和光量子论的提出，推动了物理学理论的革命。1915年爱因斯坦发表了广义相对论。他所作的光线经过太阳引力场要弯曲的预言,由亚瑟·斯坦利·爱丁顿的日全食观测结果所证实。爱因斯坦和相对论在西方成了家喻户晓的名词,同时也招来了德国和其他国家的沙文主义者、军国主义者和排犹主义者的恶毒攻击。爱因斯坦因在光电效应方面的研究,被授予1921年诺贝尔物理学奖。

✧ Life Story

Albert Einstein was born in the German Empire, when Adolf Hitler came to power in 1933, he was visiting the United States, did not go back to Germany, where he had been a professor at the Berlin Academy of Sciences. He settled in the U.S., becoming an American citizen in 1940. On the eve of World War II, he **endorsed**(支持)a letter to President Franklin D. Roosevelt alerting him to the potential development of "extremely powerful bombs of a new type" and recommending that the U.S. begin similar research. Einstein supported defending the Allied forces, but largely **denounced**(谴责)the idea of using the newly discovered **nuclear**(原子能的)fission as a weapon.

阅读辅助

出生于德国的爱因斯坦,辗转生活于米兰,苏黎世等不同地方,纳粹党攫取德国政权后,爱因斯坦是科学界首要的迫害对象,幸而当时他在美国讲学,未遭毒手。之后定居于美国。为支持反法西斯战争,他写信给罗斯福总统提醒他原子军备的危险性也建议美国应该着手发展,但是同时也对反对原子军备滥用论调提出支持。

(美)影响世界的励志名人 **Section 6-2**

❖ Spark Words

The armament race between the U.S.A. and U.S.S.R., originally supposed to be a preventive measure, **assumes**（假定）hysterical character. On both sides, the means to mass destruction are perfected with feverish haste - behind the respective walls of secrecy. The H-bomb appears on the public horizon as a probably **attainable**（可达到的）goal.

If successful, **radioactive**（有辐射的）poisoning of the atmosphere and hence annihilation of any life on earth has been brought within the range of technical possibilities. The ghostlike character of this development lies in its apparently **compulsory**（规定动作）trend. Every step appears as the unavoidable consequence of the preceding one. In the end, it beckons more and more clearly general **annihilation**（灭绝）.

> 阅读辅助
> 爱因斯坦提出了这种军备竞赛虽然是必要的但是不可以过度，否则会造成难以想象的后果，甚至可以造成人类的灭绝。

9 乔治·华盛顿 George Washington
——全世界第一位以"总统"为称号的国家元首

达人了解英美

✧ **Career**

Washington was the first President of the United States, the Commander-in-Chief of the Continental Army during the American Revolutionary War, and one of the Founding Fathers of the United States. He presided over the convention that drafted the United States Constitution, which replaced the Articles of **Confederation**（联邦）and remains the supreme law of the land.

Washington was unanimously elected President by the electors in both the 1788–1789 and 1792 elections. He oversaw the creation of a strong, well-financed national government that maintained neutrality in the French Revolutionary Wars, suppressed the Whiskey Rebellion, and won acceptance among Americans of all types. Washington established many forms in government still used today, such as the **cabinet**（内阁）system and inaugural address. His retirement after two terms and the peaceful transition from his presidency to that of John Adams established a tradition that continued up until Franklin D. Roosevelt was elected to a third term. Washington has been widely hailed as the "father of his country" – even during his lifetime.

> **阅读辅助**
>
> 乔治·华盛顿1775年至1783年美国独立战争时殖民地军的总司令,1789年成为美国第一任总统,在接连两次选举中都获得了全体选举团无异议支持,一直担任总统直到1797年。他也是一名共济会成员。在美国独立战争中率领大陆军团赢得美国独立,他拒绝了一些同僚怂恿他领导军事政权的提议,在1783年回到了他在维农山的庄园恢复平民生活。

✧ Early Life

Washington was born into the provincial gentry of Colonial Virginia; his wealthy planter family owned tobacco plantations and slaves, that he in turn inherited. Washington owned hundreds of slaves throughout his lifetime, but his views on slavery evolved. After his father and older brother died when he was young, Washington became personally and professionally attached to the powerful William Fairfax, who promoted his career as a surveyor and soldier. Washington quickly became a senior officer in the colonial forces during the first stages of the French and Indian War. Chosen by the Second Continental Congress in 1775 to be commander-in-chief of the Continental Army in the American Revolution, Washington managed to force the British out of Boston in 1776, but was defeated and almost **captured**(被俘的)later that year when he lost New York City.

> **阅读辅助**
>
> 华盛顿生于1732年,他的父亲是弗吉尼亚州一个蓄奴的大农场主,华盛顿从7岁到15岁,都没有接受过正规教育,后来在名叫威廉斯的老师那里上学。华盛顿早年在法国印第安人战争中曾担任支持大英帝国一方的殖民军军官。

✧ Affection

Washington had a vision of a great and powerful nation that would be built on republican lines using federal power. He sought to use the national government to preserve liberty, improve **infrastructure**（基础设施）, open the western lands, promote commerce, found a permanent capital, reduce regional tensions and promote a spirit of American nationalism. At his death, Washington was **eulogized**（颂扬）as "first in war, first in peace, and first in the hearts of his countrymen" by Henry Lee.

The Federalists made him the symbol of their party but for many years, the Jeffersonian continued to distrust his influence and delayed building the Washington Monument. As the leader of the first successful revolution against a **colonial**（殖民的）empire in world history, Washington became an international icon for liberation and nationalism. He isconsistently ranked among the top four presidents of the United States, according to polls of both scholars and the general public.

> **阅读辅助**
>
> 由于他扮演了美国独立战争和建国中最重要的角色，华盛顿通常被称为美国国父，并被视为美国的创立者中最重要的一位，他也在全世界成为一个典型的仁慈建国者的形象。华盛顿为未来的美国树立了许多的先例，总统不超过两任的先例被看作是华盛顿对此后的美国总统任期限制最重要的影响。

10 约翰·D. 洛克菲勒 John D. Rockefeller
——全球历史上除君主外最富有的人

达人了解英美

✧ Career

John Davison Rockefeller Sr. was a co-founder of the Standard Oil Company, which dominated the oil industry and was the first great U.S. business trust. Rockefeller revolutionized the **petroleum**（石油）industry, and along with other key contemporary industrialists such as Andrew Carnegie, defined the structure of modern **philanthropy**（慈善事业）. In 1870, he founded Standard Oil Company and actively ran it until he officially retired in 1897.

Rockefeller founded Standard Oil as an Ohio partnership with his brother and some elites. As kerosene and gasoline grew in importance, Rockefeller's wealth soared and he became the world's richest man and the first American worth more than a billion dollars, controlling 90% of all oil in the United States at his peak. Adjusting for inflation, his fortune upon his death in 1937 stood at $336 billion, accounting for more than 1.5% of the national economy, making him the richest person in history.

阅读辅助

约翰·戴维森·洛克菲勒因革新了石油工业和塑造了慈善事业现代化结构而闻名。1870年创立标准石油，在全盛期垄断了全美90%的石油市场。规模之巨大，其后继企业之一埃克森美孚在百年后的今天仍是全美第2大企业。

✧ Late-life

Rockefeller spent the last 40 years of his life in **retirement**（退休）at his estate, Kykuit, in Westchester County, New York. His fortune was mainly used to create the modern systematic approach of targeted philanthropy. He was able to do this through the creation of foundations that had a major effect on medicine, education and scientific research. His foundations pioneered the development of medical research and were instrumental in the **eradication**（消灭）of hookworm and yellow fever. Rockefeller was also the founder of both the University of Chicago and Rockefeller University and funded the establishment of Central Philippine University in the Philippines.

> **阅读辅助**
>
> 洛克菲勒在人生的后40年致力于慈善事业，主要是教育和医药领域。他在1897年结束对标准石油的直接管理。他出资成立洛克菲勒研究所资助北美医学研究，包括根除钩虫和黄热病，也对抗生素的发现帮助甚大。他也对黑人族群特别关照，斥巨资提升黑人教育。

✧ Creed

He was a devoted Northern Baptist and supported many church-based institutions. Rockefeller adhered to total **abstinence**（节制）from alcohol and tobacco **throughout**（遍及）his life. He was a faithful congregant of the Erie Street Baptist Mission Church, where he taught Sunday school, and served as a trustee, clerk, and **occasional janitor**（门警）. Religion was a guiding force throughout his life, and Rockefeller believed it to be the source of his success. Rockefeller was also considered a supporter of capitalism based in a perspective of social darwinism, and is often quoted saying "The growth of a large business is merely a survival of the **fittest**（胜任的）."

阅读辅助

洛克菲勒坚信他人生的目的是"尽力地赚钱,尽力地存钱,尽力地捐钱"。他以许多负面手段成为了空前绝后的巨富,但他私生活严谨,一生勤俭自持,终身不烟不酒。他并在晚年将大部分财产捐出资助慈善事业,开美国富豪行善之先河。

读书笔记

Section 7-1　（英）独具特色的当地节日

英国是一个古老的极具文化底蕴的国家，而悠久的历史让这个国家的节日，更具有吸引力，充满着故事性和习俗性。英国的本土节日大都是跟宗教、王室和民风有关，让我们一起来真正的领略一下这些节日背后的故事和奇特的风俗传统吧。

1 圣帕特里克节 St. Patrick's Day
——爱尔兰的国庆节

达人了解英美

✧ History

Saint Patrick's Day was made an official Christian feast day in the early 17th century and is observed by the Catholic Church, the Anglican Communion, the Eastern Orthodox Church, and Lutheran Church. The day commemorates Saint Patrick and the arrival of Christianity in Ireland, and celebrates the **heritage**（遗产）and culture of the Irish in general.

Much of what is known about Saint Patrick comes from the Declaration, which was allegedly written by Patrick himself. According to the Declaration, at the age of sixteen, he was **kidnapped**（诱拐）by Irish raiders and taken as a slave to Gaelic Ireland. It says that he spent six years there working as a shepherd and that during this time he "found God". The Declaration says that God told Patrick to flee to the coast, where a ship would be waiting to take him home. After making his way home, Patrick went on to become a priest. According to tradition, Patrick returned to Ireland to convert the **pagan**（异教徒）Irish to Christianity. The Declaration says that he spent many years evangelizing in the northern half of Ireland and converted "thousands". Tradition holds that he died on 17 March and was buried at Downpatrick. Over the following centuries, many legends grew up around Patrick and he became Ireland's foremost saint.

> **阅读辅助**
>
> 公元432年，圣帕特里克受教皇派遣前往爱尔兰劝说爱尔兰人皈依基督教。圣帕特里克临危不惧，当即摘下一棵三叶苜蓿，形象地阐明了圣父、圣子、圣灵三位一体的教义。他雄辩的演说使爱尔兰人深受感动，接受了圣帕特里克主施的隆重洗礼。461年3月17日，圣帕特里克逝世，爱尔兰人为了纪念他，将这一天定为圣帕特里克节。

◆ Celebrations

Celebrations generally involve public parades and festivals, céilithe, and the wearing of green attire or **shamrocks**（三叶草）. Christians also attend church services and the Lenten restrictions on eating and drinking alcohol are lifted for the day, which has encouraged and **prop agated**（传播）the holiday's tradition of alcohol consumption. Saint Patrick's Day is a public holiday in the Republic of Ireland, it is also widely celebrated by the Irish diaspora around the world, especially in Great Britain, Canada, the United States, Argentina, Australia and New Zealand.

In Great Britain, Queen Elizabeth The Queen Mother used to present bowls of shamrock flown over from Ireland to members of the Irish Guards, a **regiment**（大量）in the British Army consisting primarily of soldiers from both Northern Ireland and the Republic of Ireland. The Irish Guards still wear shamrock on this day, flown in from Ireland. Christian denominations in Great Britain observing his feast day include The Church of England and the Roman Catholic Church. Horse racing at the Cheltenham Festival attracts large numbers of Irish people, both residents of Britain and many who travel from Ireland, and usually coincides with St Patrick's Day.

> **阅读辅助**
>
> 这一节日起源于5世纪末期，这一天后来成为爱尔兰人的国庆节，在加拿大其他地区、英国、澳大利亚、美国和新西兰，圣帕特里克节虽然广为庆祝，但不是法定节假日。随着时代的发展，圣帕特里克节从传统的宗教仪式逐渐转变为展现各国音乐、舞蹈、美术等艺术的大舞台。参加游行表演的多是来自世界各国的艺术团体，他们精彩的表演将狂欢气氛推向了高潮。

✧ Traditions

On St. Patrick's Day it is customary to wear shamrocks and/or green clothing or accessories (the "wearing of the green"). St. Patrick is said to have used the shamrock, a three-leaved plant, to explain the Holy Trinity to the pagan Irish. The color green has been associated with Ireland since at least the 1640s, when the green harp flag was used by the Irish Catholic Confederation. Green ribbons and shamrocks have been worn on St. Patrick's Day since at least the 1680s. The wearing of the "St. Patrick's Day Cross" was also a popular custom in Ireland until the early 20th century. These were a Celtic Christian cross made of paper that was "covered with silk or ribbon of different colors, and a bunch or **rosette**（玫瑰形饰物）of green silk in the centre".

> **阅读辅助**
>
> 爱尔兰人喜欢佩带三叶苜蓿，用爱尔兰的国旗颜色——绿黄两色装饰房间，身穿绿色衣服，并向宾客赠送三叶苜蓿饰物等。圣帕特里克当年在爱尔兰传教时，就是利用三叶苜蓿向人们讲述基督教义的，现在，三叶苜蓿已经被爱尔兰人视为国花。

2 彭斯晚宴 Burns Night
——名副其实的狂欢酒筵

达人了解英美

◇ **History**

　　The first suppers were held in memoriam at Ayrshire at the end of the 18th century by Robert Burns' friends on 21 July, the anniversary of his death, and have been a regular **occurrence**（事件）ever since. The first Burns club was founded in Greenock in 1801 by merchants born in Ayrshire, some of whom had known Burns. They held the first Burns supper on what they thought was his birthday, 29 January 1802, but in 1803 they discovered in Ayrparish records that his date of birth was 25 January 1759. Since then, suppers have been held on 25 January.

　　Burns suppers are most common in Scotland and Northern Ireland, however, there has been a surge in Burns' Night celebrations in the UK events industry seeing the evening being celebrated outside their traditional confines of Burns Clubs, Scottish Societies, expatriate Scots, or aficionados of Burns' poetry. There is a particularly strong tradition of them in southern New Zealand's main city Dunedin, of which Burns' nephew Thomas was a founding father.

阅读辅助

　　专写老百姓事情的18世纪"平民诗人"罗伯特·彭斯永远是苏格兰人最钟爱的儿子。这里的人以他本人也会喜欢的方式来庆祝他的生日。"为了往昔的时光，老朋友，为了往昔的时光，再干一杯友情的酒，为了往昔的时光。"每逢18世纪英格兰民族诗人彭斯的生日，在苏格兰各地乃至欧洲的许多城市，这首歌都像幽灵似的在街头巷尾徘徊，在寒冷的夜空里低沉地萦回，伴着推杯换盏时的喊叫，伴着饕餮大餐后的呕吐，伴着彻夜不眠的彭斯之夜。

◇ Food

Burns suppers may be formal or informal. Both typically include haggis (a traditional Scottish dish celebrated by Burns in Address to a Haggis), Scotch whisky, and the recitation of Burns's poetry. Formal dinners are hosted by organizations such as Burns clubs, the Freemasons, or St. Andrews Societies and occasionally end with dancing when ladies are present. Formal suppers follow a standard format. Everyone stands as the main course is brought in. This is always a haggis on a large dish. It is usually brought in by the cook, generally while a piper plays **bagpipes**（风笛）and leads the way to the host's table, where the haggis is laid down.

阅读辅助

参加聚会的人往往会聚集在宴会厅，大吃特吃加辣根和鸡蛋沙司的风干鳕鱼和熏鳕鱼。不过这些都还只是开胃小吃。主食当然是苏格兰的本地风味菜：肉馅羊肚，就是在羊肚里填满切碎的羊肉、燕麦片、杂碎以及香料之后将羊肚封紧，然后煮成油光发亮的棕色。厨师进入大厅时，手中高举着椭圆形的大盘子；走在他两侧的是身着盛装的风笛手。

◇ Immortal Memory

One of the guests gives a short speech, remembering some aspect of Burns' life or poetry. This may be light-hearted or intensely serious. A good speaker always prepares a speech with his audience in mind, since above all the Burns' supper should be entertaining. Everyone drinks a toast to Robert

Burns.

The host will normally say a few words thanking the previous speaker for his speech and may comment on some of the points raised. This was originally a short speech given by a male guest in thanks to the women who had prepared the meal. However, nowadays it is much more wide-ranging and generally covers the male speaker's view on women. After the speeches there may be singing of songs by Burns – Ae Fond Kiss, Parcel o' Rogues, A Man's a Man, etc. – and more poetry – To a Mouse, To a Louse, Tam o' Shanter, The Twa Dugs, Holy Willie's Prayer, etc. Finally the host will call on one of the guests to give the vote of thanks, after which everyone is asked to stand, join hands, and sing Auld Lang Synebringing the evening to an end.

阅读辅助

刚开始时晚会主席致欢迎词，之后会献上彭斯的诗歌。上菜时，大家齐声朗诵苏格兰的谢恩祈祷文。到长夜结束时，参加庆典的人手挽着手，齐声高唱彭斯最著名的歌曲：《友谊地久天长》。

威尔士诗歌音乐会 *The Eisteddfod*
——英国威尔士民谣之夜

达人了解英美

◇ History

The tradition of such a meeting of Welsh artists dates back to at least the 12th century, when a festival of poetry and music was held by Rhys ap Gruffydd of Deheubarth at his court in Cardigan in 1176 but, with the decline of the **bardic**（吟游诗人的）tradition, it fell into abeyance.

The first eisteddfod can be traced back to 1176, under the auspices of Lord Rhys, at his castle in Cardigan. There he held a grand gathering to which were invited poets and musicians from all over the country. A chair at the Lord's table was awarded to the best poet and musician, a tradition that **prevails**（获胜）in the modern day National Eisteddfod. The earliest large-scale eisteddfod that can be proven beyond all doubt to have taken place, however, was the Carmarthen Eisteddfod, which took place in 1451. The next recorded large-scale eisteddfod was held in Caerwys in 1568. The prizes awarded were a **miniature**（微影）silver chair to the successful poet, a silver tongue to the best singer, and a tiny silver harp to the best **harpist**（竖琴师）. Originally, the contests were limited to professional Welsh bards who were paid by the nobility. To ensure the highest standard possible, Elizabeth I of England commanded that the bards be examined and licensed. As interest in the Welsh arts declined, the standard of the main eisteddfod deteriorated as well and they became more informal. In 1789, Thomas Jones organized an eisteddfod inCorwen, where for the first time the public were admitted. The success of this event led to a revival of interest in Welsh literature and music.

> **阅读辅助**
>
> 威尔士的音乐诗歌节，可以追溯回12世纪，是由一群威尔士的艺术家们的聚会开始的。开始的时候是由里斯勋爵赞助在他的城堡举行的，聚会汇集了来自全国各地的众多诗人，音乐家，这种庆典一直延续到今天。最早的大型音乐诗歌会是在1451年举办的，由诗人喀麦登主持。之后记录的一次大规模的集会是在 Caerwys 举行的，奖品被颁发给了一个口才最好的歌手和竖琴弹得最好的竖琴师。开始的集会仅限于贵族参与，之后伊丽莎白一世让全体民众参与。这让集会更加盛大。

◆ Organization

The National Eisteddfod is traditionally held in the first week of August and the competitions are all held in the Welsh language. The Eisteddfod Act of 1959 allowed local **authorities**（当局）to give financial support to the event. Hundreds of tents, pavilions and little stands are **erected**（竖立）in an open space to create the maes (field). The space required for this means that it is rare for the Eisteddfod to be in a city or town but instead it is held somewhere with more space. Car parking for day visitors alone requires several large fields, and many people camp on the site for the whole week.

The festival has a quasi-druidicflavor, with the main literary prizes for poetry and prose being awarded in colorful and dramatic ceremonies under the **auspices**（预兆）of the Gorsedd of Bards of the Island of Britain, complete with prominent figures in Welsh cultural life dressed in flowing **druidic**（督伊德教的）costumes, flower dances, trumpet **fanfares**（吹牛）and a symbolic Horn of Plenty.

阅读辅助

威尔士的国际音乐节通常在每个8月的第一周举行,人们大都操着一口地道的威尔士方言。随着1959年的法案将这项庆典按照官方的要求进行组织,之后每年都吸引这世界上很多热爱音乐的人们齐聚于此,他们身着各种民族服饰,载歌载舞,各种民族音乐、歌曲、诗歌使得该地区热闹非凡。

读书笔记

4　情人节 *St. Valentine's Day*
　　——爱情见证之时

达人了解英美

◇ **History**

　　St. Valentine's Day began as a **liturgical**（礼拜仪式的）celebration of one or more early Christian saints named Valentinus. Several martyrdom stories were invented for the various Valentines that belonged to February 14, and added to **latermartyrologies**（殉教史）. popular hagiographical account of Saint Valentine of Rome states that he was imprisoned for performing weddings for soldiers who were forbidden to marry and for ministering to Christians, who were persecuted under the Roman Empire. According to legend, during his imprisonment, **he healed**（治愈）the daughter of his jailer, Asterius. An embellishment to this story states that before his execution he wrote her a letter signed "Your Valentine" as a farewell. Saint Valentine's Day is an official feast day in the Anglican Communion, as well as in the Lutheran Church. The Eastern Orthodox Church also celebrates Saint Valentine's Day, albeit on July 6 and July 30, the former date in honor of the Roman presbyter Saint Valentine, and the latter date in honor of Hieromartyr Valentine, the Bishop of Interamna (modern Terni). In Brazil, the Dia de São Valentim is recognized on June 12.

> **阅读辅助**
>
> 最有名的说法是在3世纪,古罗马暴君为了充实兵力,逼令所有单身男性公民从军,不许结婚。一名叫瓦伦丁的基督教修士不理禁令,秘密替人证婚,结果被士兵逮捕,269年2月14日被绞死;为纪念瓦伦丁的勇敢精神,人们将每年的2月14日定为瓦伦丁纪念日,成了后来的"情人节"。还有一种教宗说法是在496年废除牧神节,于是把2月14日定为圣瓦伦丁日,后来成为西方的节日之一。深受西方的文化影响,这个节日也逐渐在西方以外的地方受到注重。

◆ Traditions

The day was first associated with romantic love in the circle of Geoffrey Chaucer in the High Middle Ages, when the tradition of courtly love flourished. In 18th-century England, it evolved into an occasion in which lovers expressed their love for each other by presenting flowers, offering **confectionery**(糕点糖果), and sending greeting cards. In Europe, Saint Valentine's Keys are given to lovers "as a romantic symbol and an invitation to unlock the giver's heart", as well as to children, in order to ward off epilepsy. Valentine's Day symbols that are used today include the heart-shaped outline, doves, and the figure of the winged Cupid. Since the 19th century, handwritten **valentines**(情人) have given way to mass-produced greeting cards.

Valentine's Day customs developed in early modern England and spread throughout the Anglosphere in the 19th century. In the later 20th and early 21st centuries, these customs spread to other countries, but their effect has been more limited than those of Halloween, or than aspects of Christmas, Due to a concentrated marketing effort, Valentine's Day is celebrated in some East Asian countries with Chinese and South Koreans spending the most money on Valentine's gifts.

(英)独具特色的当地节日 **Section 7-1**

阅读辅助

中世纪的时候，情人节在英国最为流行。当时还流行一些风俗，比如他们把当地未婚男女的名字分别写在纸条上，把男女的姓名分别装在不同的盒子里。然后，未婚男女就开始到装着异性姓名的盒子里抽签。当名字被抽出后，他们会互相交换礼物。女子在这一年内成为男子的"Valentine"。女子还会在男子的衣袖上绣上女子的名字，照顾和保护该女子就成为该男子的神圣职责。情人节在18世纪的英格兰首次演变成情人之间用鲜花表达他们的情感，还有糖果盒贺卡。在欧洲还有人将圣瓦伦丁的钥匙给爱人作为解锁对方的心的意思。今天的情人节使用的专有符号是心形轮廓，里面有白鸽和长着翅膀的丘比特的图。

读书笔记

5. 耶稣受难日 *Good Friday*
——纪念耶稣生命中最高潮的一周

达人了解英美

✧ Etymology

The etymology of the term "good" in the context of Good Friday is contested. Some sources claim it is from the senses pious, holy of the word "good", while others contend that it is a corruption of "God Friday". The Oxford English Dictionary supports the first **etymology**（语源）, giving "of a day or season observed as holy by the church" as an archaic sense of good, and providing examples of good tide meaning "Christmas" or "Shrove Tuesday", and Good Wednesday meaning the Wednesday in Holy Week.

In German-speaking countries, the Good Friday is generally referred as Karfreitag: Mourning Friday.

阅读辅助

许多基督徒都会觉得"Good Friday"（中文无法直译，而是根据发生的事件直接译为"耶稣受难日"或"受难日"）这个名称不太合适。既然是耶稣钉十字架的日子，理应看作是"Bad Friday"。有人相信"Good"一词从"God"变化而来，本来意思是"God's Friday"（神的星期五）。还有人相信"Good"表示由耶稣殉教带来的拯救对世人是上好的馈赠。

✧ Biblical Accounts

According to the accounts in the Gospels, the Temple Guards, guided by Jesus' disciple Judas Iscariot, arrested Jesus in the Garden of Gethsemane. Judas received money for betraying Jesus and told the guards that whomever he kisses is the one they are to arrest. Following his arrest, Jesus was brought to the house of Annas, the father-in-law of the high priest, Caiaphas. There he was **interrogated**（询问）with little result and sent bound to Caiaphas the high priest where the Sanhedrin had assembled.

Pilate authorized the Jewish leaders to judge Jesus according to their own law and execute sentencing; however, the Jewish leaders replied that they were not allowed by the Romans to carry out a sentence of death. Pilate asked what they would have him do with Jesus, and they demanded, "Crucify him". Jesus **agonized**（苦闷的）on the cross for six hours. During his last three hours on the cross, from noon to 3 pm, darkness fell over the whole land.

Joseph of Arimathea took Jesus' body, wrapped it in a clean linen shroud, and placed it in his own new tomb that had been carved in the rock in a garden near the site of **crucifixion**（苦难）. On the third day, which is now known as Easter Sunday, Jesus rose from the dead.

阅读辅助

根据福音书记载，耶稣于公元33年犹太历尼散月十四日与门徒设立纪念仪式，耶稣是在其门徒犹大的出卖后被捕的，后于上午九时左右被钉在了十字架上，于下午三时左右死去。之后整个黑暗笼罩了大地。他的圣徒将耶稣的身体放到一个干净的亚麻裹尸布里并安防的坟墓中。但是第三天时耶稣死而复生，主耶稣基督唯独吩咐门徒要纪念他的死亡。

✧ Traditions

Many other Protestant communities hold special services on this day as well. Moravians hold a Lovefeast on Good Friday as they receive Holy Communion on Maundy Thursday. The Methodist Church commemorates Good Friday with a service of worship, often based on the Seven Last Words from the Cross. It is not uncommon for some communities to hold **interdenominational**（派系间的）services on Good Friday. Some Baptist, Pentecostal, many Sabbatarian and non-denominational churches oppose the observance of Good Friday, regarding it as a papist tradition, and instead observe the Crucifixion on Wednesday to **coincide**（符合）with the Jewish sacrifice of the Passover Lamb.

> **阅读辅助**
>
> 在早期的基督教会，只有纪念耶稣复活的星期日才是举行节庆活动的圣日。到了公元4世纪，复活节之前一周的每一天都被定为圣日，其中包括耶稣受难日。圣餐礼，是为纪念耶稣受难日而举行的一种仪式。

6 圣灵降临日 *Pentecost*
——圣灵浇灌的神圣时刻

> 达人了解英美

◆ **Date**

According to the current Jewish Calendar, the date of Pentecost is fifty days from Passover. In Christian tradition Pentecost is part of the Moveable Cycle of **theecclesiastical**（神职的）year. According to Christian tradition, Pentecost is always seven weeks after Easter Sunday; that is to say, 50 days after Easter. In other words, it falls on the eighth Sunday, counting Easter Day. Since the date of Easter is **calculated**（估计）differently in the East and West, in most years the two traditions celebrate Pentecost on different days.

For some Protestants, the nine days between Ascension Day, and Pentecost are set aside as a time of fasting, and world-wide prayer in honor of the disciples' time of prayer and unity awaiting the Holy Spirit. Similarly among Roman Catholics, special Pentecost Novenas are held. The Pentecost Novena is considered the first Novena, all other Novenas offered in preparation of various festivals and Saints days deriving their practice from those original nine days of prayer observed by the **disciples**（门徒）of Christ.

> 阅读辅助
>
> 犹太教按犹太历守节期，纪念以色列人出埃及后第五十天上帝在西奈山颁给摩西《十诫》的日子；基督教的圣灵降临节的日期则定在复活节后第50天和耶稣升天节后10天。因为计算复活节的日期东西

方存在差异，但是大多选东西方计算的时间能够吻合或相近的时间庆祝节日。对于新教徒来说，与耶稣升天节相隔是9天，而五旬节则留出这个时间禁食和祈祷。

✧ Celebration

The main sign of Pentecost in the West is the color red. It symbolizes joy and the fire of the Holy Spirit. Priests or ministers, and choirs wear red **vestments**（祭坛布）, and in modern times, the custom has extended to the lay people of the **congregation**（圣会）wearing red clothing in celebration as well. Red banners are often hung from walls or ceilings to symbolize the blowing of the "mighty wind" and the free movement of the Spirit.

The celebrations may depict symbols of the Holy Spirit, such as the dove or flames, symbols of the church such as Noah's Ark and the Pomegranate, or especially within Protestant churches of Reformed and Evangelical traditions, words rather than images naming for example, the gifts and Fruits of the Spirit. Red flowers at the altar/**preaching**（讲道）area, and red flowering plants such as geraniums around the church are also typical decorations for Pentecost masses/services. These symbolize the **renewal**（复兴）of life, the coming of the warmth of summer, and the growth of the church at and from the first Pentecost. These flowers often play an important role in the ancestral rites, and other rites, of the particular **congregation**（集会）. The singing of Pentecost **hymns**（赞美诗）is also central to the celebration in the Western tradition.

Since Pentecost itself is on a Sunday, it is automatically a public holiday in Christian countries. In the United Kingdom the day is known as Whit Monday, and was a bank holiday until 1967 when it was replaced by the Spring Bank Holiday on the last Monday in May.

In the north west of England, church and chapel parades called Whit Walks take place at Whitsun. Typically, the parades contain brass bands and choirs; girls attending are dressed in white. Traditionally, Whit Fairs took place. Other customs such as morris dancing and cheese rollingare also associated with Whitsun.

阅读辅助

五旬节的主要标志是红色，它象征欢快和圣灵之火。通常神职人员和唱诗班都会穿红色衣服庆祝。还会悬挂红色条幅，庆祝活动会有表示圣灵的鸽子或者火焰，还有教会的符号如诺亚方舟和石榴。另外教堂还会装饰红色的开花植物象征着复活。英国庆祝降临节的方式有所不同，但大致内容为：去教堂聚餐；演出取材于《圣经》故事的节目，或举行群众游艺及体育活动；集体长途步行，为慈善事业募捐；教堂向群众投掷面包和干酪等，有的村庄这天屠宰一只小羊，抬着游行，跳舞，然后把小羊烤熟，将肉卖给参加活动的群众。此风俗起源久远。据说该地过去没有水源，居民祈求上天后，忽然出现一道甘泉，于是他们便杀了小羊以供献给上天。

7 女王诞辰日 Queen's Birthday
——英国举国欢庆的国庆日

达人了解英美

✧ Origin

The sovereign's birthday was first officially marked in the United Kingdom in 1748. Since then, the date of the king or queen's birthday has been determined throughout the British Empire and later the Commonwealth according to either different royal **proclamations**（宣告）issued by the sovereign or governor or by statute laws passed by the local parliament. The exact date of the celebration today varies from country to country and, except by **coincidence**（巧合）, does not fall on the day of the monarch's actual birthday, that of the present monarch being 21 April. In some cases, it is an official public holiday, sometimes coinciding with the celebration of other events. Most Commonwealth **realms**（领域）release a Birthday Honours List at this time.

It has been celebrated in the United Kingdom since 1748. There, the Queen's Official Birthday is now celebrated on the first, second, or third Saturday in June, although it is rarely the third. Edward VII, who reigned from 1901 to 1910, and whose birthday was on 9 November, in autumn, after 1908 moved the ceremony to summer in the hope of good weather. In 2013, it was celebrated on 15 June, and was on 14 June in 2014.

(英)独具特色的当地节日　　Section 7-1

> **阅读辅助**
>
> 在英国,首次的英王的寿辰庆祝是在1748年开始的。自那时候起不论是国王或是女王都由皇室和英联邦政府根据情况而定。有时候那个日期不一定是英王的真正诞辰之日。如现今的英女王寿辰一般定于6月的第一、第二或第三个星期六,把寿辰定在6月是爱德华七世的主意,这是因为那时候英国的天气较好。

◆ Celebration

The day is marked in London by the ceremony of Trooping the Colour, which is also known as the Queen's Birthday Parade. The list of Birthday Honours is also announced at the time of the Official Birthday celebrations. In British diplomatic missions, the day is treated as the National Day of the United Kingdom. Although it is not celebrated as a specific public holiday in the UK (as it is not a working day), some civil servants are given a "privilege day" at this time of year, which is often merged with the Spring Bank Holiday (last Monday in May) to create a long weekend, which was partly created to celebrate the monarch's birthday.

> **阅读辅助**
>
> 在英国本土的英女王寿辰当日,伦敦市内会举行军旗敬礼分列式,政府会公布寿辰授勋名单,宣告新获勋人士的姓名及所得勋衔。在英国的驻外外交机构,官方寿辰当日会被视作英国的国庆日。由于英女王寿辰定于星期六,并非工作日,因此不属于公众假期;出于这个原因,公务员在每年5月最后一个星期一可获得一日"优待假期"作补偿,让他们可享受一连三天的周末假期。还有一些可以将春假一起放,甚至有时会是个长达一周的假期。

8 五朔节 May Day
——古老的春之节日

达人了解英美

◇ Origins

The earliest May Day celebrations appeared in pre-Christian times, with the Floralia, festival of Flora, the Roman goddess of flowers, held April 27 during the Roman Republic era, and with the Walpurg is Night celebrations of the Germanic countries. It is also associated with the Gaelic Beltane, most commonly held on April 30. The day was a traditional summer holiday in many pre-Christian European pagan cultures. While February 1 was the first day of Spring, May 1 was the first day of summer; hence, the summer **solstice**（至）on June 25 was Midsummer.

As Europe became Christianised, the pagan holidays lost their religious character and May Day changed into a popular **secular**（世代）celebration. A significant celebration of May Day occurs in Germany where it is one of several days on which St. Walburga, credited with bringing Christianity to Germany, is celebrated.

阅读辅助

最早的五朔节庆典出现在前基督时代，同时期还有罗马花朵女神佛洛拉的节日及沃普尔吉斯之夜。同时也与凯尔特人节日Beltane有关。春天的第一天是2月1日，而5月1日则标志夏天的开始，人们所以选择这一天来庆祝这段时间的辛苦劳作。随着欧洲国家的基督化，许多异教徒庆典在欧洲的转变过程中被舍弃或被基督教化。

✧ Celebrations

Traditional English May Day rites and celebrations include Morris dancing, crowning a May Queen and celebrations involving a maypole. Much of this tradition derives from the pagan Anglo-Saxon customs held during "Þrimilci-mōnaþ" (the Old English name for the month of May meaning Month of Three Milkings) along with many Celtic traditions.

May Day has been a traditional day of festivities throughout the centuries. May Day is most associated with towns and villages celebrating springtime fertility (of the soil, livestock, andpeople) and revelry with village fetes and community gatherings. Since the reform of the Catholic **calendar**（日历）, May 1 is the Feast of St Joseph the Worker, the patron saint of workers. Seeding has been completed by this date and it was **convenient**（方便的）to give farm laborers a day off. Perhaps the most significant of the traditions is the **maypole**（五朔节花柱）, around which traditional dancers circle with ribbons.

> **阅读辅助**
>
> 传统英国五朔节仪式及庆典包括跳莫里斯舞及加冕五月女王,还有涉及五朔节花柱的活动。大部分的传统是来自异教徒的盎格鲁-撒克逊传统习俗。五朔节庆祝春季的肥沃,村庄居民聚在一起举行宴会。自从天主教历法的改革后,最著名的可能是舞者身系彩带围着五朔节花柱的传统。现在这个传统的节日成为国际性的节假日而被人们庆祝着。

✧ History

May Day was abolished and its celebration banned by puritan parliaments during the Interregnum, but reinstated with the restoration of Charles II in 1660. May 1, 1707, was the day the Act of Union came into effect, joining England and Scotland to form the Kingdom of Great Britain.

The May Day bank holiday, on the first Monday in May, was traditionally the only one to affect the state school calendar, although new arrangements in some areas to even out the length of school terms mean that Good Friday and Easter Monday, which vary from year to year, may also fall during term time. The Spring Bank Holiday on the first Monday in May was created in 1978; May Day itself – May 1 – is not a public holiday in England. In February 2011, the UK Parliament was reported to be considering **scrapping**（使解体）the bank holiday associated with May Day, replacing it with a bank holiday in October, possibly **coinciding**（同时发生）with Trafalgar Day, to create a "United Kingdom Day."

阅读辅助

五朔节曾被清教徒议会废除过，庆典也被禁止了，但随着查理二世于1660年的复辟而又再次恢复。1707年5月1日，使英格兰与苏格兰结合的联合法令生效。五朔节假日，5月的第一个星期一，从传统上来说是唯一影响到公立学校传统节日，所以一些学校试图平均学期的新安排使得原本不固定的耶稣受难节及复活节星期一公共假日也有可能落在这段时间内。于是五朔节假日于1978年创立，但是实际上它仍不是英国的公共假期。直到2011年英国议会还是考虑是否要将其取消，或改在10月的某一天和特拉法尔纪念日和在一起，创建个"英国日"。

9. 烟火节 Guy Fawkes Day
——英国最美的夜晚

达人了解英美

◆ History

Guy Fawkes Night originates from the Gunpowder Plot of 1605, a failed **conspiracy**（阴谋）by a group of provincial English Catholics to assassinate the Protestant King James I of England and replace him with a Catholic head of state. In the immediate **aftermath**（后果）of the 5 November arrest of Guy Fawkes, caught guarding a cache of explosives placed beneath the House of Lords, James's Council allowed the public to celebrate the king's survival with bonfires, so long as they were "without any danger or disorder". This made 1605 the first year the plot's failure was celebrated. Celebrating the fact that King James I had survived the attempt on his life, people lit bonfires around London, and months later the introduction of the Observance of 5th November Act enforced an annual public day of thanksgiving for the plot's failure.

阅读辅助

"盖伊福克斯之夜"，在英国已有400多年的历史。1605年，罗马天主教徒盖伊·福克斯及其同伙因为不满国王詹姆士一世的对新教徒政策，企图炸死国王，并炸毁议会大厦。但是密谋被泄露了，一个卫兵发现了盖伊·福克斯，在严刑拷打下盖伊·福克斯招供了一切。当时炸药已经放置到位了。之后国王提出允许公众燃放烟火来庆祝，之后将这个庆祝活动的日子，定为节日来感谢阴谋的失败。

✧ Celebrations

Little is known about the earliest celebrations. In **settlements**（殖民地）such as Carlisle, Norwich and Nottingham, corporations provided music and **artillery**（火炮）salutes. Canterbury celebrated 5 November 1607 with 106 pounds of gunpowder and 14 pounds of match, and three years later food and drink was provided for local **dignitaries**（显要人物）, as well as music, explosions and a parade by the local militia. Even less is known of how the occasion was first **commemorated**（纪念）by the general public, although records indicate that in Protestant Dorchester a sermon was read, the church bells rung, and bonfires and fireworks lit.

One notable aspect of the Victorians' commemoration of Guy Fawkes Night was its move away from the centers of communities, to their margins. Gathering wood for the bonfire increasingly became the province of working-class children, who solicited **combustible**（易燃物）materials, money, food and drink from wealthier neighbors, often with the aid of songs. Most opened with the familiar "Remember, remember, the fifth of November, Gunpowder Treason and Plot".

Organized entertainments also became popular in the late 19th century, and 20th-century **pyrotechnic**（烟火的）manufacturers renamed Guy Fawkes Day as Firework Night. Sales of fireworks dwindled somewhat during the First World War, but resumed in the following peace. For many families, Guy Fawkes Night became a domestic celebration, and children often **congregated**（聚集）on street corners, accompanied by their own effigy of Guy Fawkes.

阅读辅助

最早的庆祝活动甚少被人们知晓，那是在殖民地举行火炮致敬。还有一次是在1607年在坎特伯雷的庆祝活动，用了106磅的火药，当地政府提供食品和饮料以及音乐，方便人们游行庆祝。

英国将11月5日命名为"盖伊·福克斯之夜"。英格兰许多地方

> 政府会组织盛大的烟花表演，人们也会点燃篝火，把英国叛国者盖伊·福克斯的人物模型扔到火中付之一炬。在这个夜晚，一个重要的内容就是烧掉"盖伊"假人。在篝火之夜，人们还会准备丰盛的美食，称为"篝火之夜食谱"。食谱中包括太妃糖、太妃糖苹果、带皮烤土豆和加香料的热葡萄酒。

✧ Significance

Within a few decades Gunpowder Treason Day, as it was known, became the predominant English state commemoration, but as it carried strong religious overtones it also became a focus for anti-Catholic sentiment. Puritans delivered sermons regarding the **perceived**（感知）dangers of popery, while during increasingly raucous celebrations common folk burnt effigies of popular hate-figures, such as the pope. Towards the end of the 18th century reports appear of children begging for money with effigies of Guy Fawkes and 5 November gradually became known as Guy Fawkes Day. Towns such as Lewes and Guildford were in the 19th century scenes of increasingly violent class-based **confrontations**（对抗），fostering traditions those towns celebrate still, albeit peaceably. In the 1850s changing attitudes resulted in the toning down of much of the day's anti-Catholic rhetoric, and the Observance of 5th November Act was repealed in 1859. Eventually the violence was dealt with, and by the 20th century Guy Fawkes Day had become an enjoyable social commemoration, although lacking much of its original focus. The present-day Guy Fawkes Night is usually celebrated at large organized events, centered on a bonfire and **extravagant**（浪费的）firework displays.

阅读辅助

人们最初庆祝这一节日是为了维护对宗教和国家的忠诚，它是一个政治性节日。人们最初庆祝这一节日是为了维护对宗教和国家的忠诚，它是一个政治性节日，充斥着反对天主教的色彩。在几个世纪里，这个传统跨越大洋，在英国的殖民地得到传播。例如在新西兰，最晚到18世纪后，这个节日开始作为"教皇日"被庆祝。随着时代的进步，这一节日的政治色彩已不那么浓郁了，节日充满快乐和愉悦的气氛。

读书笔记

Section 7-2　（美）独具特色的当地节日

美国，是个仅有百年历史的国家。或许由于它是个年轻的移民国家，所以他们的节日有他们自己的特点，想要了解美国的本土节日就要先了解他们的民族精神——自由、自立、和自我完善等等，还要正确了解美国的价值观如"平等""竞争"等等。因为美国的特色节日大多是在这些精神和价值观基础上随着国家的发展逐渐形成的。

1. 美国独立日 *Independence Day*
——通过《独立宣言》的这一天

达人了解英美

◇ **Background**

During the American Revolution, the legal separation of the Thirteen Coloniesfrom Great Britain occurred on July 2, 1776, when the Second Continental Congress voted to approve a resolution of independence that had been proposed in June by Richard Henry Lee of Virginia declaring the United States independent from Great Britain. After voting for independence, Congress turned its attention to the Declaration of Independence, a statement explaining this decision, which had been prepared by a Committee of Five, with Thomas Jefferson as its principal author. Adams's prediction was off by two days. From the outset, Americans celebrated independence on July 4, the date shown on the much-publicized Declaration of Independence, rather than on July 2, the date the resolution of independence was approved in a closed session of Congress.

Coincidentally, both John Adams and Thomas Jefferson, the only signers of the Declaration of Independence later to serve as Presidents of the United States, died on the same day: July 4, 1826, which was the 50th **anniversary**(周年纪念日)of the Declaration. Although not a signer of the Declaration of Independence, but another Founding Father who became a President, James Monroe, died on July 4, 1831, thus becoming the third President in a row who died on the holiday.

> **阅读辅助**
>
> 美国革命期间，第二届大陆会议表决通过弗吉尼亚州的理查德·亨利·李提出的一项宣示独立决定的提案时，十三个殖民地已在法理上脱离英国。独立宣言由五人委员会准备，最终在7月4日得以通过。于是美国人就按照《独立宣言》上记录的日期7月4日庆祝美国独立。

◆ Customs

Independence Day is a national holiday marked by **patriotic**（爱国的）displays. Similar to other summer-themed events, Independence Day celebrations often take place outdoors. Independence Day is a federal holiday, so all non-essential federal institutions are closed on that day. Many politicians make it a point on this day to appear at a public event to praise the nation's **heritage**（传统）, laws, history, society, and people. Families often celebrate Independence Day by hosting or attending a picnic or barbecue and take advantage of the day off and, in some years, long weekend to gather with relatives. Decorationsare generally colored red, white, and blue, the colors of the American flag. **Parades**（游行）are often in the morning, while fireworks displays occur in the evening at such places as parks, fairgrounds, or town squares.

Independence Day fireworks are often accompanied by patriotic songs such as the national anthem "The Star-Spangled Banner" "God Bless America" "America the Beautiful" "My Country, 'Tis of Thee" "This Land Is Your Land" "Stars and Stripes Forever", and, regionally, "Yankee Doodle" in northeastern states and "Dixie" in southern states. Some of the lyrics recall images of the Revolutionary War or the War of 1812.

> 阅读辅助
>
> 在7月4日这一天，美国会举办许多活动，其中最重要的就是敲响位于费城的自由钟。在各地也会举行各项庆祝活动，像是放烟火、花车游行、节日游行、烧烤、野餐、举办音乐会、棒球赛、以及家庭聚会等。

✧ Unique or Historical Celebrations

• Held since 1785, the Bristol Fourth of July Parade in Bristol, Rhode Island is the oldest continuous Independence Day celebration in the United States.

• Since 1972, Nathan's Hot Dog Eating Contest has been held in Coney Island, Brooklyn, New York City.

• Since 1959, the International Freedom Festival is jointly held in Detroit, Michigan and Windsor, Ontario during the last week of June each year as a **mutual**（相互的）celebration of Independence Day and Canada Day).

• Numerous major and minor **league**（联盟）baseball games are played on Independence Day.

• The famous Macy's fireworks display usually held over the East River in New York City has been televised nationwide on NBC since 1976.

• Since 1970, the annual 10-kilometer Peachtree Road Race is held in Atlanta, Georgia.

• On the Capitol lawn in Washington, D.C., A Capitol Fourth, a free concert broadcast live by PBS, NPR and the American Forces Network, precedes the fireworks and **attracts**（吸引）over half a million people annually.

> 阅读辅助
>
> 美国不同地方利用自身的特色活动表示对美国独立日的庆贺。

2 马丁·路德金日 *Martin Luther King, Jr. Day*
——唯一一个纪念美国黑人的联邦假日

达人了解英美

◇ History

The idea of Martin Luther King, Jr. Day as a holiday was promoted by labor unions in contract **negotiations**（磋商）. After King's death, U.S. Representative John Conyers and U.S. Senator Edward Brooke introduced a bill in Congress to make King's birthday a national holiday. The bill first came to a vote in the U.S. House of Representatives in 1979. Soon after, the King Center turned to support from the corporate community and the general public. The success of this strategy was **cemented**（巩固）when musician Stevie Wonder released the single "Happy Birthday" to popularize the campaign in 1980 and hosted the Rally for Peace Press Conference in 1981. Six million **signatures**（签名）were collected for a petition to Congress to pass the law, termed by a 2006 article in The Nation as "the largest **petition**（请愿）in favor of an issue in U.S. history." At the White House Rose Garden on November 2, 1983, President Ronald Reagan signed a bill, proposed by Representative Katie Hall of Indiana, creating a federal holiday to honor King. It was observed for the first time on January 20, 1986.

阅读辅助

金牧师遇刺后，美国众议院会员John Conyers提出法案，设立金牧师的生日为联邦假日，缺了五票未过。投票失败之后，转向请求私人公司和公民支持，举行了和平集会请愿国会通过法律。这是

> 美国有史以来最大的一次请愿事件。1983年11月2日，美国总统里根在白宫玫瑰花园签订法案，建立联邦假日纪念金牧师。第一次放假是1986年1月20日。

◇ Alternative Names

While all states now observe the holiday, some did not name the day after King. For example, in Utah, the holiday was known as "Human Rights Day" until 2000, when the Utah State Legislature voted to change the name of the holiday from Human Rights Day to Martin Luther King Jr. Day. In that same year, Governor Michael O. Leavitt signed the bill officially naming the holiday "Martin Luther King Jr. Day". In Alabama, Martin Luther King Jr. Day is known as "Robert E. Lee/Martin Luther King Birthday". In Arizona, Martin Luther King, Jr. Day is known as "Martin Luther King Jr./Civil Rights Day". In Idaho, Martin Luther King, Jr. Day is known as "Martin Luther King Jr.-Idaho Human Rights Day". In New Hampshire, its official name is "Martin Luther King Jr. Civil Rights Day".

> **阅读辅助**
> 虽然现在美国所有的州都放此假日，但有些州并没有以金牧师命名。在犹他州，直到2000年州议院投票改名，这个假日称为"人权节"，在弗吉尼亚州，它的名字是"李－杰克森－金纪念日"。

◇ King Day of Service

The national Martin Luther King Day of Service was started by former Pennsylvania U.S. Senator Harris Wofford and Atlanta Congressman John, who co-authored the King Holiday and Service Act. The federal legislation challenges Americans to transform the King Holiday into a day of citizen action volunteer service in honor of Dr. King. The federal legislation was signed into law by President Bill Clinton on August 23, 1994. Since 1996, Wofford's former state office director, Todd Bernstein, has been directing the annual Greater Philadelphia King Day of Service, the largest event in the nation honoring Dr. King.

Several other universities and organizations around the U.S., such as Arizona State University, Greater DC Cares and City Year, participate in the Dr. Martin Luther King Jr. Day of Service. In honor of MLK, hundreds of Volunteer Centers, and volunteers across the country **donate**（捐赠）their time to make a difference on this day.

> **阅读辅助**
>
> 前宾夕法尼亚州参议员 Harris Wofford 和亚特兰大众议员 John Lewis 提议联邦法案 "King Holiday and Service Act"，建议把这个假日作为一个为公民服务的时间，以此纪念金牧师。1994年8月23日由总统比尔·克林顿签为法律。从1996年开始，费城地区的服务日是全美国最大的服务活动。

3　复活节 *Easter Day*
——象征着重生与希望的节日

达人了解英美

◇ Origin

Easter, also called Pasch or Resurrection Sunday, is a festival and holiday celebrating the resurrection of Jesus Christ from the dead, described in the New Testament as having occurred three days after his crucifixion by Romans at Calvary. It is the culmination of the Passion of Christ, preceded by Lent, a forty-day period of fasting, prayer, and penance.

The week before Easter is called Holy Week, and it contains the days of the Easter Triduum, including Maundy Thursday, commemorating the Last Supper and its preceding foot washing, as well as Good Friday, commemorating the **crucifixion**（苦难）and death of Jesus. In western Christianity, Eastertide, the Easter Season, begins on Easter Sunday and lasts seven weeks, ending with the coming of the fiftieth day, Pentecost Sunday. In Orthodoxy, the season of Pascha begins on Pascha and ends with the coming of the **fortieth**（第四十）day, the Feast of the **Ascension**（耶稣升天）.

阅读辅助

耶稣被钉死在十字架上，第三天身体复活，复活节因此得名。复活节是基督宗教最重大的节日，复活节前日即复活节前的星期六。在天主教徒心中，是等待耶稣基督自死中复活的日子。当日天主教会不举行弥撒，直到晚上才举行隆重的至圣之夜逾越节守夜礼（Easter Vigil），庆祝基督战胜罪恶和死亡，为人类带来救恩和希望。

✧ Custom

Easter is linked to the Jewish Passover by much of its symbolism, as well as by its position in the calendar. In many languages, the words for "Easter" and "Passover" are identical or very similar. Easter customs vary across the Christian world, and include sunrise services, exclaiming the Paschal greeting, clipping the church, and decorating Easter eggs, a symbol of the empty tomb. The Easter lily, a symbol of the **resurrection**（复活）, traditionally decorates the chancel area of churches on this day and for the rest of Eastertide. Additional customs that have become associated with Easter and are observed by both Christians and some non-Christians include egg hunting, theEaster Bunny, and Easter parades. There are also various traditional Easter foods that vary **regionally**（地域性地）.

> **阅读辅助**
>
> 在西方，与复活节相关的物品有复活节兔和复活节彩蛋。传说复活节彩蛋都是兔子的蛋（但事实上，兔子其实是不下蛋的，所以复活节彩蛋其实都是鸡蛋），有些人喜欢在蛋上画各种各样的鬼脸或花纹。而这些民间风俗都不是起源于基督教的。

✧ Celebrate

In countries where Christianity is a state religion, or where the country has large Christian population, Easter is often a public holiday. As Easter is always a Sunday, many countries in the world also have Easter Monday as a public holiday. Some retail stores, shopping malls, and restaurants are closed on Easter Sunday. Good Friday, which occurs two days before Easter Sunday, is also a public holiday in many countries, as well as in 12 U.S. states. Even in states where Good Friday is not a holiday, many financial institutions, stock markets, and public schools are closed. Few banks that are normally open on regular Sundays are closed on Easter.

In the United States, because Easter falls on a Sunday, which is already a non-working day for federal and state employees, it has not been designated as a federal or state holiday. Easter parades are held in many American cities, involving festive strolling processions, with the New York City parade being the best known.

> **阅读辅助**
>
> 在多数西方国家里，复活节一般要举行盛大的宗教游行，在美国至少政府法定假日里是没有复活节的。可能因为总是在周日的缘故，在美国从来没有因为这个节放过假。

◆ Easter Eggs

Easter eggs are specially decorated eggs given out to celebrate the Easter holiday. The custom of the Easter egg may have existed in the early Christian community of Mesopotamia, who stained eggs red in memory of the blood of Christ, shed at his crucifixion. In later traditions the egg is also a symbol of the empty tomb. The oldest tradition is to use dyed chicken eggs, but a modern custom is to **substitute**（替代）eggs made from chocolate, or plastic eggs filled with candy such as jellybeans.

Many Americans follow the tradition of coloring hard-boiled eggs and giving baskets of candy. The Easter Bunny is a popular legendary anthropomorphic Easter gift-giving character **analogous**（类似的）to Santa Claus in American culture. On Easter Monday, the President of the United States holds an annual Easter egg roll on the White House lawn for young children. Easter eggs are a widely popular symbol of new life in Poland and other Slavic countries' folk traditions. A batik-like decorating process known as pisanka produces intricate, brilliantly-colored eggs. The celebrated House of Fabergé workshops created exquisite jewelled eggs for the Russian Imperial Court.

阅读辅助

复活节彩蛋是为了给人们带来快乐——确实如此！这些彩蛋精美漂亮且富有装饰性，它们代表着人们的美好心愿，并与你分享季节更替的喜悦。

读书笔记

4 华盛顿诞辰日 *Washington's Birthday*
——美国的"总统日"

达人了解英美

◆ **History**

The federal holiday honoring George Washington was originally implemented by an Act of Congress in 1879 for government offices in Washington and expanded in 1885 to include all federal offices. As the first federal holiday to honor an American president, the holiday was celebrated on Washington's actual birthday, February 22. On January 1, 1971, the federal holiday was shifted to the third Monday in February by the Uniform Monday Holiday Act. This date places it between February 15 and 21, which makes the name "Washington's Birthday" in some sense a **misnomer** (误称), since it never occurs on Washington's actual birthday, either February 11, or February 22.

An early draft of the Uniform Monday Holiday Act would have renamed the holiday to "Presidents' Day" to honor the birthdays of both Washington and Lincoln, which would explain why the chosen date falls between the two, but this proposal failed in committee, and the bill was voted on and signed into law on June 28, 1968, keeping the name as Washington's Birthday. By the mid-1980s, with a push from advertisers, the term "Presidents' Day" began its public appearance. In Washington's adopted hometown of Alexandria, Virginia, celebrations are held throughout the month of February.

> **阅读辅助**
>
> 美国独立前，人们每年都要为英国国王庆祝诞辰。宣布独立后，美国人民转而庆祝华盛顿将军的生日。原先就是指名庆祝华盛顿生日，而美国的第16任总统林肯是在2月份出生，就提议把"华盛顿诞辰纪念日"改为"总统节"，同时庆祝这两位总统的2月生日。

◇ Traditions

Today, the February holiday has become well known for being a day in which many stores, especially car dealers, hold sales. Consequently, some schools, which used to close for a single day for both Lincoln's and Washington's birthday, now often close for the entire week as a "mid-winter recess". The federal holiday Washington's Birthday honors the accomplishments of the man known as "The Father of his Country". Celebrated for his leadership in the founding of the nation, he was the Electoral College's **unanimous**（无异议的）choice to become the first President; he was seen as a unifying force for the new republic and set an example for future holders of the office.

The holiday is also a **tribute**（贡物）to the general who created the first military badge of merit for the common soldier. Revived on Washington's 200th birthday in 1932, the Purple Heart medal is awarded to soldiers who are injured in battle. As with Memorial Day and Veterans Day, Washington's Birthday offers another opportunity to honor the country's veterans. Community celebrations often display a **lengthy**（冗长的）heritage. Washington's hometown of historic Alexandria, Virginia, hosts a month-long tribute, including the longest running George Washington Birthday parade, while the community of Eustis, Florida, continues its annual "George Fest" celebration begun in 1902. Since 1862 there has been a tradition in the United States Senate that George Washington's Farewell Address be read on his birthday. Citizens had asked that this be done in light of the approaching

Civil War. The annual tradition continues with the reading of the address on or near Washington's Birthday.

> **阅读辅助**
>
> 现在华盛顿诞辰日已成为联邦各州的法定节日,届时各州都普遍举行隆重的公众仪式、盛大宴会等庆祝活动。美国人在这一天还喜欢吃樱桃馅饼,玩纸制小斧,这一习俗来源于华盛顿幼小时用斧砍坏樱桃树后向其父诚实认错的故事。

5 美国阵亡将士纪念日 *Memorial Day*
——展现爱国情操的重要节日

达人了解英美

◇ **History**

The practice of decorating soldiers' graves with flowers is an ancient custom. Soldiers' graves were decorated in the U.S. before and during the American Civil War. A claim was made in 1906 that the first Civil War soldier's grave ever decorated was in Warrenton, Virginia, on June 3, 1861, implying the first Memorial Day occurred there. Though not for Union soldiers, there is **authentic**（真正的）documentation that women in Savannah, Georgia, decorated Confederate soldiers' graves in 1862. In 1863, the cemetery dedication at Gettysburg, Pennsylvania, was a ceremony of commemoration at the graves of dead soldiers. Local historians in Boalsburg, Pennsylvania, claim that ladies there decorated soldiers' graves on July 4, 1864. As a result, Boalsburg promotes itself as the birthplace of Memorial Day.

Following President Abraham Lincoln's assassination in April 1865, there were a variety of events of commemoration. The sheer number of soldiers of both sides who died in the Civil War, more than 600,000, meant that burial and memorialization took on new cultural significance. Under the leadership of women during the war, an increasingly formal practice of decorating graves had taken shape. In 1865, the federal government began creating national military cemeteries for the Union war dead. The first widely-publicized observance of a Memorial Day-type observance after the Civil War was in Charleston, South Carolina, on May 1, 1865. During the war, Union soldiers who were prisoners of war had been held at the Hampton Park Race Course in Charleston; at least 257 Union prisoners died there and were **hastily**（匆忙地）buried in unmarked graves.

> **阅读辅助**
>
> 1866年，在南北战争结束后不久，有人提议全城商铺关门一天，为在战争中牺牲的将士们默哀。这一提议得到了人们的支持，同一年5月5日，该镇正式举办了纪念活动，人们将花圈十字架放在士兵的墓碑前。同一天，乔纳森·洛根将军宣布5月30日将会是一个纪念在战争中牺牲的士兵的日子。

◇ Name and Date

The preferred name for the holiday gradually changed from "Decoration Day" to "Memorial Day", which was first used in 1882. It did not become more common until after World War II, and was not declared the official name by Federal law until 1967. On June 28, 1968, the Congress passed the Uniform Monday Holiday Act, which moved four holidays, including Memorial Day, from their traditional dates to a specified Monday in order to create a convenient three-day weekend. The change moved Memorial Day from its traditional May 30 date to the last Monday in May. The law took effect at the federal level in 1971. After some initial confusion and **unwillingness**（不情愿）to comply, all 50 states adopted Congress' change of date within a few years. Memorial Day endures as a holiday which most businesses observe because it marks the unofficial beginning of summer.

> **阅读辅助**
>
> 最初被称为装饰日，老兵和市民一起，在这一天为那些为国捐躯的将士们扫墓，1873年，纽约州政府开始官方承认纪念阵亡将士，当然这个日期得到了北方各州的认可。南方并不认同这一天，于是各自公祭，为了让更多的人能够方便的纪念这一天，联邦政府将其定为国家节日，并将日期定为5月的最后一个星期一。

◇ Traditions

On Memorial Day, the flag of the United States is raised **briskly**（尖刻地）to the top of the staff and then solemnly lowered to the half-staff position, where it remains only until noon. It is then raised to full-staff for the **remainder**（残余）of the day. The half-staff position remembers the more than one million men and women who gave their lives in service of their country. At noon, their memory is raised by the living, who resolve not to let their sacrifice be in vain, but to rise up in their stead and continue the fight for liberty and justice for all.

The National Memorial Day Concert takes place on the west lawn of the United States Capitol. The concert is broadcast on PBS and NPR. Music is performed, and respect is paid to the men and women who gave their lives for their country. For many Americans, the central event is attending one of the thousands of parades held on Memorial Day in large and small cities all over the country. Most of these feature marching bands and an overall military theme with the National Guard and other servicemen participating along with veterans and military vehicles from various wars.

> **阅读辅助**
>
> 这一天最重要的活动为纪念在战争中死去的美军将士。人们将在士兵的墓碑前放上花圈和旗帜，政府部门将会降下半旗，一些小镇将会组织游行队伍，人们会穿上南北战争时期的军人服装。美国总统或副总统会在阿灵顿国家公墓主持纪念活动并发表演说。

6 感恩节 Thanksgiving Day
——是美国人民独创的一个古老节日

达人了解英美

◆ **Background**

Thanksgiving Day has been an annual holiday in the United States since 1863. Not everyone sees Thanksgiving Day as a cause for celebration. Each year since 1970, a group of Native Americans and their supporters have staged a protest for a National Day of Mourning at Plymouth Rock in Plymouth, Massachusetts on Thanksgiving Day. American Indian Heritage Day is also observed at this time of the year.

There are claims that the first Thanksgiving Day was held in the city of El Paso, Texas in 1598. Another early event was held in 1619 in the Virginia Colony. Many people trace the origins of the modern Thanksgiving Day to the harvest celebration that the Pilgrims held in Plymouth, Massachusetts in 1621. However, their first true thanksgiving was in 1623, when they gave thanks for rain that ended a **drought**（缺乏）. These early thanksgivings took the form of a special church service, rather than a feast.

In the second half of the 1600s, thanksgivings after the harvest became more common and started to become annual events. However, it was celebrated on different days in different communities and in some places there were more than one thanksgiving each year. George Washington, the first president of the United States, **proclaimed**（公告）the first national Thanksgiving Day in 1789.

> **阅读辅助**
>
> 源于1620年，五月花号船满载英国受迫害的清教徒到达美洲。当年冬天，不少人饥寒交迫，染病身亡。在印第安人帮助下，新移民学会了狩猎、种植玉米、南瓜，并在来年迎来了丰收。他们邀请印第安人庆祝节日，感谢其帮助。联合国总部于感恩节当天放假。

◆ Custom

Thanksgiving Day is traditionally a day for families and friends to get together for a special meal. The meal often includes a turkey, stuffing, potatoes, **cranberry**（蔓越橘）sauce, gravy, pumpkin pie, and vegetables. Thanksgiving Day is a time for many people to give thanks for what they have.

Thanksgiving Day parades are held in some cities and towns on or around Thanksgiving Day. Some parades or festivities also mark the opening of the Christmas shopping season. Some people have a four-day weekend so it is a popular time for trips and to visit family and friends.

> **阅读辅助**
>
> 在风俗习惯上食俗有：吃烤火鸡、南瓜饼红莓苔子果酱、甜山芋、玉蜀黍；活动有：玩蔓越桔竞赛、玉米游戏、南瓜赛跑；举行化装游行、戏剧表演或体育比赛等集体活动，并有相应的假期2天，在远方的人们都会回家与亲人团聚。现在还形成了豁免火鸡、黑色星期五购物等习惯。

◆ Historical Menus

According to what traditionally is known as "The First Thanksgiving", the 1621 feast between the Pilgrims and the Wampanoag at Plymouth Colony contained turkey, waterfowl, venison, fish, lobster, clams, berries, fruit, pumpkin, and squash. William Bradford noted that, "besides waterfowl, there was great store of wild turkeys, of which they took many." Many of the foods that were included in the first feast (except, notably, the seafood) have since gone on to become staples of the modern Thanksgiving dinner.

The use of the turkey in the USA for Thanksgiving precedes Lincoln's **nationalization**（国有化）of the holiday in 1863. Alexander Hamilton proclaimed that no "Citizen of the United States should refrain from turkey on Thanksgiving Day", and many of the Founding Fathers (particularly Benjamin Franklin) had high regard for the wild turkey as an American icon, but turkey was uncommon as Thanksgiving fare until after 1800. By 1857, turkey had become part of the traditional dinner in New England.

> **阅读辅助**
>
> 感恩节的晚宴是美国人一年中很重视的一餐。这一餐的食物非常之丰富。在餐桌上，火鸡和南瓜饼都是必备的。感恩节的传统食品还有甜山芋、玉蜀黍、南瓜饼、红莓苔子果酱、自己烘烤的面包及各种蔬菜和水果等。

7 万圣节 *Halloween*
—— "Trick or treat" 捣蛋鬼们的狂欢节

达人了解英美

✧ Origin

The original source of Halloween is believed to be of pagan tradition, although many believe the Christian celebrations came first. These festivals often honored gods of fruits, such as the Roman Pomona. Others, like the festival of Parentalia, may have honored the deceased.

There were several legends associated with Samhain due to the believed opening of the underworld: The body parts of those who had died since the last Halloween would become **animated**（活生生的）and possess the living. This is why many observers would **extinguish**（熄灭）fire inside of their house and purposely make it very cold so that spirits would not be drawn there.

Halloween also borrows elements from the Christian tradition. The name comes from All Hallows Eve, the day that Christians spent honoring the deceased and the saints. As a Holy Day of Obligation, some observers honor those in purgatory by ringing bells. Many Halloween traditions come from a mixture of these Christian and pagan traditions. The influx of Irish and Scottish immigrants during the 19th century brought the celebration to America. The traditions and imagery of Halloween are largely adopted from horror stories and gothic works—ghosts, vampires, other monsters, haunted houses, skeletons.

> **阅读辅助**
>
> 万圣夜起源于不列颠凯尔特人的传统节日，在10月的最后一天，他们相信这是夏天的终结，冬天的开始，这一天是一年的重要标志，是最重要的节日之一，被称为"死人之日"，或者"鬼节"。这一天各种恶鬼出没，死去人们的灵魂也会离开身体，在世间游走，这一天的晚上也就格外危险。为了吓走邪恶的鬼魂，凯尔特人会戴上面具。

✧ Special Object

Jack-o-lanterns were carved to light nighttime paths and protect from these evil spirits. The carved pumpkin's namesake comes from the legend that a boy named Jack paraded through the town with a pumpkin in which he'd trapped the devil. The devil curses Jack upon his release and **condemns**（谴责）him to spend forever in hell. When the gates open on Halloween, Jack would escape hell to wreak **havoc**（浩劫）upon the town. The Jack-o-Lanterns were supposed to trick Jack into thinking it held the devil, scaring him off.

The practice of dressing up in costumes and begging door to door for treats on holidays dates back to the Middle Ages and includes Christmas **wassailing**（痛饮）. Trick-or-treating resembles the late medieval Christian practice of souling, when poor folk would go door to door on Hallowmas, receiving food in return for prayers for the dead on All Souls Day. It originated in Ireland and Britain, although similar practices for the souls of the dead were found as far south as Italy.

> **阅读辅助**
>
> 杰克灯是万圣夜最广为人知的象征物。在英国和爱尔兰，当地人原本在挖空的芜菁中燃点蜡烛造成杰克灯，但移民到美国的人很快便采用南瓜代替，因为南瓜比较大和容易在上面雕刻图案。万圣夜的主要活动是"不给糖就捣蛋"。

◇ Traditions

Trick-or-Treating is the practice of children dressing up in costume to ring doorbells for candy. When the door opens, they will say, "Trick or treat? Give me something good to eat," which is sometimes followed by, "if you don't, I don't care, I'll pull down your underwear!"

Some children may opt to collect for charity, such as the UNICEF coin boxes that observers can donate change into as the child collects candy. Children will often dress in a Halloween **costume**（装束）, such as a witch or a ghost. They may choose instead to dress of as a fictional or real figure they admire. For example, they may choose to emulate figures like Batman and Abraham Lincoln rather than something with an evil theme.

In the theme of a festival, carnival-esque gamers were held, many with pagan origins—bobbing for apples, not tossing peels over your shoulder. Activities related to divination or ghost hunting. Those interested in this aspect may hold a séance or explore **haunted**（闹鬼的）houses. Recreational activities like hay rides and corn mazes.

> **阅读辅助**
>
> 除了孩子们的Trick or treat之外，还有一些节日特色游戏，其中最常见的就是"咬苹果"，还有说鬼故事及看恐怖片是万圣夜派对中常见的活动。

◇ Food

Making and eating candied apples is popular. Apples are harvested right before Halloween. Especially Irish-Americans, observers may eat a type of fruit cake containing a coin. Those who received the piece with the coin were given good luck for the rest of the year.

On All Hallows' Eve, many Western Christian denomination encourage **abstinence**（禁食）, giving rise to a variety of vegetarian foods associated with this day. Because in the Northern Hemisphere Halloween comes in the wake of the yearly apple harvest, caramel or taffy apples are common Halloween treats made by rolling whole apples in a sticky sugar syrup, sometimes followed by rolling them in nuts.

阅读辅助

由于万圣夜临近苹果的丰收期，太妃糖苹果（toffee apples）成为应节食品。万圣节的传统食物是苹果汁、爆玉米花、南瓜馅饼和女巫状的香料生姜饼等。

8 圣诞节 Christmas Day
——美国庆祝圣人诞生的节日

达人了解英美

✧ Christmas Story

It is believed that Jesus was born sometime between 7 and 2 BC. Two of the four **canonical**（牧师礼服）gospels mention his birth, although it is not believed to have actually taken place on the date of Christmas. Rather, the holiday began to take place during the time of the winter solstice in order to distract from and absorb the pagan festivals associated the time of year.

Christians celebrate the birth of Jesus and the fulfillment of the Messianic **prophecy**（预言）. The two **biblical**（圣经的）accounts from Luke and Matthew have evolved into a popular tradition of the tale, stating that Joseph and Mary traveled to Bethlehem on a donkey in order to take part in a census. The couple approached an inn, but there was no room, so the couple was put up in a stable with a manger and farm animals. The baby Jesus was then born and was placed in the manger. Jesus was visited first by shepherds in surrounding fields that were told by angles of Jesus's birth and to go and see the child. Jesus was also visited by three wise men, guided to the nativity with a star, followed by other **astrologers**（占星家）and scholars who had noticed the star.

The celebration of Christmas on December 25th has been observed since the fifth century. During World War I, a truce was observed on Christmas Eve in 1914 and 1915.

> **阅读辅助**
>
> 据说耶稣是因着圣灵成孕，由童女马利亚所生的。神更派遣使者加伯列在梦中晓谕约瑟，把那孩子起名为"耶稣"，意思是要他把百姓从罪恶中救出来。后人为纪念耶稣的诞生，便定十二月二十五为圣诞节，年年望弥撒，纪念耶稣的出世。

✧ Secular Traditions

Santa Claus: In America, Santa Claus is a Christmas figure that brings toys to children on Christmas Eve. He is **stationed**（驻扎）in the North Pole, where he works all year with his elves as helpers to make toys to bring boys and girls on Christmas Eve. Many children will send Santa a list of things they want for Christmas or visit Santa at the mall. On Christmas Eve, Santa loads up the toys in a red sack into his sleigh, which is pulled by twelve reindeer. The reindeer are led by Rudolph, a **reindeer**（驯鹿）with a bright red nose that can guide the reindeer throughout the world at night. Rudolph used to be **teased**（取笑）by the other reindeer for his red nose, but this stopped when it was put to good use on Christmas Eve. Santa visits each child's house on Christmas Eve, leaving their gifts under the tree or by the fireplace. He also stuffs stockings that each child hangs over the fireplace with treats, **trinkets**（小玩意儿）, and other goodies. Many children leave out cookies and milk for Santa to enjoy as he leaves presents. On Christmas morning, children will joyfully awaken and make their way to the fireplace and Christmas tree in order to see what Santa brought them. Many families open Christmas presents on Christmas Day but some may exchange gifts of Christmas Eve.

Christmas Trees: The tradition of Christmas Trees comes from the pagan ritual observed during the winter **solstice**（至日）in which involved tree worship carried out through decorating trees. The tradition of decorating a tree for Christmas likely came from Germany during the nineteenth century, which then spread to England and other areas. The pagan involvement of plants has also evolved into the tradition of using holly and mistletoe in Christmas decorations. If observers find themselves **underneath**（在……的下面）hanging mistletoe, they are expected to kiss. Many contemporary observers decorate the Christmas tree on Christmas Eve, although most will decorate the tree before this. The tree will be decorated with **ornaments**（装饰品）, lights, ribbons, and other decorations with an angel or star on top in honor of nativity story.

Christmas Lights: Many observers will decorate their homes and communities with Christmas Lights. This practice comes from the tradition of decorating Christmas trees with candles in Germany during the 18th century. Christmas trees are still decorated with lights along with households and the exteriors of houses, which may feature **elaborate**（精心制作的）designs and patterns.

> 阅读辅助
>
> 圣诞树是圣诞节庆祝中最有名的传统之一。用灯烛和装饰品把枞树或洋松装点起来的常青树，作为圣诞节庆祝活动的一部分。圣诞老人是一个叫做尼古拉斯，他死后被尊为圣徒，是一位身穿红袍、头戴红帽的白胡子老头。每年圣诞节他驾着鹿拉的雪橇从北方而来，由烟囱进入各家，把圣诞礼物装在袜子里挂在孩子们的床头上或火炉前。

✧ Celebration

Some families celebrate by holding a meal, exchanging gifts, attending a religious service, and going to parties and gatherings of friends and family. It is largely seen as a time to appreciate loved ones. Most workers and students in the United States will have Christmas off even though it is not considered a public holiday.

There are many other different traditions of Christmas. Observers may form groups of carolers to sing Christmas songs throughout the neighborhood. Some may mark the holiday with volunteer work with **shelters**（庇护所）or soup kitchens.

Most church services will feature Advent **wreaths**（花环）and candles and a recreation of the nativity scene. Some churches hold a Midnight Mass. Services will not only celebrate the story of the nativity but the overall significance of Jesus Christ, as it is viewed as the coming of the Savior, a very joyous event. Passages from the nativity story will often be read along with the singing of the many religious songs and hymns associated with the holiday. Songs will often feature themes from the nativity story, such as the messenger angels and the stable.

> 阅读辅助
>
> 圣诞习俗数量众多，大部分人熟悉的圣诞符号及活动，如圣诞树、圣诞火腿、圣诞柴、冬青、槲寄生以及互赠礼物，都是基督教传教士从早期 Asatru 异教的冬至假日 Yule 里吸收而来。

读书笔记